RECESSIONS: PROSPECTS AND DEVELOPMENTS

RECESSIONS: PROSPECTS AND DEVELOPMENTS

NEREA M. PÉREZ
AND
JUNE A. ORTEGA
EDITORS

Nova Science Publishers, Inc.
New York

For permission to use material from this book please contact us:
Telephone 631-231-7269; Fax 631-231-8175
Web Site: http://www.novapublishers.com

LIBRARY OF CONGRESS CATALOGING-IN-PUBLICATION DATA

Recessions : prospects and developments / Nerea M. Pérez and June A. Ortega (editors).
p. cm.
Includes bibliographical references and index.
ISBN 978-1-60456-866-0 (hardcover : alk. paper)
1. Recessions. 2. Business cycles. 3. Economic forecasting. I. Pérez, Nerea M. II. Ortega, June A.
HB3716.R43 2009
338.5'42--dc22

2008037509

Published by Nova Science Publishers, Inc. ✢ New York

CONTENTS

PREFACE

A critical consideration in understanding business cycles is the amplification and propagation of shocks to the economic system. Many recessions seem to arise without a clearly identifiable cause or at least one of significant magnitude to justify an economy-wide recession. How can a small shock cause large changes in the economy? What are the mechanisms that amplify a modest shock such that a serious recession ensues? Despite the persistent search for a mechanism for business cycle amplification and propagation, much research in business cycles seems to ignore the likely role of the financial system. If a shock to the economy inhibits the capital allocation capability of an economy, then a seemingly mild shock may be amplified through its impact on new investment thereby snuffing out economic growth and causing a recession. This book provides new research on the field of recessions from around the globe.

As explained in Chapter 1, a recession is one of several discrete phases in the overall business cycle. The term may often be used loosely to describe an economy that is slowing down or characterized by weakness in at least one major sector like the housing market. When used by economists, "recession" means a significant decline in overall economic activity that lasts more than a few months. The National Bureau of Economic Research (NBER) business cycle dating committee is the generally recognized arbiter of the dates of the beginnings and ends of recessions. As with all statistics, it takes some time to compile the data, which means they are only available after the events they describe. Moreover, because it takes time to discern changes in trends given the usual month-to-month volatility in economic indicators, and because the data are subject to revision, it takes some time before the dating committee can agree that a recession began at a certain date. It can be a year or more after the fact that the dating committee announces the date of the beginning of a recession.

At the moment, there seems to be a growing sentiment that the U.S. economy is in, or is headed into, a recession. All that seems necessary for the word "recession" to be heard in public discourse is for economic growth to slow, for the unemployment rate to rise, or for there to be some turmoil in a sector of the economy large enough to affect large numbers of households. The term may often be used loosely to describe an economy that is slowing down or characterized by weakness in at least one major sector like the housing market. When economists use the term, however, they try to do so consistently. Recessions typically have common characteristics and so economists try to identify the beginning and ending dates of recessions in order to further their overall understanding of the economy.

Economic fluctuations are the central topic in which macroeconomists disagree. The classical tradition, strongly based on the theory of real business cycles (RBC) of Kydland and Prescott (1982) and Long and Plosser (1983), believes that cycles are the result of exogenous disturbances on technology or public expenditures and of the impact these have over the choices of private agents concerning the allocation of their time between labor and leisure. Thus, fluctuations exist even though markets work efficiently and agents are rational and adopt an optimizing behavior.

On the contrary, Keynesian economics, that include prominent contributions like the ones by Samuelson and Solow (1960) or Mankiw (1985), have tended to see periods of expansion and periods of recession as the result of the intrinsic behavior of markets: coordination failures, less than perfect information, less than rational expectations and price sluggishness contribute to the lack of market clearing, which is considered the primary source underlying the fluctuation in time of macro variables. In this perspective of business cycles, these are eminently endogenous arising from the nonlinear relation between aggregate variables even if such variables are assumed as fully deterministic.

As the consensus between classics and Keynesians began to grow stronger, with the so called neo-classical synthesis or new Keynesian economics paradigm, the understanding of business cycles started to share some common traits; classical economists have incorporated in their models price stickiness and Keynesians began to look at microfoundations. In Chapter 2, we discuss the literature on exogenous and endogenous cycles and search for common grounds. A brief review of how the two paradigms have evolved is presented and, on a second stage, a model that integrates both perspectives is formulated. In this model, fluctuations are intrinsically endogenous but they tend to fade away in the long term unless an external stochastic process relating one of the model's parameters is added.

As presented in Chapter 3, the U.S. economy has faced some bad news lately. The housing boom has come to an abrupt halt, and housing sales and house building have been falling at double digit rates. Problems in housing markets have spread to financial markets, causing a "liquidity crunch" in August 2007, and calm has not been restored since. Financial institutions have written off large losses because of falling asset values, particularly for mortgage-backed securities. Commodity prices have been rising, and the price of crude oil has recently topped $120 per barrel. While each of these factors might not be enough to cause a recession in isolation, their cumulative effect could be great enough to push the economy into recession. In light of this news, it is perhaps unsurprising that consumer confidence is at a five-year low.

In response to these events, Congress has enacted an economic stimulus package (P.L. 110-185) and the Federal Reserve has aggressively cut interest rates and lent directly to the financial system to spur economic growth. Despite these actions, a recent survey of private sector forecasters put the chance of a recession in 2008 at 60%.

A look at the available data suggests that economic growth has slowed considerably, but it is too soon to tell if the economy has entered a recession. Typically, the NBER does not announce that the economy has entered a recession until the recession is well under way, for good reason. Recessions are defined as prolonged and sustained declines in economic activity, so by definition, a persistent downturn cannot be identified until it has persisted. Any decline in economic activity at this point is only nascent. Growth was slow in the last two quarters for which data are available, but remained positive. During the onset of the liquidity crunch, economic growth was an unusually high 4.9% in the third quarter of 2007.

Employment declined slightly in the first four months of 2008. The same forecasters who believe there is a one in two chance of recession also predict that growth will average 1.4% in 2008.

Given the lags between policy changes and their effects on the economy, the economy has not yet felt the full impact of the stimulus package and the Federal Reserve's actions.

Efforts to reduce the inflation volatility caused by inflationary shocks have been accompanied in many countries by higher output gap volatility and prolonged recessions. The empirical relationship known as the Phillips curve summarizes the trade-off between stabilizing inflation and stabilizing the output gap faced by the monetary authority. If the Phillips curve is not a structural feature of the economy, but only a reduced-form relationship, the policymaker can in principle influence the recessionary impact of inflation stabilization. Chapter 4 examines the impact of the Canadian inflation targeting policy adopted in 1991 on the inflation-output gap trade-off, and the role it played in the ensuing recession. We document that the empirical relationship between the output gap and the inflation rate in Canada changed after the shift to the inflation targeting regime, and show that the shift in the inflation process and in the inflation-output trade-off can be explained as the result of the inflation targeting monetary policy. Using a sticky price-sticky wage model and data on output, inflation, exchange and interest rates, we build the historical series of exogenous shocks that affected the economy since 1991, and compare the Phillips curve relationship and inflation's time series properties under the inflation targeting regime with its counterfactual under the previous monetary policy. The results show that: (i) the shifts in the inflation dynamics and inflation-output gap trade-off since 1991 would not have happened under the pre-1991 monetary policy; (ii) the disinflation in the early 1990s occurred at the cost of a significant output loss. Therefore, while inflation targeting allowed the policymaker to lower the recessionary impact of inflation stabilization on average, conditional on the vector of shocks that affected the economy it was among the causes of the 1992-1994 recession.

Chapter 5 employs a number of economic and financial variables and their combinations to forecast recessions for Canada and the USA. These variables include real gross domestic product (GDP), industrial production, M1 money supply, spread between long term bond rates and risk free rates, Treasury bill rates, short-term bond rates, longterm bond rates, TSE300 stock prices index for Canada, and S&P500 stock price index for USA. The relationship between these economic and financial variables and recessions 1 — 10 quarters ahead out of sample is modeled using artificial neural networks (ANN) that are considered to be a highly flexible functional form of nonlinear models. The forecast approximated from these models are evaluated using SCORE accuracy measure of recession predictions.

From the fourteen ANN models that are approximated from the seven economic and financial or indicator variables and their combinations for each of the forecast horizons (i.e. 1 — 10 quarters ahead), the single indicator variables stock price index, Treasury bill rates, industrial production, short term bond rates, long term bond rates, and the spread between long term bond rates and Treasury bill rates are the candidate variables for predicting Canadian recessions. However, when these indicator variables are used for real time forecast of future recessions for Canada, no single indicator variable predicted Canadian recessions beyond 2005:Q2 which is the last observation in all the series. However, short term bond rate predicted American recessions two quarters ahead, whereas industrial production growth predicted American recessions one, three and four quarters ahead, although the combined indicator variables are able to predict American recessions up to nine quarters ahead.

Forecasting when a recession is approaching is important for policy makers and market participants. The focus of Chapter 6 is on predicting binary recession events rather than predicting output growth itself. This article includes a review of the econometric methods used in the literature to forecast recessions. The main predictors used in the literature are examined. In particular, considerable research used financial variables as predictors since they are forward-looking variables and have the main advantage of being instantaneously available and precisely measured. The main financial variables that have been identified as leading indicators of future expansions and contractions include: interest rates, and in particular interest rate spread such as the term spreads (the difference between long-term interest rates and short-term interest rates) and default spreads (the difference between the interest rates on matched maturity with different degrees of default risk), and stock returns. I review the empirical evidence of predicting recessions for the United States and for selected developed countries. The term spread appears to contain important predictive content for future recessions and to outperform other indicators although its predictability has diminished in the most recent period.

As presented in Chapter 7, the mysterious and relatively less predictable cyclical fluctuations are known as 'Business Cycle' – one of the blackist in many black boxes in Economics. The patterns and ordering of the cyclical effects may vary for different economies. They depend on the socio-economic and political structure of the countries. The corporate arrangements, ownership structures, cash flows and employment are always affected in the recessions. The industrial and financial institutions – particularly, insurance companies, banks and securities firms - should always plan for their business with consideration of the patterns of business cycles.

In the Expert commentary, we draw heavily from our prior work, outlining the underlying economic logic of the risk premium as a propagation mechanism and providing empirical support for our view. We describe this analysis conceptually and refer the interested reader to Fuerst (2006) for additional technical details. In addition, we discuss issues addressed in companion research, Bian and Fuerst (2008).

In: Recessions: Prospects and Developments
Editors: N.M. Pérez and J.A. Ortega, pp. 1-5
ISBN: 978-1-60456-866-0

Chapter 1

WHAT IS A RECESSION, WHO DECIDES WHEN IT STARTS, AND WHEN DO THEY DECIDE?*

Brian W. Cashell
Macroeconomic Policy
Government and Finance Division

Abstract

A recession is one of several discrete phases in the overall business cycle. The term may often be used loosely to describe an economy that is slowing down or characterized by weakness in at least one major sector like the housing market. When used by economists, "recession" means a significant decline in overall economic activity that lasts more than a few months. The National Bureau of Economic Research (NBER) business cycle dating committee is the generally recognized arbiter of the dates of the beginnings and ends of recessions. As with all statistics, it takes some time to compile the data, which means they are only available after the events they describe. Moreover, because it takes time to discern changes in trends given the usual month-to-month volatility in economic indicators, and because the data are subject to revision, it takes some time before the dating committee can agree that a recession began at a certain date. It can be a year or more after the fact that the dating committee announces the date of the beginning of a recession.

At the moment, there seems to be a growing sentiment that the U.S. economy is in, or is headed into, a recession. All that seems necessary for the word "recession" to be heard in public discourse is for economic growth to slow, for the unemployment rate to rise, or for there to be some turmoil in a sector of the economy large enough to affect large numbers of households. The term may often be used loosely to describe an economy that is slowing down or characterized by weakness in at least one major sector like the housing market. When economists use the term, however, they try to do so consistently. Recessions typically have common characteristics and so economists try to identify the beginning and ending dates of recessions in order to further their overall understanding of the economy.

---

* This report is excerpted from CRS Report RS22793; Dated January 23, 2008.

What is a Recession?

A recession is one of several discrete phases in the overall business cycle. The beginning of a recession is known as a business cycle "peak," and the end of a recession is referred to as a business cycle "trough." In 1946, Arthur Burns and Wesley Mitchell published a study of business cycles and offered a definition intended as a guide for further study:

> Business cycles are a type of fluctuation found in the aggregate economic activity of nations that organize their work mainly in business enterprises: a cycle consists of expansions occurring at about the same time in many economic activities, followed by similarly general recessions, contractions, and revivals which merge into the expansion phase of the next cycle.[1]

This definition requires both expansions and recessions to be apparent in *many economic activities* at about the same time, which would seem to exclude an economy exhibiting weakness in a single market.

More recently, economists at the National Bureau of Economic Research (NBER), issued a memo with a slightly more precise definition:

> A recession is a significant decline in economic activity spread across the economy, lasting more than a few months, normally visible in real GDP, real income, employment, industrial production, and wholesale-retail sales. A recession begins just after the economy reaches a peak of activity and ends as the economy reaches its trough. Between trough and peak, the economy is in an expansion. Expansion is the normal state of the economy; most recessions are brief and they have been rare in recent decades.[2]

This is the generally accepted view among economists of what constitutes an economic recession. There is also a commonly cited "rule of thumb" that is referred to in the press. That rule is that a recession is two consecutive quarterly declines in real gross domestic product (GDP). But this rule does not always apply. For example, there was a recession beginning in March 2001 and ending in November 2001 that was not characterized by two successive quarterly declines in real GDP.

In any case, an important distinction is that a recession is a period of declining output and not just a period of slower economic growth. It is possible for GDP growth to be positive yet so slow that the unemployment rate rises. This is sometimes referred to as a "growth recession."

Who Decides When the U.S. Economy is in a Recession?

Among economists, the NBER is the generally accepted arbiter of business cycle turning points.[3] The NBER is a private nonprofit and nonpartisan organization that was founded in 1920. In the beginning its focus was on the macroeconomy, business cycles, and long-term growth, but now it seeks to promote research on a wide variety of topics. For many years, the NBER itself determined the dates of swings in the business cycle.

In 1978, however, a separate *business cycle dating committee* was formed. The members of the committee are appointed by the president of the NBER, and they are now responsible for determining the dates of the beginnings and ends of recessions.[4] The current members of this committee are as follows:

- Robert Hall, Chair - Director of NBER's Program of Research on Economic Fluctuations and Growth,
- Martin Feldstein — President of NBER,
- Jeffrey Frankel — Director of NBER's Program on International Finance and Macroeconomics,
- Robert J. Gordon — NBER Research Associate, and Professor at Northwestern University,
- Christina and David Romer — Co-Directors of NBER's Program on Monetary Economics, and
- Victor Zarnowitz — NBER Research Associate and Professor Emeritus at the University of Chicago.

If There Is a Recession, When Will We Know When It Started?

The most important indicator of economic conditions is growth in real GDP. GDP is a quarterly measure, and thus there is a time lag between the first month that is reflected in the data and the release of the data. For example, the first release of data for the first calendar quarter of a given year does not occur until late April. The data from that release is subject to revision in each of the next two months and may be revised later on as well. It is not inconceivable that a first release of data that showed a decline in real GDP would later be revised to show an increase. Even so, those using the rule of thumb that two successive quarterly declines in real GDP constitutes a recession would have to wait for the release of the second quarter data in August to establish that a recession began at the start of the year.

Because of the time lag associated with the release of GDP data, and because business cycle turning points are associated with months rather than quarters, the dating committee relies on a number of monthly economic indicators. Among the more important monthly indicators the committee looks at are personal income, employment, and industrial production. Even in the case of monthly indicators, it may require several months of data to establish a change in trends.

When there is a recession, not all of the economic indicators will show a change in trend at the same time. Historically, some indicators such as housing starts and the stock market tend to slow or decline in advance of a recession, and some like the unemployment rate tend to react to changing conditions with a lag.

With all statistics it takes some time to compile the data which means they are only available after the events they describe. Moreover, because it takes time to discern changes in trends given the usual month-to-month volatility in economic indicators, and because the data are subject to revision, it takes some time before the dating committee can agree that a recession (or an expansion) began at a certain date. Table 1 shows, for recent business cycle peaks and troughs, the date of the turning point and the date when the committee issued a release identifying the date of the turning point.

Table 1. Dates of Recent Business Cycle Turning Points and Dates They Were Announced by the NBER

Turning Point	Date of Turning Point	Date Turning Point Was Announced by NBER	Months After Turning Point
peak	January 1980	June 3, 1980	5
trough	July 1980	July 8, 1981	12
peak	July 1981	January 6, 1982	6
trough	November 1982	July 8, 1983	8
peak	July 1990	April 25, 1991	9
trough	March 1991	December 22, 1992	21
peak	March 2001	November 26, 2001	8
trough	November 2001	July 17, 2003	20

Source: National Bureau of Economic Research.

The longest delay between the beginning of a new phase of the business cycle and its announcement was when a recession was found to have ended in March 1991 but was not announced until 21 months had passed. The shortest delay was five months after the expansion ended in January 1980. Of the eight examples shown here, three were not announced until at least a year had elapsed.

Rhetorical and Analytical Significance

While all recessions have unique characteristics, they also have many common aspects. Thus, they are the object of economic analysis both individually and collectively. Because they are undesirable, economists study them in the hope that they can advise policymakers how to avoid them. To do so, it is important to agree on a chronology, and it may not be an inconvenience to economists that it takes time to establish one.

Policymakers, on the other hand, are more concerned with the present and the immediate future. If they hope to avert or mitigate the consequences of recession, they cannot wait for an "official" declaration. By then the recession is likely to be history.

Although there can be a significant delay between the onset of a recession and the dating committee determination, there is often little doubt that the economy is, or has been, in recession well before the announcement. For policy to have mitigating effects, it must occur quickly. Policymakers may not have the luxury of holding themselves to as strict a definition of recession as economic analysts.

References

[1] Arthur F. Burns and Wesley C. Mitchell, *Measuring Business Cycles*, National Bureau of Economic Research, 1946, p. 3.
[2] Business Cycle Dating Committee, Memo, National Bureau of Economic Research, January 7, 2008, 3 pp. Available on the Internet at [http://www.nber.org/cycles/jan08bcdc_memo.html].
[3] The NBER website is at [http://www.nber.org].
[4] A working paper published by the Bureau of Economic Analysis found that "[t]he NBER dating committee's methodology appears to be very robust." See Bruce T. Grimm, "Alternative Measures of U.S. Economic Activity in Business Cycles and Business Cycle Dating," Bureau of Economic Analysis Working Paper 2005-05, August 2005, 14 pp.

In: Recessions: Prospects and Developments
Editors: N.M. Pérez and J.A. Ortega, pp. 7-44
ISBN: 978-1-60456-866-0

Chapter 2

BUSINESS CYCLES IN ECONOMIC THEORY: EXOGENOUS OR ENDOGENOUS?

Orlando Gomes*
Escola Superior de Comunicação Social [Instituto Politécnico de Lisboa] and Unidade de Investigação em Desenvolvimento Empresarial – Economics Research Center [UNIDE/ISCTE - ERC]

Abstract

Economic fluctuations are the central topic in which macroeconomists disagree. The classical tradition, strongly based on the theory of real business cycles (RBC) of Kydland and Prescott (1982) and Long and Plosser (1983), believes that cycles are the result of exogenous disturbances on technology or public expenditures and of the impact these have over the choices of private agents concerning the allocation of their time between labor and leisure. Thus, fluctuations exist even though markets work efficiently and agents are rational and adopt an optimizing behavior.

On the contrary, Keynesian economics, that include prominent contributions like the ones by Samuelson and Solow (1960) or Mankiw (1985), have tended to see periods of expansion and periods of recession as the result of the intrinsic behavior of markets: coordination failures, less than perfect information, less than rational expectations and price sluggishness contribute to the lack of market clearing, which is considered the primary source underlying the fluctuation in time of macro variables. In this perspective of business cycles, these are eminently endogenous arising from the nonlinear relation between aggregate variables even if such variables are assumed as fully deterministic.

As the consensus between classics and Keynesians began to grow stronger, with the so called neo-classical synthesis or new Keynesian economics paradigm, the understanding of business cycles started to share some common traits; classical economists have incorporated in their models price stickiness and Keynesians began to look at microfoundations. In this chapter, we discuss the literature on exogenous and endogenous cycles and search for common grounds. A brief review of how the two paradigms have evolved is presented and, on

---

* Orlando Gomes; address: Escola Superior de Comunicação Social, Campus de Benfica do IPL, 1549-014 Lisbon, Portugal. Phone number: + 351 93 342 09 15; fax: + 351 217 162 540. E-mail: ogomes@escs.ipl.pt.
Acknowledgements: Financial support from the Fundação Ciência e Tecnologia, Lisbon, is gratefully acknowledged, under the contract No POCTI/ECO/48628/2002, partially funded by the European Regional Development Fund (ERDF).

a second stage, a model that integrates both perspectives is formulated. In this model, fluctuations are intrinsically endogenous but they tend to fade away in the long term unless an external stochastic process relating one of the model's parameters is added.

1. Introduction

Economists tend to disagree about the causes of the observed fluctuations in aggregate economic activity. This chapter addresses this discussion, putting in confrontation the two main theories that try to explain the mechanics underlying the recurrent expansions and contractions found at the macro level. Afterwards, inspired by the recent attempts to find a unifying theoretical framework, a model of business cycles with elements from both views is proposed. These two perspectives relate to a classical approach in which market efficiency plays a central role, and a Keynesian view, where nominal frictions and inertia in goods and labor markets furnish a convincing explanation for such aggregate fluctuations.

The first perspective was well accepted until the great depression in the 1930s. At that time, economists had developed powerful microeconomic tools and the wonders that free trade was presenting in terms of increased prosperity led to a widespread belief that cycles were relatively unimportant and that they resulted fundamentally from real shocks on the supply side. It was believed that demand has little to do with the way the economic system performs over time. The great depression and the Keynesian revolution in the economics profession changed such belief. The years that followed have completely dismissed the microeconomic concepts as a sound basis for the understanding of business cycles. Fiscal and monetary policy and the behavior and expectations of private agents took the central stage on the explanation of the short run performance of the economic system. The most important implication was that the concept of invisible hand lost credibility on an aggregate level. Economists, and the general public, started to wonder whether households and firms, acting rationally, could ever lead the overall economic system to an equilibrium result only disturbed by the own dynamism of the markets. The intervention of the government became essential to dominate and control 'animal spirits', that, if left alone, could disrupt the economy through phenomena likely to arise when collective action is not regulated (e.g., herd behavior, crashes or bubbles).

The contemporaneous debate about the most reasonable view on macroeconomic fluctuations was initiated by the rational expectations revolution of the 1970s and the aggregative general equilibrium models that followed. The resulting theory, the real business cycles theory, is discussed in section 2. The enormous success of this approach in academic circles could not, however, hide some of its shortcomings; we might argue that recessions and expansions are possible to model under market clearing and in the absence of any public policy (mainly, monetary policy), but when looking at reality we cannot just ignore such factors. Even if one attributes to real shocks (e.g., technological ones) the main role in explaining cycles, we cannot overlook that such occurs in a world where markets do not function perfectly and where the government often intervenes even when such is not desirable from a strict economic efficiency perspective.

From the benchmark RBC model, i.e., from the dynamic stochastic general equilibrium model that reproduces cycles if an exogenous disturbance is accounted for, one may depart a little or a lot, in order to introduce Keynesian elements to the explanation of cycles. Section 3 addresses some of such departures, which have as a common point the idea that the macroeconomic system may be modelled in such a way that fluctuations arise as endogenous, i.e., explained by the nonlinear relation between aggregates, and without the need of taking any exogenous influence.

The purpose of this text is not only to assess the two conflicting views, which by the way are progressively less conflicting as the most relevant arguments of both are beginning to be jointly considered, but to sketch a possible modelling structure that reunites both approaches. We begin, in sections 2 and 3, by looking at the most relevant features of exogenous and endogenous business cycles theories. In section 4, we briefly discuss the main features of observed business cycles. Then one may discuss the validity of different theoretical interpretations. Sections 5 and 6 deal with a dynamic model of cycles. This is an RBC model in the sense that it uses the benchmark utility maximization general equilibrium model, but it generates endogenous cycles by assuming a disequilibrium component that makes the markets not to clear immediately; market inefficiency tends to be overcome in the long term and as a result, cycles tend to fade away in the absence of any external shock. Thus, we introduce a perturbation as the ones generally taken in RBC theory.

2. The RBC Theory

The classical view of economics, under which prices are flexible and adjust instantly to clear markets given the rational behavior and expectations of private agents, has dominated macroeconomic thought in the 60 and 70 decades of the twentieth century. To this contributed the work of some of the most prominent economists ever: Friedman and Schwartz (1963), Phelps (1968), Sargent and Wallace (1975) and Lucas (1976), just to cite a few, offered a perspective about aggregate phenomena strongly based on microeconomic optimization principles and in which general equilibrium prevails most of the time. Such a conception of the economic reality although appealing from a scientific point of view, seemed somehow limited on its ability to explain short run fluctuations. In fact, if markets are always in equilibrium and resources are fully employed with maximum efficiency, one can only expect the economy to follow the potential trend of growth, without observing any significant departure from this trend.

Despite the argument of incompatibility between well behaved markets and aggregate fluctuations, the application of the classical economics principles to the study of business cycles gained a crucial contribution in the beginning of the 1980s, with the brilliant work of the 2004 Nobel laureates Finn Kydland and Edward C. Prescott. In the words of Rebelo (2005), the merits of the work of Kydland and Prescott (1982) are essentially three:

(*i*) they are able to incorporate a reasonable and convincing explanation for business cycles into the benchmark representative agent intertemporal optimization model; in other words, they have demonstrated that dynamic general equilibrium analysis is compatible with the replication of business fluctuations. This is relevant because it allows for undermining the Keynesian view under which the explanation of cycles is incompatible with a scenario of competitive markets and rational expectations;

(*ii*) as a consequence of introducing the analysis of cycles into general equilibrium models, it became possible to jointly analyze cycles and growth. The intertemporal optimization model is, above all, a framework to explain growth. A representative agent maximizes the intertemporal utility of consumption and, in this way, it is generated an output time path that converges to a long run state of positive or zero growth (depending on the properties of the production function). As Romer (1996, page 151) emphasizes, the benchmark growth model, i.e., the Ramsey model, 'is the natural Walrasian baseline model of the aggregate economy'. Thus, the analysis by Kydland and Prescott (1982) may be interpreted as a modification of the benchmark competitive growth setup in order to explain temporary deviations from the growth trend;

(*iii*) the model may be calibrated using values of parameters that describe reasonable economic conditions in order to generate time series that can be compared with the economic aggregates' time series observed in reality. This kind of comparison has proved successful, i.e., there are important similarities between real world business cycles and the ones the model allowed to reproduce [see, in what concerns the empirical validation of this class of models, Rotemberg and Woodford (1996) and King and Rebelo (1999)].

The literature strand initiated by Kydland and Prescott (1982) has gained the designation of real business cycles (RBC) theory. The mechanism allowing for generating business cycles in RBC models functions in two steps: first, a second argument is attached to the intertemporal utility function: besides consumption, it is assumed that the representative individual also withdraws utility from leisure. Such an assumption introduces labor market considerations into the optimization problem; by optimizing the allocation of their time between leisure and work, households will furnish into the productive system varying quantities of the labor input. If no stochastic component is added to the model, the labor allocation share, as well as the other assumed variables, converges to some long term fixed point steady state.

The second step, the one that turns possible the introduction of persistent in time fluctuations, is related to the presence of real shocks affecting the economy. In the original formulation, these shocks are technological ones; however, the source of business fluctuations may be other, for instance, changes in the level of public expenditures. The argument seems reasonable: external technology shocks, or external disturbances of any other kind, stimulate the production capabilities turning more attractive (in terms of real wage) the participation in the labor force. Hence, whenever a technology enhancement takes place, the value of labor rises and individuals replace leisure time by work time. If the shock is a one time event, the system will converge in the long run to a fixed point, i.e., the effects of the perturbation tend to fade away; however, economic history gives us reasons to believe that technology improvements are recurrent and systematic through time, and therefore a new incentive to rise labor participation will always come around, making perpetual cyclical motion to set in.

Note that the previous reasoning is strongly founded on the Walrasian notion of market clearing not only in terms of the functioning of the goods market, but also in what concerns the labor market. At this level, some doubts can be cast over the true applicability of this type of model to real economies. There is no strong evidence, in any developed country, pointing to such flexible labor markets capable of allowing to promptly change the amount of working hours as a result of any technological novelty in the production process.

The RBC theory produces interesting results in what concerns the capacity to replicate the patterns of observed business cycles. Phenomena as the strong volatility of investment, the pro-cyclicity of almost all aggregate real variables or the persistence of fluctuations are compatible with the mechanics of RBC models. This is the strongest point of the theory; a point so appealing that it has generated a huge amount of related literature following 1982. Immediately after, Long and Plosser (1983) have highlighted another contribution of the theory besides the meaningful properties of the simulated time series of the economic aggregate variables. This contribution relates to the evidence that RBC models are able to reproduce the co-movement of different sectors of the economy, which is something one clearly observes when looking at business cycles in practice. Such an argument was further developed in Christiano and Fitzgerald (1998) and Greenwood, Hercowitz and Krusell (1997). A similar line of investigation was followed by Backus and Kehoe (1992), Baxter (1995) and Ambler, Cardia and Zimmermann (2004). These address international business cycles co-movements at the light of RBC; once again, the model reveals promising in terms of compatibility with observed data.

Other authors search for equally important contributions of the theory. For instance, Burnside, Eichenbaum and Rebelo (1993), Burnside and Eichenbaum (1996), King and Rebelo (1999) and Jaimovich (2004) address the importance of technology shocks in producing cycles. These authors basically restate the relevance of innovation to cycles, even though they correct the original formulation by making a clear distinction between true technology shocks and the ones relating to a broader notion of total factor productivity.

Another relevant implication of the theory is thoroughly discussed in King, Plosser and Rebelo (1988) and King (1991). This relates to the property that positive technology shocks rise hours worked. Above, we have called the attention for this concern. Looking at the structure of labor markets, one does not encounter reasons to believe in the existence of sufficient flexibility to turn these markets into the main vehicle of propagation of technology shocks. The unrealistically high elasticity of labor supply required to generate cycles is one of the most uncomfortable assumptions underlying the RBC theory and one that is not yet completely resolved.

The RBC models are also excellent laboratories for testing public policy. Fiscal policy in RBC models has been studied in Christiano and Eichenbaum (1992), Baxter and King (1993) and McGrattan (1994), among others. The overall result is that the inclusion of taxes and public expenditures in RBC models improves their forecasting ability, but fiscal shocks (in tax rates or government spending) cannot play the role of a major source of business fluctuations. Concerning monetary policy, the works by Bernanke, Gertler and Gilchrist (1999), Christiano, Eichenbaum and Evans (1999), Smets and Wouters (2003) and Altig, Christiano, Eichenbaum and Linde (2005), among others, emphasize the role of nominal frictions (sticky prices and wages) in the economy; in this perspective, nominal forces may shape the economy's response to technology shocks and, therefore, the way monetary authorities exert influence over the private economy through the manipulation of the interest rate, must be taken seriously as an important mechanism behind the cyclical evolution of macro aggregates.

The consideration of price and wages stickiness in RBC models implies that these models begin to incorporate some new Keynesian features and, thus, they begin to change relatively to what was indeed their initial purpose: to explain fluctuations under a purely competitive general equilibrium framework characterized by instantaneous market clearing and rational expectations. The new RBC models, as the ones by Ellison and Scott (2000), Ireland (2003) and Christiano, Eichenbaum and Evans (2005), continue to argue that cycles are essentially driven by exogenous disturbances, although they incorporate market frictions and new forms of addressing expectations (e.g., learning mechanisms). The aim of the new analyses is the same as ever: to reproduce in a more realistic way the business cycles.

One of the attempts to conciliate nominal frictions with the RBC main arguments is explored in Kurz, Jin and Motolese (2005). These authors use the concept of 'rational belief equilibrium' (RBE) to introduce additional elements of realism into the RBC approach. The concept of RBE is known from the literature since the work of Kurz (1994, 1996, 1997), Kurz and Motolese (2001) and Kurz, Jin and Motolese (2003). The cited authors begin by emphasizing the idea that the equilibrium theory underlying RBC models leaves no place for monetary policy. In their words (page 2019), '*money is neutral and monetary policy has no social function*' if the three main underlying assumptions of the RBC theory are seriously taken into account: (*i*) markets are not subject to frictions, i.e., perfect competition holds; (*ii*) prices are completely flexible; (*iii*) the agents' behavior is driven by rational expectations.

The Keynesian view on cycles, which Kurz and his co-authors call the 'dynamic new Keynesian theory', maintains the third assumption of the classical approach and dismisses the other two: markets are not fully competitive (monopolistic competition replaces the competitive scenario) and prices are sluggish to adjust. Following the literature on sticky prices, which is founded on the work of Taylor (1980), Calvo (1983), Yun (1996) and Clarida, Gali and Gertler (1999), the new Keynesian literature has also known some success on explaining the rational of cycles. Cycles are, in this view, not eminently caused by real disturbances but by nominal frictions; these frictions underlie a Phillips curve relation that is in the centre of the Keynesian approach to fluctuations.

The sticky prices approach to business cycles is hard to classify in terms of our discussion of exogenous vs endogenous cycles. It clearly departs from the RBC exogenous disturbances approach but the occurrence of cycles continues to need some external trigger. Basically, exogenous shocks continue to cause fluctuations, however these are amplified by the incorrect firms' price setting.

Returning to the argument of Kurz, Jin and Motolese (2005), this is related to the idea that new Keynesians search for more consequent views on fluctuations through price rigidity and market imperfections, but neglect the role of expectations by taking the strong assumption of rational expectations. Rather than doing this, it is possible to preserve the assumptions of market competition and price flexibility (taking, thus, a standard RBC model), but removing at the same time the rational expectations assumption. The authors consider that agents have heterogeneous beliefs and this suffices for making money a non neutral entity, attributing to monetary policy an influent role concerning the stabilization of cycles. Besides demonstrating the usefulness of central bank intervention, the referred study attains the relevant result of replicating better the empirical business cycles properties than the RBC original model [in concrete, Kurz and his co-authors compare their results with the results of the benchmark model as presented in King and Rebelo (1999); in the appendix to this chapter, we make reference to such benchmark results].

The main merit of the pointed study is that the better fit to empirical data is accomplished by changing solely the formulation of expectations, maintaining simultaneously the rest of the basic framework, namely the general equilibrium intertemporal model where productivity shocks and optimal decisions concerning the workforce allocation are the driving factors of cycles.

Independently of the version of the model we consider, it is a well accepted fact that models with real shocks as the primary source of aggregate fluctuations are capable of explaining some of the most striking facts concerning the evolution over time of macro variables. It is also true that, despite the fact that the RBC models account well for observed fluctuations and are elegant logical frameworks that serve to explain without ambiguities a process of cycles through shocks over a system that is otherwise stable, these models are, nevertheless, subject to relevant criticism. Although the RBC theory continues to be the dominant paradigm concerning the analysis of aggregate fluctuations, the truth is that this theory is for the explanation of cycles as the Solow (1956) growth model is for the explanation of long term growth. In both theories, the phenomenon that is intended to be explained is the result of an exogenous process of technological development or productivity growth. After all, RBC models just attribute the cause of cycles to something that is outside the scope of economic analysis.

In the appendix in the end of the chapter, we develop the basic structure of the RBC model. We not only present the equations of motion underlying the fluctuations mechanism, but we also use a standard parameters' calibration in order to replicate cycles' main features. The facts referred to in section 4 are accounted for in this modelling exercise.

3. The EBC Theory

Contrasting with the RBC approach to cycles, a relevant part of the Keynesian macroeconomics tradition highlights the existence of a set of market inefficiencies or frictions that lead to intrinsic nonlinear relations between economic aggregates which translate on fluctuations that are endogenous, i.e., that occur without the need of assuming any external shock. This tradition goes back to the accelerator-multiplier model of Kalecki (1935), Samuelson (1939), Kaldor (1940), Hicks (1950) and Goodwin (1951).

The development of sophisticated mathematical tools in the decades that followed, allowed for the search of new insights on the relation between macro variables. The work by Stutzer (1980), Benhabib and Day (1981), Day (1982) and Deneckere and Pelikan (1985), among many others, initiated a research on models that intrinsically generate periodic or a-periodic cycles without the need of assuming any stochastic components. This literature has received the designation of endogenous business cycles (EBC) literature. The term EBC contrasts with RBC. The extent in which one and the other view of the business cycles differ varies with the goals of the analysis. While some authors have searched for nonlinearities in Walrasian market clearing models, others have departed from this kind of market structure associating the economic fluctuations to different types of market imperfections.

The line of analysis under which nonlinearities and chaotic motion are compatible with market clearing specifications was developed, among others, by Nishimura and Yano (1995), Nishimura, Shigoka and Yano (1998) and Boldrin, Nishimura, Shigoka and Yano (2000). These authors found nonlinear dynamics in general equilibrium models for extreme conditions such as unrealistically high discount rates and non conventional types of production functions. Because the referred models are optimal growth models that do not consider any exogenous shock and still they reproduce business fluctuations, the authors have no doubt in classifying them as EBC models; this is explicitly done in Mitra, Nishimura and Sorger (2006), who, despite the differences, clearly highlight the basic point in common: both RBC and EBC models are Pareto efficient, i.e., in both cases the business cycles arise from optimal programs. The interesting point is that without departing from the standard assumptions of optimal growth theory, periodic and a-periodic motion arise as the result of optimal control problems. Nevertheless, this kind of EBC is far from producing the same appealing results as the RBC theory in what respects the comparison between time series generated from the model and the observed in practice aggregate fluctuations.

The large majority of works relating EBC departs from the market clearing scenario and take the notion of market disequilibrium as a central argument of the analysis. At this level, we should distinguish as well two different approaches. The first continues to be based upon the basic framework of utility maximization, and introduces some kind of mechanism that produces a departure from a purely competitive scenario. The second approach abandons the optimal growth Ramsey model and discusses cycles and growth considering an array of market inefficiencies, including agent heterogeneity, information biases and nominal rigidities.

On the EBC models based on the RBC structure, the central idea relates to the consideration of an externality affecting the production of final goods. If each firm in the economy benefits from the economy wide level of existing inputs, then it suffers a positive externality that, through aggregation, generates an economy wide production function exhibiting increasing returns to scale. Two types of models have been developed to show that this production function under economies of scale leads to endogenous fluctuations (the frameworks are such that when some parameter of the model is changed, the system is likely to cross a bifurcation line, making the system to pass from a state of stability to a state that locally is classified as unstable but that from a global dynamics point of view corresponds to a region of cycles of multiple possible periodicities).

The first type of models relies on the framework of overlapping generations (OLG). OLG models capable of producing endogenous fluctuations were developed, following the pioneer discussion by Grandmont (1985), by a group of economists where one can include Cazzavillan, Lloyd-Braga and Pintus (1998), Aloi, Dixon and Lloyd-Braga (2000), Aloi, Lloyd-Braga and Whitta-Jacobsen (2003), Cazzavillan and Pintus (2006) and Lloyd-Braga, Nourry and Venditti (2007). In this case, the analysis is essentially focused on finding local bifurcation points, but there is not a thorough investigation of the global properties of the specified dynamic systems; this implies that it is suggested the existence of cycles (they may occur when the system changes its qualitative nature, that is, when it passes through a bifurcation point), but their properties are not fully dissected.

The second type of models works with the Ramsey growth model, as the RBC theory, and includes, as main references, Christiano and Harrison (1999), Schmitt-Grohé (2000), Guo and Harrison (2001), Guo and Lansing (2002) and Coury and Wen (2006). This group of authors realizes that local dynamic analysis of the standard growth model with externalities tends to be incomplete and gives misleading information. A indeterminacy or a saddle-path local equilibrium result can hide a global nonlinear long run behavior; therefore, most of the cited works address the study of global dynamics of maximization utility models.

Once again, the weakest point in the analysis relates to its poor performance when calibrated to explain observed business cycles. In particular, the degree of aggregate returns to scale that is necessary to assume to match some of the observed fluctuations' properties is unrealistically high [this is true since the beginning, that is, since the pioneer work by Christiano and Harrison(1999)], and therefore the empirical relevance of this kind of models is seriously compromised. The same happens for instance in Guo and Lansing (2002), who examine the role of the government tax policy over the growth model with externalities; to generate cycles, these authors needed to assume highly unrealistic parameter values for tax rates.

An interesting line of research is pursued by Schmitt-Grohé (2000). This paper focuses on trying to find on the EBC formulation the explanatory power that the RBC models miss, that is, the proposed exercise is to take the stylized facts on business cycles that standard RBC models have more difficulty in explaining and to try to attach them to the reasoning underlying EBC models; in this way, one could support the idea that fluctuations are part exogenous and part endogenous. The result is not satisfactory, though. The author does not encounter, for empirically realistic calibrations of the chosen framework, in an EBC perspective, the elements that seem to be missing in the existing RBC models.

Let us now abandon the growth model structure for the analysis of cycles and focus on a perspective of endogenous cycles with a much more Keynesian flavour. In Flaschel, Franke and Semmler (1997) it is argued that instead of being completely rational, having full information and being able to optimize over large horizons, the economic agents are subject to making mistakes and to form expectations in a non rationally perfect manner. As a result, the agents face a complex and uncertain environment that drives the economic system away from the market equilibrium that in a classical perspective is achieved automatically given the capacity of prices to adjust instantly. Thus, cycles are, in this view, inherently attached to an out of equilibrium state that persists over time.

Adopting this view of reality, where frictions are recurrent and excess demand and excess supply outcomes are not simply transitory, opens the door to multiple interpretations of cyclical motion. In fact, this view is one under which the economic system is above all a complex body that should not be oversimplified; otherwise, one will just lose track of its most appealing properties and ends up with a conceptual framework with too little explanatory power.

The complex view of economics is debated in Kirman (2004). The argument is that aggregate phenomena should not be understood as the behavior of some average or representative agent (in fact, this is what the RBC view of cycles does). The interaction of heterogeneous agents is complex and produces phenomena like herd behavior, crashes or bubbles; oversimplifying such interaction means failing to achieve the most essential purpose of macroeconomics: to understand the reasons and consequences of collective behavior. The message is this: no simple and straightforward correspondence exists between individual and aggregate regularities.

Starting with the work of Brock and Hommes (1997, 1998) on adaptive belief systems applied to economics and finance, there is a huge amount of literature on how persistent heterogeneous behavior may result on endogenous fluctuations. Although some of this literature deals with business cycles, we do not intend to survey it here [see Hommes (2006) for such a survey]; we just reemphasize that once we let go from the representative agent benchmark framework, the doors for encountering new and appealing explanations for fluctuations become wide open.

While some of the studies on nonlinear macrodynamics are relevant theoretical exercises but lack the ability to reproduce real world business fluctuations, recent work on disequilibrium theory has been able to encounter a balance between relevant theory and applicability. Some of this literature includes Chiarella and Flaschel (2000), Asada, Chiarella and Flaschel (2003), Chiarella, Flaschel and Franke (2005), Raberto, Teglio and Cincotti (2006), Hallegatte, Ghil, Dumas and Hourcade (2007) and Hallegatte and Ghil (2007). The models developed in the cited studies involve considering a wide set of macro relations, that allow to simultaneously characterize the several macro markets (goods, labor, money and foreign exchange).

The disequilibrium may be present in one market and, through a contagion effect, affect all the economy, or it may be pervasive on the economy. Nevertheless, at least the labor market can easily be pointed as a market where market clearing is difficult to attain and, thus, it seems reasonable to accept the assumptions underlying the Keynesian perspective on endogenous cycles. In Hallegatte, Ghil, Dumas and Hourcade (2007), for instance, business cycles correspond to a chaotic behavior that is visible in the long term evolution of the most relevant economic variables; in this case, the source of fluctuations is the investment-profit instability; this instability does not lead to an explosive dynamic result because the amplitude of the instability is constrained by the increase in labor costs and the inertia that characterizes the installed production capacity.

In synthesis, we have looked at several different interpretations of what an EBC model is. Some interpret it as the nonlinear long term motion that arises from the interconnection of a large set of economic relations involving the whole of the macroeconomic markets; in this perspective, agents do not necessarily behave in a same way and intertemporal optimization is not a requirement. Furthermore, rational expectations are not a prerequisite as well. Given the large amount of parameters involved in the analysis it becomes relatively easy to encounter a calibration capable of reproducing satisfactorily the historical data, as the RBC models do.

Others prefer to stay closer to the classical interpretation of fluctuations by continuing to assume the dynamic equilibrium growth framework; the finding that an externality in the production of final goods is all that is needed to generate endogenous cycles in an otherwise conventional deterministic Ramsey growth model became an extremely appealing idea, but some difficulties were encountered when it was necessary to attach the model's results to the observed cyclical motion. Finally, another group of authors have insisted that the original growth model is able, per se, to generate endogenous fluctuations without the necessity of giving up on any of the strong assumptions that allow to build the intertemporal utility maximization problem subject to constraints on capital accumulation.

4. And What About the Facts?

It was stressed in the previous sections that the main item that allows to give credibility to a theory of cycles is its capability to explain a large set of stylized facts that one encounters when observing how the time series of the main economic aggregates evolve over time. These facts have been thoroughly discussed in the literature. We address them briefly in the next paragraphs. We rely essentially on the presentation by King and Rebelo (1999) and Dosi, Fagiolo and Roventini (2006). The most striking fact is that fluctuations have common features across time and space. Despite differences in government policies, households' preferences and behavior, firms' structure and many other factors, it is indeed amazing the similarities that today's cycles have relatively to fluctuations that occurred one century ago, and that cycles in one part of the globe resemble cycles in a country on a completely different geographical area.

Stylized facts can be grouped in three categories: volatility, co-movement and persistence.[1] In terms of volatility, it is widely accepted that:

1) Investment is considerably more volatile than output (about three times more volatile);
2) Private consumption of non-durables is less volatile than output;
3) Private consumption of durables is more volatile than output;
4) Government expenditures are less volatile than output;
5) Both the volatility of employment and the volatility of hours worked are similar to the volatility of output (thus, hours worked per person are less volatile than output);
6) Labor productivity and the real wage are less volatile than output.

In what concerns co-movement, the most important observation is that economic aggregates share a high degree of co-movement, i.e., they are strongly pro-cyclical. Obviously, the unemployment rate is anti-cyclical, while relevant a-cyclicity is found in real wages, government expenditures and the stock of physical capital; these three aggregates have very low degrees of correlation with output.

Relating co-movement, it is yet important to stress that investment and consumption tend to be coincident variables, i.e., variables that are pro-cyclical with output without any lag, while employment is found to be a lagging variable.

Finally, persistence is a property shared by all macroeconomic aggregates, i.e., sudden changes in the direction followed by the time series of economic variables are not common; technically, we might say that the serial correlation displayed by any of the previously referred aggregates tends to be strong.

Dosi, Fagiolo and Roventini (2006) also address a set of microeconomic facts relating to cycles, namely the ones concerning to the nature of firms' investment decisions, the characteristics of innovation processes and the dispersion of productivity. However, these are not so consensual, because their empirical testing is difficult and because several kinds of idiosyncrasies make them not so pervasive as the relating aggregate facts.

From an empirical standpoint, it is also relevant to access the reasonability of assuming exogenous shocks to the economy. After all, giving a clear answer to the doubt of what is the true extent of the relevance of shocks over observed fluctuations may constitute an argument in support of RBC or EBC. King and Rebelo (1999) cast some doubts on the relevance of technology shocks. They argue that although productivity / technology shocks are central to the RBC argument, these disturbances would need to be larger and more persistent than one observes in practice in order to generate fluctuations similar to the ones that effectively occur. Therefore, technology shocks can account only for a part of the observed business cycles. This does not put in check the supply side explanation of fluctuations; it just calls the attention for the need to consider other potential sources of supply shocks, that should be jointly analyzed with the ones triggered by productivity fluctuations. The most frequent candidates to include in the array of supply disturbances relate to measures of fiscal policy and government spending, on one hand, and shocks on inputs prices (like the price of oil), on the other hand.

[1] See the appendix to this chapter for a discussion of these stylized facts at the light of the RBC benchmark model.

A last point that deserves our attention in this section relates to the cross-country evidence on cycles. In the beginning of the section, we have stated that one of the most striking facts relating business fluctuations is that geography seems not to play a decisive role in shaping economic fluctuations. Putting it simple, we might say that business cycles are all alike regardless from the location on the globe one is considering. Such a statement is, of course, exaggerated. Cycles resemble each other because effectively one often encounters the same type of volatility, a strong correlation between the path of output and the trajectories of other macro variables and a persistence pattern in the evolution of the main economic aggregates. Nevertheless, there are relevant idiosyncrasies easily depicted when comparing output time series of different countries in similar time periods.

For instance, Mejia-Reyes (2004) compares the business cycles of seven countries in the American continent. The author does not find relevant coincidences in the aggregate performance of the economies, except when comparing the short run evolution of the United States and the Canadian economies. The withdrawn conclusion is that there is not a significant contagion effect of a leading country over the others in terms of generating phases of expansion and recession; simultaneously, one should also reject the idea that macroeconomic policies are internationally coordinated. This conclusion is corroborated in the study by Bowden and Martin (1992), who compare the post-second world war evolution of the United States and the Australian economies: The findings are that there are striking differences; while the United States business cycle is a well defined cycle, the Australian one is more diffuse, lacking coherence between the relevant macro indicators. Also Artis, Kontolemis and Osborn (1997) point to asymmetries when studying the behavior of macro variables in the G7 economies and in the economies of a number of selected European countries.

Although it is relatively easy finding evidence of lack of coordination in business fluctuations across national economies, the most common view is that there is a co-existence between a country-specific component of cycles and a world component of fluctuations. This is stressed, among others, by Gregory, Head and Raynauld (1997) and Kose, Otrok and Whiteman (2003). Such evidence is compatible with the intuition that there are region-specific factors determining part of the economic performance, but international linkages are relevant and allow to seriously consider a 'world business cycle' with well shaped properties concerning volatility, co-movement and persistence. As a result, the path pursued by the theory, i.e., building a generic theory of cycles that one can apply to every economy in every time period, does not constitute a mere conceptual exercise; it can be seen as the basis to understand the fundamentals of fluctuations, being these fundamentals in the essence of any observed aggregate time series evolution over time.

A good economic theory of business cycles must accomplish two things: first, it should be able to reproduce the basic business cycles stylized facts one has presented (for model's calibrations close to what one encounters in developed economies); second, it must achieve the first goal under reasonable and appealing assumptions about the way the economy works. Therefore, it is not surprising the disagreement on the interpretation of cycles that the economic theory has witnessed: two competing views of the world were able to reproduce the same basic facts; hence, which one of the views one should accept as valid? We answer this question by saying that both perspectives have some admissible assumptions. Combining them, one may build a stronger theory for the understanding (and prediction) of economic cycles. The following sections propose a framework with such characteristics.

5. An Application: Utility Maximization with Market Inefficiency

The discussion on the merits and flaws of distinct theories of cycles seems to raise the necessity of a unifying framework, one capable of resorting to the optimization framework of the RBC theory and simultaneously include the most relevant Keynesian elements. One attempt to make such conciliation is explored in this section. We take the utility maximization setup and consider a technology shock, on one hand, and, on the other hand, we consider a setup of market disequilibrium. After the model is presented, we calibrate it in order to discuss the reasonability of the generated business cycles.

The aim is not to reproduce stylized facts in such a systematic way as the RBC setup discussed in appendix, but fundamentally to illustrate how a growth-cycles framework can contain endogenous and exogenous components, being both of them essential for the perpetuation of business fluctuations. The chosen setup has several relevant differences relatively to the benchmark RBC model. First, we will explore an endogenous growth model where the production function is of the AK type (this contrasts with the neoclassical structure of the growth model underlying the RBC framework); as a consequence, we eliminate the labor-leisure choice, making it unfeasible to derive cycles' results relating the labor market. The utility function will be just a simple logarithmic function with a single argument: consumption.

Furthermore, we choose to work with ratios that are expected to be constant in the steady state; this implies that we can look directly to these stationary ratios and no detrending process is adopted. Finally, we consider technology shocks, but differently from what is considered in the appendix to the chapter about the RBC structure, we assume that the deterministic part of the innovation process does not grow in time; this is just a simplifying assumption, in order not to take simultaneously a growth process that is endogenous and intrinsic to the model's dynamics and a further, exogenous, source of long term growth.

To the just described simplified and modified version of the RBC growth framework, we add a mechanism of market disequilibrium, in which demand and output do not have to coincide in every moment, i.e., instantaneous market clearing is absent.

The model explores further the framework proposed in Gomes (2008). Consider a representative agent that maximizes the expected consumption utility from t=0 to an infinite horizon in the future. The agent's objective function is

$$U_0 = E_0 \sum_{t=0}^{+\infty} \left[\beta^t \cdot u(c_t)\right] \tag{1}$$

In equation (1), $\beta \in (0,1)$ corresponds to the intertemporal discount factor and $u(c_t)$ is the instantaneous utility function. Variable $c_t \in \mathbb{R}_+$ respects to real consumption. The consumption variable, as all the subsequent real variables to define, may be understood as a level variable or a per capita variable, since we do not consider population growth.

We adopt the functional form $u(c_t)=\ln(c_t)$; this fulfils the basic requirements of standard utility analysis: the function is continuous and differentiable and marginal utility is positive and diminishing ($u'>0$ and $u''<0$). The considered economy is constrained by a conventional capital accumulation equation,

$$k_{t+1} - k_t = i_t - \delta k_t,\ k_0 \text{ given.} \tag{2}$$

with k_t, $i_t \in \mathbb{R}_+$ the levels of accumulated physical capital and investment, respectively. Parameter $\delta \geq 0$ refers to the rate of capital depreciation. Besides equation (2), the representative consumer's problem is subject to two additional constraints, which introduce the assumption of absence of instantaneous market clearing. The presentation of these two equations is based on the framework of Hallegatte, Ghil, Dumas and Hourcade (2007), who develop an eight dimensional non equilibrium model (they include, in their analysis, besides the goods market, also monetary and labor markets). One of such equations relates to the dynamics of a goods inventory variable, $h_t \in \mathbb{R}$ .This serves to characterize cases of overproduction ($h_t>0$), in which there is an excess supply or a selling lag, and cases of underproduction ($h_t<0$), in which there is excess demand or a delivery lag. The motion of this variable is given by the difference between output ($y_t \in \mathbb{R}_+$) and demand ($d_t \in \mathbb{R}_+$),

$$h_{t+1} - (1+g) \cdot h_t = y_t - d_t,\ h_0 \text{ given.} \tag{3}$$

In the assumed economy, that lacks the role of the government and foreign economic relations, then $d_t=c_t+i_t$. Parameter g is introduced because we choose to work with an endogenous growth framework. In this framework, we may define a market clearing steady state as the state in which $y_t=d_t$. Therefore, parameter g is, according to equation (3), the market clearing steady state rate of growth of the goods inventory. If hypothetically such a steady state was achieved, all real variables (i.e., c_t, i_t, k_t, y_t, d_t, h_t) would grow at the same rate g. Such a result would be obtained in the absence of any disturbance over the model's parameters. Hence, it is an expected result but not the one that will effectively be observed. In this sense, g arises as the expected steady state growth rate of the economy (of its main aggregates). If one preferred to address a neo-classical growth setup instead of an endogenous growth environment, then $g=0$ [as in the referred paper by Hallegatte and co-authors].

The second equation refers to the motion of the price level. This is modelled as a function of the inventories per unit of demand. The intuition is the following: positive inventories are synonymous of overproduction and, thus, if they are in fact positive, prices will tend to fall to re-establish the macroeconomic equilibrium; negative inventories mean underproduction and in this case prices will have to rise in order to create the possibility of recovering equilibrium. The equation is

$$p_{t+1} - p_t = -\theta \cdot p_t \cdot \frac{h_t}{d_t},\ p_0 \text{ given, or } \pi_t = -\theta \cdot \frac{h_t}{d_t}. \tag{4}$$

with $\theta>0$ the degree of sensitivity of changes in inventories over prices; variable $p_t \in \mathbb{R}_+$ corresponds to the price level and $\pi_t \equiv (p_{t+1} - p_t)/p_t$ is the inflation rate.

In order to simplify the analysis, we take the reasonable assumption that monetary authorities are able to keep the price level stable at some inflation target, given the manipulation of the nominal interest rate. As a result, we just assume $\pi_t=\pi^*$, with π^* some positive and close to zero inflation rate level. By assuming that the inflation is a constant positive value, we are saying, according to equation (4), that inventories are always negative, i.e., a situation of underproduction subsists in the economy as long as the central bank chooses to keep inflation above zero.

The inflation rate is also a control variable for the representative agent (this has the capacity to choose the price evolution that best serves the goal of intertemporal utility maximization; after all, it is the private agent, i.e., the interaction between the representative consumer and the representative firm, who selects how prices will change). In practical terms, the optimization of price evolution will not exert any influence on the role of the central bank in controlling inflation, as we shall see when solving the optimal control problem below.

Because we assume an endogenous growth setup, the aggregate production function must exhibit constant marginal returns to physical capital, i.e., $y_t = XA_t k_t$., with X a positive constant (the deterministic part of the technology state) and A_t the random component of the state of technology. As in the RBC models, we assume that the evolution of A_t in time is subject to a Markov process, $\ln A_{t+1} = \rho \cdot \ln A_t + \varepsilon_{t+1}$, with $\rho \in (0,1)$ and $\varepsilon_t \sim iid(0, \sigma^2)$.

The maximization problem one has to solve consists on maximizing (1), given dynamic constraints (2) and (3) and the static relation between inflation, inventories and demand in (4). Considering co-state variables $p_t^y, p_t^h \in \mathbb{R}$ that relate to each one of the state variables y_t and h_t, the current value Hamiltonian function is presented,

$$H(y_t, h_t, c_t, \pi_t, p_t^y, p_t^h) = u(c_t) - \beta p_{t+1}^y \cdot \left[XA_t \cdot \left(\frac{\theta}{\pi_t} \cdot h_t + c_t \right) + \delta y_t \right] + \beta p_{t+1}^h \cdot \left[y_t + \left(g + \frac{\theta}{\pi_t} \right) \cdot h_t \right] \tag{5}$$

The first-order optimality conditions are:

$$H_c = 0 \Rightarrow 1/c_t = XA_t \beta p_{t+1}^y \tag{6}$$

$$H_\pi = 0 \Rightarrow XA_t p_{t+1}^y = p_{t+1}^h \tag{7}$$

$$\beta p_{t+1}^y - p_t^y = -H_y \Rightarrow (1-\delta) \cdot \beta p_{t+1}^y - p_t^y = -\beta p_{t+1}^h \tag{8}$$

$$\beta p_{t+1}^h - p_t^h = -H_h \Rightarrow \left(1 + g + \theta/\pi^*\right) \cdot \beta p_{t+1}^h - p_t^h = XA_t \cdot (\theta/\pi^*) \cdot \beta p_{t+1}^y \tag{9}$$

$$\lim_{t \to +\infty} y_t \beta^t p_t^y = 0 \text{ (transversality condition)} \tag{10}$$

$$\lim_{t \to +\infty} h_t \beta^t p_t^h = 0 \text{ (transversality condition)} \tag{11}$$

Considering (6), (7) and (8), the dynamics of consumption comes,

$$\frac{c_{t+1}-c_t}{c_t}=\beta\cdot(1+XA_t-\delta)-1 \tag{12}$$

Equation (11) reveals that in the absence of disturbances in technology, the growth rate of consumption is constant over time. Defining the steady state as the long run scenario in which the disturbance term is absent, the steady state growth rate of consumption is:

$$g_c=\beta\cdot(1+X-\delta)-1 \tag{13}$$

with A=1 the steady state level of the stochastic part of the technology index. All real variables will grow in the steady state at rate $g=\beta\cdot(1+X-\delta)-1$, in accordance with the previous discussion and the known properties of endogenous growth models.

To proceed with the analysis, let us define the following ratios, which are stationary in the long term, $\varphi_t\equiv h_t/y_t$ and $\psi_t\equiv c_t/y_t$. The following difference equations are derived from the previous dynamic rules,

$$\varphi_{t+1}=\frac{1+\beta\cdot(1+X-\delta)\cdot\varphi_t+\theta\cdot\varphi_t/\pi^*}{1-\delta-XA_t\cdot(\theta\cdot\varphi_t/\pi^*+\psi_t)} \tag{14}$$

$$\psi_{t+1}=\frac{\beta\cdot(1+XA_t-\delta)}{1-\delta-XA_t\cdot(\theta\cdot\varphi_t/\pi^*+\psi_t)}\cdot\psi_t \tag{15}$$

Solving $\overline{\varphi}\equiv\varphi_{t+1}=\varphi_t$ and $\overline{\psi}\equiv\psi_{t+1}=\psi_t$, a unique steady state solution is obtained, $(\overline{\varphi},\overline{\psi})=\left(-\frac{\pi^*}{\theta};\frac{1-\beta}{X}\cdot(1+X-\delta)\right)$.

The steady state growth rates of output and goods inventory can be withdrawn from constraints (2) and (3), $g_y=X\cdot\left(-\frac{\theta}{\pi^*}\cdot\overline{\varphi}-\overline{\psi}\right)-\delta$ and $g_h=1/\overline{\varphi}+\theta/\pi^*+g$. Replacing the found steady state ratios, it is true that both g_y and g_h grow in the steady state at the same rate as consumption, i.e., rate (13). In what concerns the remaining aggregate variables, equation (4) indicates that for a constant inflation rate, the goods inventory – demand ratio is constant, and thus demand effectively grows at the same rate as the goods inventory; in the steady state, g_d, i.e., the growth rate of demand, is identical to growth rate (13). Obviously, if consumption and demand grow at a same rate, investment must grow at exactly that rate. In this way, one confirms that all relevant variables grow at rate (13).

To understand the dynamics of the system, let us linearize it in the neighbourhood of the equilibrium point and present the obtained system in matrix form,

$$\begin{bmatrix} \varphi_{t+1} - \overline{\varphi} \\ \psi_{t+1} - \overline{\psi} \end{bmatrix} = \begin{bmatrix} 1 + \dfrac{\theta / \pi^* - X}{\beta \cdot (1 + X - \delta)} & -\dfrac{A\pi^* / \theta}{\beta \cdot (1 + X - \delta)} \\ \dfrac{1-\beta}{\beta} \cdot \dfrac{\theta}{\pi^*} & \dfrac{1}{\beta} \end{bmatrix} \cdot \begin{bmatrix} \varphi_t - \overline{\varphi} \\ \psi_t - \overline{\psi} \end{bmatrix} \quad (16)$$

Each element of the Jacobian matrix in (16) corresponds to the derivative of each one of equations (14) and (15) relatively to each one of the endogenous variables of the system. These derivatives are, then, evaluated in the expected market clearing steady state.

From the matrix in (16), it is straightforward to obtain its trace and determinant, which are $Tr(J) = \dfrac{1+\beta}{\beta} + \dfrac{\theta / \pi^* - X}{\beta \cdot (1 + X - \delta)}$; $Det(J) = \dfrac{1}{\beta} + \dfrac{\theta / \pi^* - \beta X}{\beta^2 \cdot (1 + X - \delta)}$, and to apply the well known stability conditions for two dimensional discrete time systems:

i) $1 + Tr(J) + Det(J) = 2 \cdot \dfrac{1+\beta}{\beta} + \dfrac{1}{\beta \cdot (1 + X - \delta)} \cdot \left(\dfrac{1+\beta}{\beta} \cdot \dfrac{\theta}{\pi^*} - 2X \right) > 0$;

ii) $1 - Tr(J) + Det(J) = \dfrac{1-\beta}{\beta} \cdot \dfrac{1}{\beta \cdot (1 + X - \delta)} \cdot \dfrac{\theta}{\pi^*} > 0$;

iii) $1 - Det(J) = -\dfrac{1-\beta}{\beta} - \dfrac{\theta / \pi^* - \beta X}{\beta^2 \cdot (1 + X - \delta)} > 0$.

The second condition holds for any positive inflation rate target. Further stability results are revealed once we compute the following relation between trace and determinant: $Det(J) = -\dfrac{1 + \beta X - \delta}{\beta^2 \cdot (1 + X - \delta)} + \dfrac{1}{\beta} \cdot Tr(J)$. This relation is valid only for $Tr(J) > 1 + \dfrac{1-\delta}{\beta \cdot (1 + X - \delta)}$ and $Det(J) > \dfrac{1-\delta}{\beta \cdot (1 + X - \delta)}$, in order to guarantee $\theta / \pi^* > 0$. Because both trace and determinant must be positive, the first stability condition is also automatically satisfied (the corresponding bifurcation line does not cross the first quadrant of the trace-determinant relation). Therefore, stability will hold as long as the third condition is satisfied; this requires $0 < \theta / \pi^* < \beta \cdot [\beta X - (1-\beta) \cdot (1-\delta)]$; if $\theta / \pi^* > \beta \cdot [\beta X - (1-\beta) \cdot (1-\delta)]$, then the system is unstable, i.e., the system does not converge to the long run equilibrium locus. Recall that the equilibrium locus is, in the approached case of expected steady state, a result in which all variables grow at a same constant rate and the goods market clears.

The stability condition may be presented as a monetary policy requirement. Rearranging the above stability result, we can state that the inflation target must be set at a value above a given combination of parameter values, if one wants the economy to converge to such a stable outcome: $\pi^* > \theta / \{\beta \cdot [\beta X - (1-\beta) \cdot (1-\delta)]\}$. Figure 1 presents the eventual location of the system in the trace-determinant diagram; one observes that different values of parameters may either lead to two eigenvalues of the Jacobian matrix inside the unit circle (stability) or to two complex eigenvalues with real parts with modulus higher than unity.

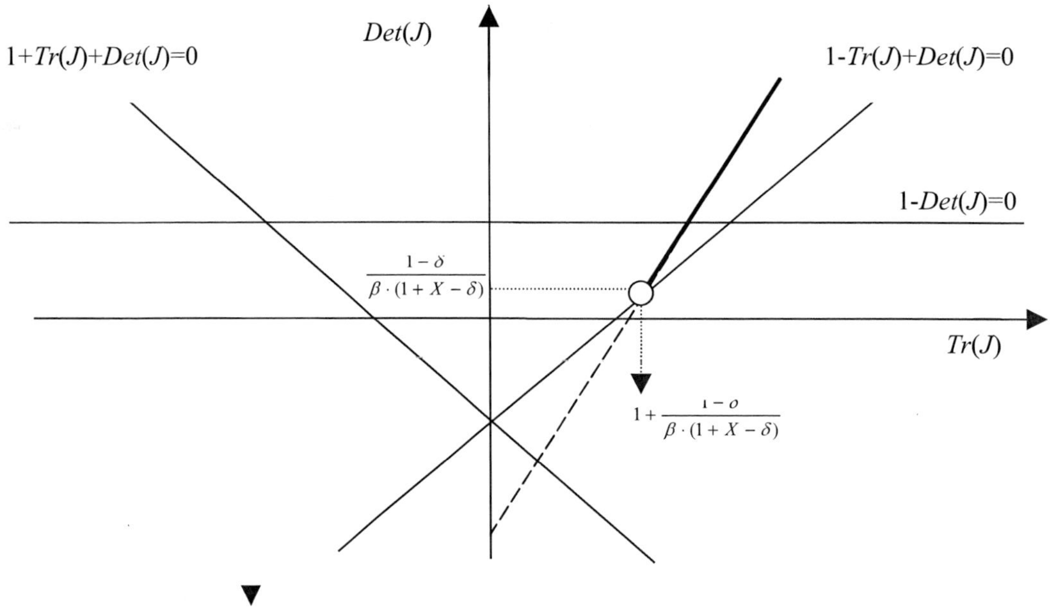

Figure 1. Trace-determinant diagram in the local analysis of the disequilibrium model.

Figure 1 reveals some innovations relatively to the conventional endogenous growth model with instantaneous market clearing. While this latter one typically has a unique possible stability outcome, independently of parameter values (this is a saddle-path stable result), in our non equilibrium model we find two possible outcomes (stability or instability), which will be obtained for different parameter values; it is the relation between the values of the inflation rate, the price sensitivity parameter, the intertemporal discount factor, the capital depreciation rate and the deterministic technology index, that generate a stability or an instability long term outcome. It is this innovation in terms of possible dynamic results in the endogenous growth model that will allow for generating perpetual cycles when one introduces a disturbance term. The logic of the argument we will use is that the introduced shock makes the system to cross repeatedly up and down the line 1-*Det*(*J*)=0 in figure 1, i.e., the system will oscillate between phases of stability and instability, implying a perpetual motion around a fixed point without, however, ever reaching such point or without ever departing infinitely from that point.

In the following section, we address the presence of cycles and their perpetuation in the long run. We will consider an economic scenario in which the deterministic part of the system locates inside the stable area. This will imply that there will exist cycles in the short run and that they tend to disappear as the economy evolves, since the economic system tends to a long term fixed point market clearing result (the dynamic outcome is, in this case, a stable focus). Once we introduce the possibility of technology disturbances over a model's calibration allowing for stability, we are enabling the possibility that in some moments the system will cross to the instability side. Thus, moments of stability and moments of instability will alternate in time, turning it possible that the aggregates true evolution sometimes depart and sometimes approach the underlying growth trend.

6. The Dynamics of Perpetual Cycles – A Numerical Example

The analysis of cyclical motion that is developed in this section involves essentially the observation of how the two considered ratios, the inventories-output ratio and the consumption-output ratio, evolve over time, in the presence of a technology disturbance term. We can also observe how the economy's growth rate behaves and look at the movement of the demand-output ratio (under a stable deterministic outcome this just converges to 1).

The mechanism underlying the perpetuation of cycles is the following: we assume a combination of parameters that allows, in the absence of the disturbance term, for stability (the system will locate inside the inverted triangle in figure 1; this triangle has correspondence on the unit circle). Stability corresponds, in this case, to an oscillating and convergent pattern of evolution that culminates in a long term stable outcome. The existence of shocks implies that for some time moments the system passes to the instability side and, therefore, instead of having fluctuations of decreasing volatility that will fade away in the long run, in some time periods instability provokes an increasing volatility. As a result of this pattern of evolution, cycles tend to be perpetuated in time.

The main idea is that we are combining features relating to both interpretations of the causes of cycles. The fluctuations are endogenous in the sense that they are the result of the intrinsic nature of the relation between aggregates, however these cycles tend to be progressively less accentuated and the long term result is one of fixed point stability. Knowing that the previous result is valid for a combination of parameters allowing for stability, we then add a disturbance term that makes the system to alternate between periods of stability and periods of instability, i.e., periods of cycles of decreasing volatility and periods of increasing volatility. As a result of this pattern of evolution, cycles tend to be perpetuated in time and these remain inside some finite bounds.

For the parameters that are common to the RBC analysis (see appendix), we choose the same values, namely β=0.988, δ=0.025, ρ=0.979. Because we need only a small disturbance to generate cycles, we will work with a small standard deviation value (recall that this relates to the white noise associated with the Markov process that defines the evolution of technology in time): σ=0.001. The price sensitivity parameter in equation (4) is set at θ=0.0007. The level of technology is selected in order to guarantee a steady state growth rate of 1% per quarter (i.e., g=0.01); this level of technology satisfies $g = \beta \cdot (1 + X - \delta) - 1$, that is, X=0.0473. Finally, the inflation rate target must be such that the system is stable. Recalling that $\pi^* > \theta / \{\beta \cdot [\beta X - (1-\beta) \cdot (1-\delta)]\}$, in the present case one must have π^*>0.0202. We should work with a value of inflation slightly above 2%; let π^*=2.3%.

With the previous calibration, we will compare results about the specified ratios in the presence and in the absence of the technology shock. Besides those ratios, we will keep in mind that $\dfrac{d_t}{y_t} = -\dfrac{\theta}{\pi^*} \cdot \varphi_t$ and that the growth rate of output is $g_y = \left(\dfrac{d_t}{y_t} - \psi_t \right) \cdot XA_t - \delta$.

The demand-output ratio will converge, in the absence of the stochastic disturbance, to unity;

that is, market clearing prevails in a deterministic or expected long term scenario. The growth rate will converge to the specified constant value, which in the present case is 1%.

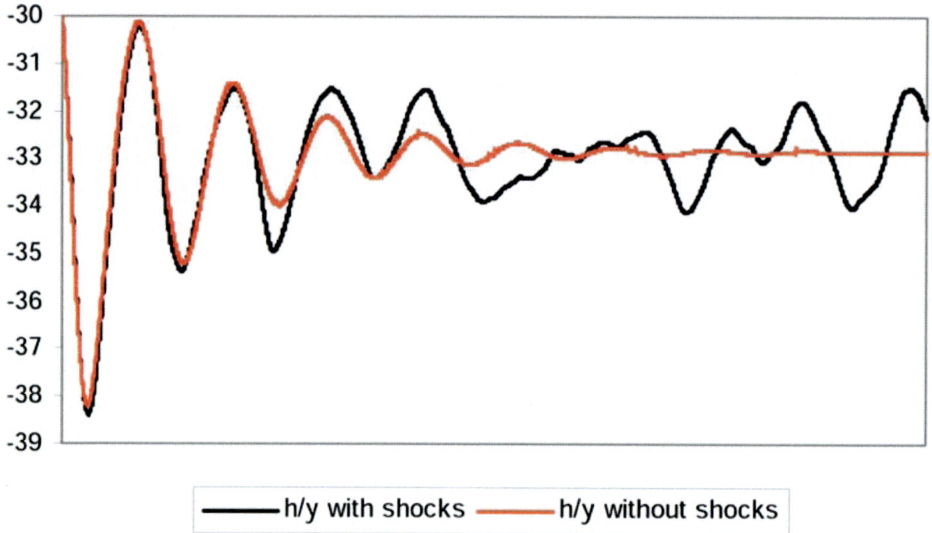

Figure 2. Inventories-output ratio time series in the disequilibrium model.

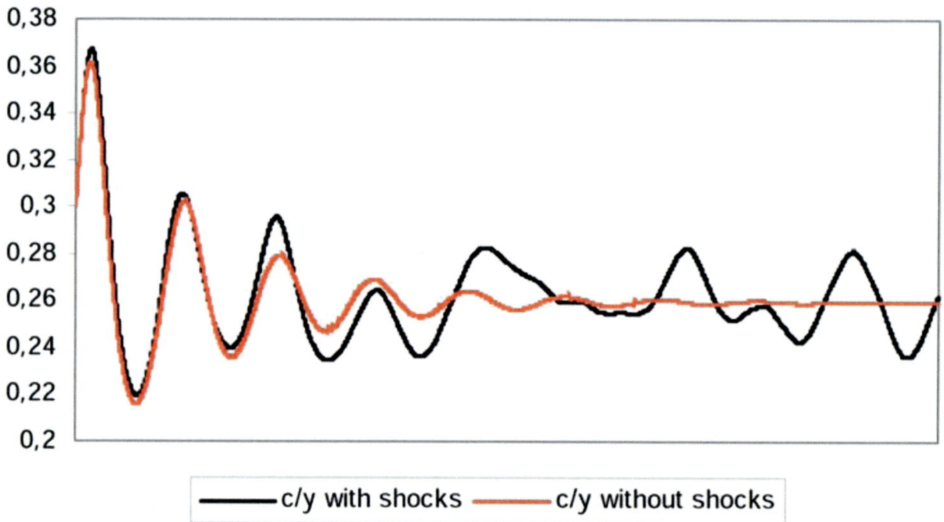

Figure 3. Consumption-output ratio time series in the disequilibrium model.

To perceive the results that one obtains, we undertake essentially a graphical analysis. Figures 2 to 5 represent, respectively, the inventories-output ratio, the consumption-output ratio, the demand-output ratio and the growth rate of output through time, from an initial moment t=0 and considering the following 3,000 observations. Each figure displays simultaneously the time path of each one of the referred entities in the absence of the productivity disturbance and in the presence of such disturbance. We verify that while the non-disturbances time series tend to a constant long run locus, the introduction of the disturbance implies the perpetuation of cycles.

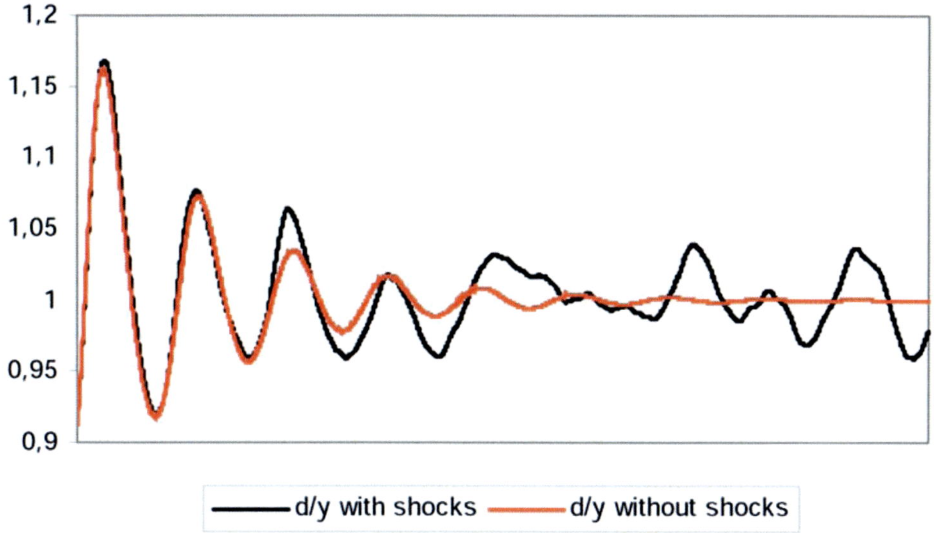

Figure 4. Demand-output ratio time series in the disequilibrium model.

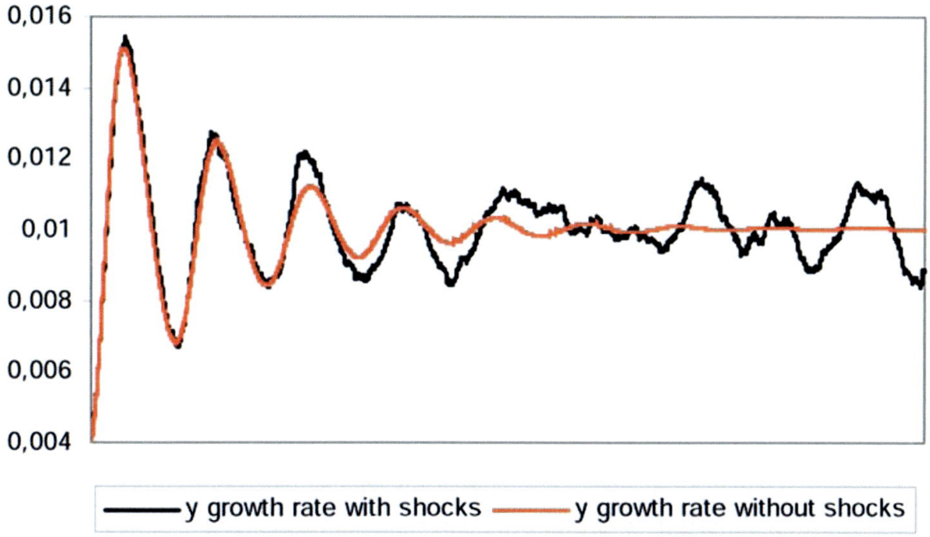

Figure 5. Output growth rate time series in the disequilibrium model.

Notice, in figures 2 to 5, that initially there is an almost perfect coincidence between time paths, i.e., the transitional dynamics behavior is almost identical whether we consider or we do not consider the productivity disturbance. As one proceeds to a long term situation, the convergence of the no shocks series continues, while the perpetual fluctuations of the series involving shocks becomes evident.

Figure 5 reveals that the long run growth rate of the economy oscillates around 1% but will not rest in this value, if technology is subject to a random evolution. Figure 4 gives an important clue about the reason why cycles are perpetuated in this framework; the idea is that technology shocks provoke a permanent market disequilibrium, i.e., output and demand will have different values even in the steady state, and this disequilibrium does not allow to reach a fixed point long term result with the main economic aggregates remaining in constant values. Therefore, we might say that fluctuations arise in a two step mechanism: first, the consideration of a non instantaneous market clearing framework implies that the convergence to an eventual steady state occurs through cyclical motion; second, the introduction of the productivity disturbance leads to an everlasting result of absence of market clearing. The systematic misalignments between output and demand will then mean that none of the assumed ratios will converge to a fixed point steady state.

7. Concluding Remarks

Despite the idiosyncrasies that characterize each country and each time period in what concerns economic performance, a common feature is generically evidenced: all economies are constantly subject to business cycles. Periods of expansion alternate with periods of recession, and such behavior is not only a feature unique to output or income but it is extensible to all the economic aggregates that somehow affect our every day life. Fluctuations in employment, consumption, investment, price level and interest rates introduce uncertainty and penalize individuals when they have to make decisions concerning the future.

To understand why such cycles are persistent and many times almost immune to stabilization policies is a relevant theme of debate that economists are compelled to address. Economists have chosen to focus their attention in two distinct views. In this chapter, such views were confronted. Basically, the discussion about cycles corresponds to a broader debate about how one should understand macroeconomics. Mankiw (2006) surveys the different views on macroeconomic themes, and he is automatically forced to separate macroeconomics into the classical perspective, the one that believes that the general equilibrium market clearing model is able to give all the answers including an almost perfect description of the observed business cycles, and the Keynesian perspective, where market imperfections play a leading role in establishing a set of complex economic relations that involve nonlinearities capable of generating endogenous complicated dynamics.

Therefore, the debate on this chapter is essentially a presentation of distinct arguments to explain the same group of facts. The RBC theory has, on its side, the ability to reproduce extremely well observed fluctuations just by taking an exogenous stochastic process over an otherwise simple and elegant general equilibrium optimal control problem. The endogenous cycles perspective avoids giving to an external element the main role on the explanation of such a relevant economic phenomenon and relies on the view that the economy is a complex system where the interaction among thousands or millions of individual decisions cannot, in principle, produce a well behaved invisible hand outcome; on the contrary, nonlinearities should be found as the direct result of such complexity.

The apologists of the endogenous cycles literature stress that the fundamental mistake that classical economists make relates to the oversimplified way in which the aggregation of individual decisions and actions is taken. It is emphasized that the behavior of a large group of agents is not reducible to the behavior of the average or representative individual and, therefore, it does not matter much if the simulations of equilibrium models are able to generate time series with features similar to the empirical time paths of the economic aggregates; the argument is that it is useless to obtain meaningful results that are the outcome of considering unreasonable assumptions, like the ideas that markets are in every moment in an equilibrium position and that real disturbances are the only admissible cause of fluctuations in the economy.

In an attempt to illustrate a possible way to combine and reconcile both views about fluctuations, we have proposed in section 5 a theoretical structure that combines elements of both perspectives. The model begins by being a classical structure, i.e., we consider an optimal control problem, where a representative agent maximizes the intertemporal utility of consumption. Then, we add an endogenous fluctuations feature by assuming a market disequilibrium mechanism; we avoid considering instantaneous market clearing, and as a result the economy will converge to or diverge from an endogenous growth steady state where the goods market can eventually reach a market clearing outcome. Thus, we have a typical endogenous growth model, where a given constant and positive growth rate is common to the assumed economic variables, but where transitional dynamics are disturbed by the absence of automatic goods market equilibrium.

The framework generates two possible stability outcomes: the underlying system is stable for a relatively high inflation rate, and it is unstable otherwise. Stability is, in this case, a result that implies cycles of decreasing volatility (stable focus) and instability will have correspondence on time paths where cycles of increasing volatility are evidenced (unstable focus). Consequently, the market disequilibrium mechanism generates cycles, and one may assert that fluctuations are endogenously generated. Nevertheless, if no other ingredient is introduced into this logical set of arguments, the long run will just be a state where cycles vanish (stability means convergence to a steady state fixed point result; instability will imply a complete divergence from any long term feasible outcome). The presence of everlasting business cycles, i.e., perpetual motion around the steady state outcome, is then achieved by introducing the external productivity shock given by the technology Markov process. In synthesis, the proposed framework is able to endogenously generate cycles through the assumption of a market inefficiency; however, such cycles only are persistent in time if a systematic real disturbance is able to throw the system in appreciation from the stable area into the unstable area and vice-versa across successive time periods.

Appendix. The Analytics of the RBC Model

a. The Non-Equilibrium Optimal Control Problem

Consider a model economy, where a representative agent maximizes expected intertemporal utility. The arguments of the utility function are two, and these correspond to the control variables of the problem: real consumption, $C_t \in \mathbb{R}_+$, and the share of available time allocated to leisure activities, $1-\ell_t \in (0,1)$. Obviously, $\ell_t \in (0,1)$ is the share of time that the representative agent dedicates to working hours. The lifetime expected utility of the agent in t=0 is given by function U_0,

$$U_0 = E_0 \sum_{t=0}^{+\infty} \left[b^t \cdot u(C_t, 1-\ell_t) \right] \qquad (i)$$

In equation (i), parameter $b \in (0,1)$ corresponds to the discount factor and the expectations operator E_0 is introduced in order to translate the idea that the maximization of utility is conditioned upon the available information at time zero. Notice that an infinite horizon is taken into account, what is reasonable in the sense that discounting turns far away utility levels negligible in the overall utility of the agent. We also assume a constant population level and, therefore, consumption, as defined above (and as all the variables to define below), can be interpreted indistinctly as a level variable or a per capita variable. The instantaneous utility function $u(\cdot):\mathbb{R}_+ \rightarrow \mathbb{R}$ obeys to the conventional properties of utility: it is a continuous, twicely differentiable function, with a positive first order derivative and a negative second derivative in order to each one of the arguments. Thus, marginal utility is positive and diminishing, concerning both consumption and leisure.

The maximization of U_0 is subject to a resource constraint that describes the process of capital accumulation. By definition, the capital stock in moment t+1 corresponds to the capital stock at t, $K_t \in \mathbb{R}_+$, plus investment in t, $I_t \in \mathbb{R}_+$, less a depreciation term, with $\delta \geq 0$ the rate of depreciation:

$$K_{t+1} = K_t + I_t - \delta K_t,\ K_0 \text{ given.} \qquad (ii)$$

Demand is defined, in the assumed economy where the government and foreign trade relations are absent, simply as the sum of consumption and investment, i.e.,

$$D_t = C_t + I_t \qquad (iii)$$

The RBC model assumes that the goods market clears instantly, and therefore demand and output are always balanced. Output is defined in terms of the corresponding neo-classical production function,

$$Y_t = A_t \cdot F(K_t, \ell_t \cdot X_t) \qquad (iv)$$

In expression (iv), one implicitly assumes that the level of population is normalized to 1, so that the labor input is just the share of working hours [this assumption was also implicitly present in utility function (i)]. Variable $A_t \in \mathbb{R}_+$ is a random productivity shock and $X_t \in \mathbb{R}_+$ is the deterministic component of productivity. Productivity is assumed to grow at rate γ-1, such that

$$X_{t+1} = \gamma \cdot X_t,\ X_0 \text{ given}, \gamma > 1 \qquad (v)$$

The productivity shock will be such that ln(A_t) follows an order 1 autoregressive process; in particular, we consider

$$\ln A_{t+1} = \rho \cdot \ln A_t + \varepsilon_{t+1},\ A_0 \text{ given.} \qquad (vi)$$

Parameter ρ is a positive value below unity and ε_t is a white noise stochastic variable: $\varepsilon_t \sim iid(0,\sigma^2)$. Thus, we are just assuming that $\ln(A_t)$ follows a Markov process. The long term expected value of A is 1, because $\ln(A_t)$ converges to zero if one neglects the white noise term.

Production function F: $\mathbb{R}_+ \times \mathbb{R}_+ \rightarrow \mathbb{R}_+$ is a neo-classical production function, i.e., it is a continuous and twicely differentiable function with positive and diminishing marginal returns regarding each one of its arguments. It is also a homogeneous function of degree one.

The various real variables are presentable as variables per productivity unit, i.e., per unit of X_t. This allows to eliminate the growth trend on the analysis of the steady state. Thus, let $c_t \equiv C_t/X_t$, $k_t \equiv K_t/X_t$, $i_t \equiv I_t/X_t$, $y_t \equiv Y_t/X_t$. The expected sequence of utility functions becomes

$$U_0 = E_0 \sum_{t=0}^{+\infty} \left[(b\gamma)^t \cdot u(c_t, 1-\ell_t) \right] \qquad (vii)$$

We will designate the new discount factor by $\beta \equiv b\gamma$ and also consider that $\beta \in (0,1)$.

The state constraint to which the maximization of (*vii*) is subject to is presentable as

$$\gamma \cdot k_{t+1} = y_t - c_t + (1-\delta) \cdot k_t \qquad (viii)$$

The inspection about the presence of cycles in the proposed growth model requires assuming specific functional forms for the utility function in (*vii*) and for the production function (*iv*). Relatively to the utility function, we consider an additively separable increasing and concave function in both arguments, of the form

$$u(c_t, 1-\ell_t) = \ln c_t + \theta \cdot \ln(1-\ell_t) \qquad (ix)$$

with $\theta > 0$ the degree of relevance that the representative agent attributes to leisure relatively to consumption in terms of the utility result.

The production function is a standard Cobb-Douglas production function. Letting $\alpha \in (0,1)$ be the output-capital elasticity, the output-productivity ratio comes

$$y_t = A_t k_t^{\alpha} \ell_t^{1-\alpha} \qquad (x)$$

b. Optimality Conditions and the Steady State

The optimal program [i.e., the maximization of the intertemporal flow of functions (*vii*) subject to the constraint relating capital accumulation] can be solved in order to obtain a dynamic equation regarding the motion of the consumption variable and an expression giving the optimal working hours share as a relation between the other endogenous variables. Remind that c_t and ℓ_t are the control variables of the problem and assume that p_t is the shadow-price of physical capital. The following is the current value Hamiltonian function of the problem:

$$H(k_t, p_t, c_t, \ell_t) = u(c_t, 1-\ell_t) + \frac{\beta}{\gamma} \cdot p_{t+1} \cdot \left[y_t - c_t - (\gamma + \delta - 1) \cdot k_t \right] \qquad (xi)$$

The first-order optimality conditions are:

$$H_c = 0 \Rightarrow c_t^{-1} = \frac{\beta}{\gamma} \cdot p_{t+1} \qquad (xii)$$

$$H_\ell = 0 \Rightarrow \theta \cdot (1-\ell_t)^{-1} = \frac{\beta}{\gamma} \cdot p_{t+1} \cdot (1-\alpha) \cdot A_t k_t^{\alpha} \ell_t^{-\alpha} \qquad (xiii)$$

$$\beta \cdot p_{t+1} - p_t = -H_k \Rightarrow \left[1 + \alpha \cdot A_t k_t^{-(1-\alpha)} \ell_t^{1-\alpha} - \delta \right] \cdot \frac{\beta}{\gamma} \cdot p_{t+1} = p_t \qquad (xiv)$$

$$\lim_{t \to +\infty} k_t \beta^t p_t = 0 \text{ (transversality condition)} \qquad (xv)$$

Resorting to equations (*xii*) and (*xiv*), the optimal motion of consumption will be given by

$$c_{t+1} = \frac{\beta}{\gamma} \cdot c_t \cdot \left[1 + \alpha \cdot A_{t+1} k_{t+1}^{-(1-\alpha)} \ell_{t+1}^{1-\alpha} - \delta \right] \qquad (xvi)$$

Equation (*xiii*) may be rewritten as a static relation between consumption, the labor share, the capital stock and the technology disturbance variable,

$$c_t = \frac{1-\ell_t}{\theta} \cdot (1-\alpha) \cdot A_t k_t^{\alpha} \ell_t^{-\alpha} \qquad (xvii)$$

Having derived the optimality conditions, the optimal plan is defined as the sequences $\{k_t\}_{t=0}^{+\infty}$, $\{c_t\}_{t=0}^{+\infty}$, $\{\ell_t\}_{t=0}^{+\infty}$ that obey directly to conditions (*viii*), (*xvi*) and (*xvii*) and that satisfy also all the other analytical relations that were established (namely, the initial conditions and the transversality condition).

The problem has a unique stationary state. This occurs for A_t=A, with A=1 the expected long term value of the technology shack variable. In this point, the values of the variables of the problem are presentable explicitly.

We begin by addressing inputs' prices. The steady state rental price of capital is $\bar{r} + \delta$, with $\bar{r}$ the steady state real interest rate. The rental price of capital corresponds to the marginal product of capital, i.e., $r_t + \delta = \alpha A_{t+1} k_{t+1}^{-(1-\alpha)} \ell_{t+1}^{1-\alpha}$. From (*xvi*), one withdraws the following steady state result:

$$\bar{r}+\delta=\gamma/\beta-(1-\delta) \tag{xviii}$$

The other input price is the wage rate. The real wage rate corresponds to the marginal product of labor, that is, $w_t=(1-\alpha)\cdot A_t k_t^{\alpha}\ell_t^{-\alpha}$. The long term value is

$$\bar{w}=(1-\alpha)\cdot A^{1/(1-\alpha)}\cdot\left(\frac{\alpha}{\bar{r}+\delta}\right)^{\alpha/(1-\alpha)} \tag{xix}$$

The following ratios are straightforward to compute:

$$\frac{\bar{k}}{\bar{\ell}}=\left(\frac{\alpha A}{\bar{r}+\delta}\right)^{1/(1-\alpha)} \tag{xx}$$

$$\frac{\bar{c}}{\bar{k}}=\frac{\bar{r}+\delta}{\alpha}-(\gamma+\delta-1) \tag{xxi}$$

$$\frac{\bar{c}}{1-\bar{\ell}}=\frac{1-\alpha}{\theta}\cdot A^{1/(1-\alpha)}\cdot\left(\frac{\alpha}{\bar{r}+\delta}\right)^{\alpha/(1-\alpha)} \tag{xxii}$$

Quotients (*xx*) to (*xxii*) allow to find a constant steady state value for consumption,

$$\bar{c}=\frac{A^{1/(1-\alpha)}\cdot\left(\frac{\alpha}{\bar{r}+\delta}\right)^{\alpha/(1-\alpha)}}{\frac{\theta}{1-\alpha}+\frac{\bar{r}+\delta}{(\bar{r}+\delta)-\alpha\cdot(\gamma+\delta-1)}} \tag{xxiii}$$

Other steady state values, namely concerning output and investment, may be displayed in relation to the capital stock value,

$$\bar{y}=\frac{\bar{r}+\delta}{\alpha}\cdot\bar{k} \tag{xxiv}$$

$$\bar{i}=(\gamma+\delta-1)\cdot\bar{k} \tag{xxv}$$

With the analysis of the steady state, one has concluded that the transformed economy (i.e., the economy in which variables are addressed as values per productivity unit) rests, in fact, over a non-growing stationary state. Since variable X_t grows at a constant rate in time, the original economy (all the relevant original variables) will grow at a constant positive rate in time. The only considered variables that do not grow in the steady state are the real interest rate, the labor share and the wage rate. These are the ones not divided by the productivity variable.

c. Transitional Dynamics

To study the characteristics of cycles under the proposed setup, one has to analyze the local properties of the system composed by equations (*viii*), (*vi*) and (*xvi*). This requires the log-linearization of the model around the steady state values previously encountered. Log-linearized consumption corresponds to $\hat{c}_t = \ln(c_t / \overline{c})$; a similar notation is used for all the other variables.

The following relations are directly obtained from the previously presented and derived conditions:

$$\hat{k}_{t+1} = \frac{\overline{r}+\delta}{\alpha\gamma}\cdot\left[\hat{A}_t + \alpha\hat{k}_t + (1-\alpha)\cdot\hat{\ell}_t\right] - \frac{1}{\gamma}\cdot\frac{\overline{c}}{\overline{k}}\cdot\hat{c}_t + \frac{1-\delta}{\gamma}\cdot\hat{k}_t \tag{xxvi}$$

$$\hat{c}_{t+1} = \hat{c}_t + \frac{\beta}{\gamma}\cdot(\overline{r}+\delta)\cdot\left[\hat{A}_{t+1} + (1-\alpha)\cdot(\hat{\ell}_{t+1} - \hat{k}_{t+1})\right] \tag{xxvii}$$

$$\hat{\ell}_t = \frac{1-\overline{\ell}}{\alpha + (1-\alpha)\cdot\overline{\ell}}\cdot\left[\hat{A}_t + \alpha\hat{k}_t - \hat{c}_t\right] \tag{xxviii}$$

$$\hat{y}_t = \hat{A}_t + \alpha\hat{k}_t + (1-\alpha)\cdot\hat{\ell}_t \tag{xxix}$$

$$\hat{w}_t = \hat{A}_t + \alpha\cdot(\hat{k}_t - \hat{\ell}_t) \tag{xxx}$$

$$\hat{r}_t = \frac{\overline{r}+\delta}{\overline{r}}\cdot\left[\hat{A}_{t+1} + (1-\alpha)\cdot(\hat{\ell}_{t+1} - \hat{k}_{t+1})\right] \tag{xxxi}$$

$$\hat{i}_t = \frac{\overline{y}}{\overline{y}-\overline{c}}\cdot\hat{y}_t - \frac{\overline{c}}{\overline{y}-\overline{c}}\cdot\hat{c}_t \tag{xxxii}$$

The variable in which the disturbance terms is involved will have its loglinearized version directly withdrawn from the respective definitions, i.e.,

$$\hat{A}_t = \ln(A_t / A) = \ln(A_t) \text{ (because } A=1) \tag{xxxiii}$$

Basically, one has two dynamic equations, (*xxvi*) and (*xxvii*). These form the conventional system of growth models where one can evaluate the relation between capital accumulation and the path of consumption. This is known to be a saddle-path relation, i.e., a unique stable path exists in the two-dimensional space formed by these two variables. Thus, to evaluate the model's dynamics, one has to assume that the saddle-path is followed. We proceed with the computation of such trajectory.

In this computation, we have to include as endogenous variable the technology. Because the rule of motion of this variable is stable (it converges to the steady state value), we will have a three dimensional system with a two-dimensional stable region. In this way, the stable trajectory may be presented as consumption being a linear function of the other two variables (capital and technology). The three-dimensional system in the steady-state vicinity is

$$\begin{bmatrix} \hat{k}_{t+1} \\ \hat{A}_{t+1} \\ \hat{c}_{t+1} \end{bmatrix} = J \cdot \begin{bmatrix} \hat{k}_{t} \\ \hat{A}_{t} \\ \hat{c}_{t} \end{bmatrix} \qquad (xxxiv)$$

Jacobian matrix J is a 3×3 square matrix, with its elements being given by the derivative of each t+1 variable relatively to each t variable. These elements are:

$$\frac{\partial \hat{k}_{t+1}}{\partial \hat{k}_t} = \frac{\bar{r}+\delta}{\gamma} \cdot \frac{1}{\alpha + (1-\alpha)\cdot \bar{\ell}} + \frac{1-\delta}{\gamma};$$

$$\frac{\partial \hat{k}_{t+1}}{\partial \hat{A}_t} = \frac{\bar{r}+\delta}{\alpha\gamma} \cdot \frac{1}{\alpha + (1-\alpha)\cdot \bar{\ell}};$$

$$\frac{\partial \hat{k}_{t+1}}{\partial \hat{c}_t} = 1 - \frac{\bar{r}+\delta}{\alpha\gamma} \cdot \frac{1}{\alpha + (1-\alpha)\cdot \bar{\ell}} - \frac{1-\delta}{\gamma};$$

$$\frac{\partial \hat{A}_{t+1}}{\partial \hat{k}_t} = \frac{\partial \hat{A}_{t+1}}{\partial \hat{c}_t} = 0; \frac{\partial \hat{A}_{t+1}}{\partial \hat{A}_t} = \rho;$$

$$\frac{\partial \hat{c}_{t+1}}{\partial \hat{k}_t} = \zeta_1\zeta_2 \cdot (1-\alpha)\cdot \bar{\ell} \cdot \frac{\partial \hat{k}_{t+1}}{\partial \hat{k}_t};$$

$$\frac{\partial \hat{c}_{t+1}}{\partial \hat{A}_t} = \zeta_1\zeta_2 \cdot \left[\rho - (1-\alpha)\cdot \bar{\ell} \cdot \frac{\partial \hat{k}_{t+1}}{\partial \hat{A}_t}\right];$$

$$\frac{\partial \hat{c}_{t+1}}{\partial \hat{c}_t} = \zeta_1 \cdot \left[1 - \zeta_2 \cdot (1-\alpha)\cdot \bar{\ell} \cdot \frac{\partial \hat{k}_{t+1}}{\partial \hat{c}_t}\right].$$

Constants ζ_1 and ζ_2 are: $\zeta_1 \equiv \left[1+\frac{(1-\alpha)\cdot(1-\overline{\ell})}{\alpha+(1-\alpha)\cdot\overline{\ell}}\cdot\frac{\beta}{\gamma}\cdot(\overline{r}+\delta)\right]^{-1}$ and $\zeta_2 = \frac{\beta}{\gamma}\cdot(\overline{r}+\delta)\cdot\frac{1}{\alpha+(1-\alpha)\cdot\overline{\ell}}$.

From the Jacobian matrix, one withdraws three eigenvalues by solving the characteristic equation. The obtained values must be: $\lambda_1 = \rho$, $\lambda_2 \in (-1,1)$, $\lambda_3 \notin (-1,1)$. Thus, two eigenvalues lie inside the unit circle. The associated eigenvectors are $p_i = (p_{1i} \quad p_{2i} \quad p_{3i})'$, i=1,2. The stable trajectory will be:

$$\hat{c}_t = (p_{31} \quad p_{32})\cdot\begin{pmatrix} p_{11} & p_{12} \\ p_{21} & p_{22} \end{pmatrix}^{-1}\cdot\begin{bmatrix} \hat{k}_t \\ \hat{A}_t \end{bmatrix} \qquad (xxxv)$$

To address the business cycles properties of the model, we will resort to the dynamic relations (*xxvi*) and (*vi*), and to a group of static relations that includes (*xxxv*) and (*xxviii*), among other relations concerning the economy's aggregates. The analysis of the model requires a calibration (the use of concrete values for the various parameters that are close to the ones measured in practice). After recovering the original variable from the log-linearized series, one has to remove the underlying growth trend of the variables [this is usually done by using the Hodrick-Prescott (HP) filter].[2] The series one will analyze correspond to the percentage difference between the value of the aggregate in logs and the detrended series.

d. Calibration and the Results of the Benchmark RBC Model

In pursuing a numerical analysis of cycles under the established framework, we follow the same set of goals of King and Rebelo (1999), i.e., we are basically concerned with how well the model's simulation results fit the observed data in terms of three fundamental properties of the business cycle: volatility, co-movement and persistence (see section 4 in the body of the chapter). The stylized facts about volatility are well known; having output volatility as our reference, it is widely accepted that in developed countries private consumption tends to be less volatile than output, while investment is more volatile (more precisely, investment is typically three times more volatile than output). Concerning other aggregates, evidence shows that the real wage rate displays low volatility, while total hours worked has almost the same volatility as output. Labor productivity is less volatile than output. These facts about volatility relate to the contemporaneous relation between aggregates.

Concerning co-movement, the evidence reveals that macroeconomic time series are generally pro-cyclical. This is true for almost all variables, except, considering the variables that are relevant in our analysis, the real wage and the capital stock, which are eminently a-

[2] The HP filter add-in used in the computation that follows is a freeware program written by Kurt Annen and available at www.web-reg.de. The calculus of the stationary series using the HP filter requires considering a value for a smoothing parameter. For quarterly data, the value generally considered is 1,600. This is the value we use.

cyclical. Pro-cyclicity is translated on the significant contemporaneous correlation with output.

Finally, cycles are persistent. Analytically, one measures the degree of first-order serial correlation for each one of the time series of macro aggregates and conclude that autocorrelation is close to one. This implies that the evolution of the variables is relatively smooth; there are no sudden jumps from a situation of recession to an expansionary phase.

Our benchmark will be table 1 in King and Rebelo (1999), that we reproduce below. This table presents, for each one of the relevant variables of the analysis the standard deviation, the first-order autocorrelation and the contemporaneous correlation with output, for the American economy in the period 1947-1996. A basic role of the RBC analysis is to compare the properties of the simulated data with the values in table 1.

Table 1. Volatility, persistence and co-movement in business cycles - estimates for the US economy (all variables are measured in logs, except the real interest rate).

	Standard deviation	Relative standard deviation	First-order auto-correlation	Contemporaneous correlation with output
Y_t	1.81	1.00	0.84	1.00
C_t	1.35	0.74	0.80	0.88
I_t	5.30	2.93	0.87	0.80
ℓ_t	1.79	0.99	0.88	0.88
Y_t/ℓ_t	1.02	0.56	0.74	0.55
w_t	0.68	0.38	0.66	0.12
r_t	0.30	0.16	0.60	-0.35
A_t	0.98	0.54	0.74	0.78

To proceed, we need to calibrate the model. Once again, we resort to King and Rebelo (1999, table 2), to consider the following parameter values: γ=1.004, b=0.984, (and, thus, β=$b\gamma$=0.988), θ=3.48, α=0.333, δ=0.025, ρ=0.979, σ=0.0072. By following the procedure previously described, i.e., by assuming the log-linearized variables and by applying the HP filter, we reach a set of time series that reflect the cyclical properties of the various aggregates (More precisely, the aggregates in table 1).

Our results are not exactly equal to the ones in King and Rebelo (1999, table 3), but they are extremely close [the differences are related to how one computes the stable trajectory and, consequently the saddle expression for consumption; in our case, a linearized expression, (*xxxv*), is derived; nevertheless, the small differences tend to work in favour of our results, in the sense that they are closer to the ones in the statistics of table 1]. Table 2 presents our RBC results. The values in brackets correspond to the percentage difference between the obtained values and the ones in the paper by King and Rebelo; with the exception of the interest rate standard deviation and correlation with output, the results are identical or almost identical.

With table 2, one observes that the original RBC model reproduces fairly well the main characteristics of business cycles. As in reality, the model's results show that investment is three times more volatile than output, while consumption is less volatile than output. The results on the volatility of the wage rate and total worked hours also encounter some compatibility with the statistics in table 1. Concerning persistence, the found degree of autocorrelation does not deviate significantly from what real data shows, and, concerning co-movement, we confirm that most time series are strongly correlated with output.

Table 2. Volatility, persistence and comovement in the RBC model.

	Standard deviation	Relative standard deviation	First-order auto-correlation	Contemporaneous correlation with output
Y_t	1.44 (3.60%)	1.00 (0%)	0.75 (4.17%)	1.00 (0%)
C_t	0.63 (3.28%)	0.44 (0%)	0.81 (2.53%)	0.95 (1.06%)
I_t	4.26 (4.16%)	2.95 (0%)	0.74 (4.23%)	0.99 (0%)
ℓ_t	0.70 (4.48%)	0.48 (0%)	0.73 (2.82%)	0.97 (0%)
Y_t/ℓ_t	0.78 (4.00%)	0.54 (0%)	0.78 (2.63%)	0.98 (0%)
w_t	0.78 (4.00%)	0.54 (0%)	0.78 (2.63%)	0.98 (0%)
r_t	0.06 (20.00%)	0.04 (0%)	0.73 (2.82%)	0.62 (-34.74%)
A_t	0.98 (4.26%)	0.68 (0%)	0.75 (4.17%)	1.00 (0%)

Figures *a*1 to *a*3 illustrate graphically these business cycles properties by presenting the detrended time series of the various variables in relation to output. Figure *a*1 relates output with consumption and investment; figure *a*2 relates the output time series with the series of the labor share and output by labor unit; and figure *a*3 performs this comparison with the cyclical components of the wage rate and the interest rate.

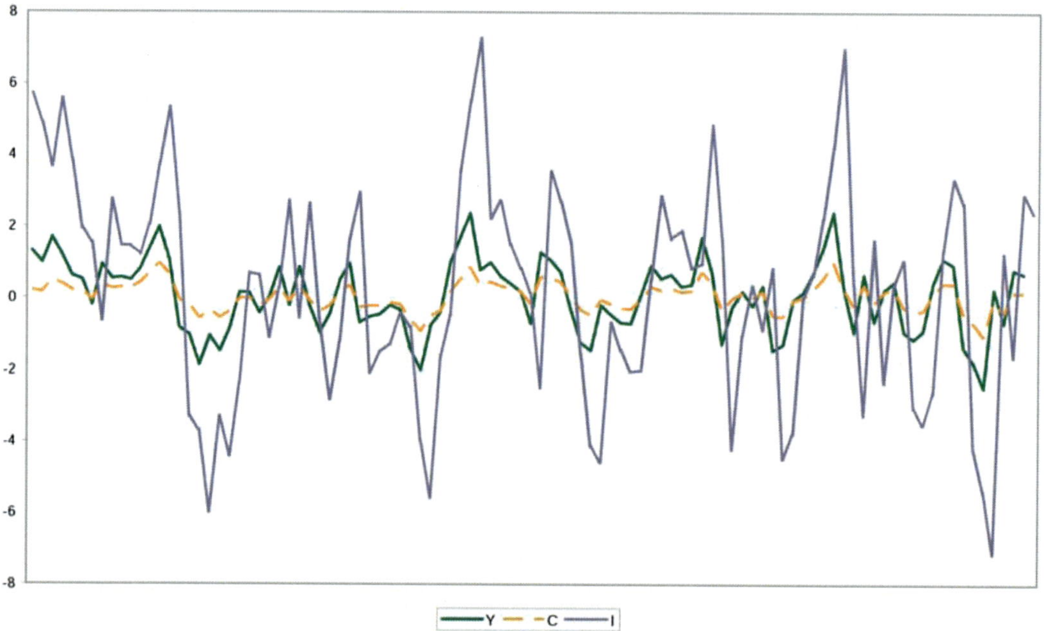

Figure *a*1. Output, consumption and investment detrended time series.

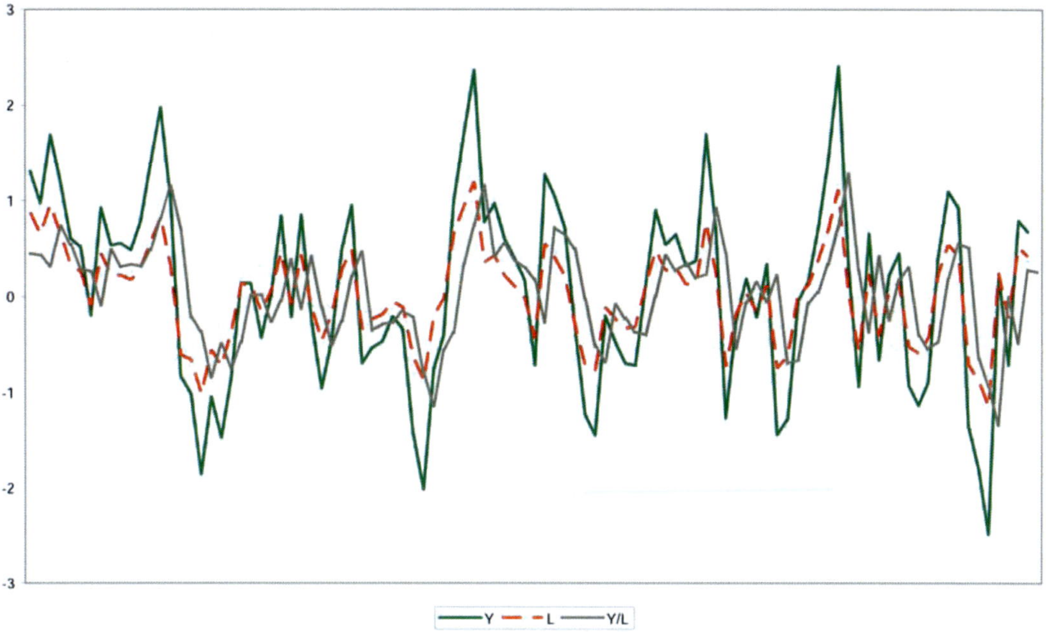

Figure *a*2. Output, labor share and output per labor unit detrended time series.

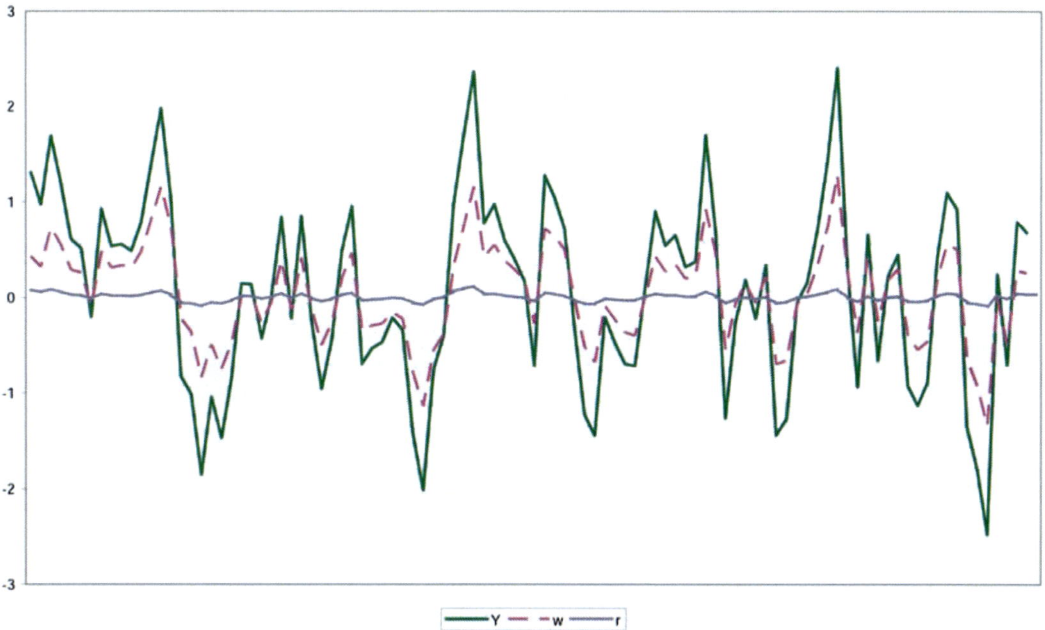

Figure *a*3. Output, wage rate and interest rate detrended time series.

References

[1] Aloi, M.; T. Lloyd-Braga and H. J. Whitta-Jacobsen (2003). "Endogenous Business Cycles and Systematic Stabilization Policy." *International Economic Review*, vol. 44, pp. 895-915.

[2] Aloi, M.; H. D. Dixon and T. Lloyd-Braga (2000). "Endogenous Fluctuations in an Open Economy with Increasing Returns to Scale", *Journal of Economic Dynamics and Control*, vol. 24, pp. 97-125.

[3] Altig, D.; L. J. Chrsitiano, M. Eichenbaum and J. Linde (2005). "Firm-Specific Capital, Nominal Rigidities and the Business Cycle." *NBER working paper* nº 11034.

[4] Ambler, S.; E. Cardia and C. Zimmermann (2004). "International Business Cycles: What are the Facts?" *Journal of Monetary Economics*, vol. 51, pp. 257-276.

[5] Artis, M. J.; Z. G. Kontolemis and D. R. Osborn (1997). "Business Cycles for G7 and European Countries." *Journal of Business*, vol. 70, pp. 249-279.

[6] Asada, T.; C. Chiarella and P. Flaschel (2003). "Keynes-Metzler-Goodwin Model Building: The Closed Economy." *UTS School of Finance and Economics Working Paper* No. 124.

[7] Backus, D. and P. Kehoe (1992). "International Evidence on the Historical Properties of Business Cycles." *American Economic Review*, vol. 82, pp. 864-888.

[8] Baxter, M. (1995). "International Trade and Business Cycles." in G. Grossman and K. Rogoff (eds.) *Handbook of International Economics*, vol. 3, Amsterdam: Elsevier Science Publishers, pp. 1801-1864.

[9] Baxter, M. and R. King (1993). "Fiscal Policy in General Equilibrium." *American Economic Review*, vol. 83, pp. 315-334.

[10] Benhabib, J. and R. H. Day (1981). "Rational Choice and Erratic Behaviour." *Review of Economic Studies*, vol. 48, pp. 459-471.

[11] Bernanke, B.; M. Gertler and S. Gilchrist (1999). "The Financial Accelerator in a Quantitative Business Cycle Framework." in J. Taylor and M. Woodford (eds.), *Handbook of Macroeconomics*, Amsterdam, New York and Oxford: Elsevier Science, North-Holland, pp. 1341-1393.

[12] Boldrin, M.; K. Nishimura; T. Shigoka and M. Yano (2001). "Chaotic Equilibrium Dynamics in Endogenous Growth Models." *Journal of Economic Theory*, vol. 96, pp. 97-132.

[13] Bowden, R. J. and V. L. Martin (1992). "No, Business Cycles are not All Alike: the United States and Australia Compared." *Australian Economic Papers*, vol. 31, pp. 385-398.

[14] Brock, W. A. and C. H. Hommes (1997). "A Rational Route to Randomness." *Econometrica*, vol. 65, pp.1059-1095.

[15] Brock, W. A. and C. H. Hommes (1998). "Heterogeneous Beliefs and Routes to Chaos in a Simple Asset Pricing Model." *Journal of Economic Dynamics and Control*, vol. 22, pp. 1235-1274.

[16] Burnside, C. and M. Eichenbaum (1996). "Factor Hoarding and the Propagation of Business Cycle Shocks." *American Economic Review*, vol. 86, pp. 1154-1174.

[17] Burnside, C.; M. Eichenbaum and S. Rebelo (1993). "Labor Hoarding and the Business Cycle." *Journal of Political Economy*, vol. 101, pp. 245-273.

[18] Calvo, G. (1983). "Staggered Prices in a Utility Maximizing Framework." *Journal of Monetary Economics*, vol. 12, pp. 383-398.
[19] Cazzavillan, G.; T. Lloyd-Braga and P. Pintus (1998). "Multiple Steady-States and Endogenous Fluctuations with Increasing Returns to Scale in Production." *Journal of Economic Theory*, vol. 80, pp. 60-107.
[20] Cazzavillan, G. and P. Pintus (2006). "Endogenous Business Cycles and Dynamic Inefficiency." *University of Venice Economics working paper* n° 37_06.
[21] Chiarella, C. and P. Flaschel (2000). *The Dynamics of Keynesian Monetary Growth: Macro Foundations*. Cambridge, UK: Cambridge University Press.
[22] Chiarella, C.; P. Flaschel and R. Franke (2005). *Foundations for a Disequilibrium Theory of the Business Cycle*. Cambridge, UK: Cambridge University Press.
[23] Christiano, L. J. and S. Harrison (1999). "Chaos, Sunspots and Automatic Stabilizers." *Journal of Monetary Economics*, vol. 44, pp. 3-31.
[24] Christiano, L. J. and M. Eichenbaum (1992). "Current Real-Business-Cycle Theories and Aggregate Labor-Market Fluctuations." *American Economic Review*, vol. 82, pp. 430-450.
[25] Christiano, L. J. and T. J. Fitzgerald (1998). "The Business Cycle: It's Still a Puzzle." *Federal Reserve Bank of Chicago Economic Perspectives*, vol. 22, pp. 56-83.
[26] Christiano, L. J.; M. Eichenbaum and C. Evans (1999). "Monetary Policy Shocks: What Have We Learned and to What End?" in M. Woodford and J. Taylor (eds.), *Handbook of Macroeconomics*, vol. 1A, Amsterdam, New York and Oxford: Elsevier Science, North-Holland, pp. 65-148.
[27] Christiano, L. J.; M. Eichenbaum and C. Evans (2005). "Nominal Rigidities and the Dynamic Effects of a Shock to Monetary Policy." *Journal of Political Economy*, vol. 111, pp. 1-45.
[28] Clarida, R.; J. Gali and M. Gertler (1999). "The Science of Monetary Policy: A New Keynesian Perspective." *Journal of Economic Literature*, vol. 37, pp. 1661-1707.
[29] Coury, T. and Y. Wen (2006). "Global Indeterminacy and Chaos in Standard RBC Models." *University of Oxford and Cornell University working paper*.
[30] Day, R. H. (1982). "Irregular Growth Cycles." *American Economic Review*, vol. 72, pp.406-414.
[31] Deneckere, R. and S. Pelikan (1986). "Competitive Chaos." *Journal of Economic Theory*, vol. 40, pp. 13-25.
[32] Dosi, G.; G. Fagiolo and A. Roventini (2006). "An Evolutionary Model of Endogenous Business Cycles." *Computational Economics*, vol. 27, pp. 3-34.
[33] Ellison, M. and A. Scott (2000). "Sticky Prices and Volatile Output." *Journal of Monetary Economics*, vol. 46, pp. 621-632.
[34] Flaschel, P.; R. Franke and W. Semmler (1997). *Dynamic Macroeconomics: Instability, Fluctuations and Growth in Monetary Economies*. Cambridge, MA: the MIT Press.
[35] Friedman, M. and A. Schwartz (1963). *A Monetary History of the United States, 1867-1960*. Princeton: Princeton University Press.
[36] Gomes, O. (2008). "Endogenous Growth, Price Stability and Market Disequilibria." Forthcoming in the Proceedings of the conference *The Institutional and Social Dynamics of Growth and Distribution* (Lucca, Italy -2007).
[37] Goodwin, R. M. (1951). "The Nonlinear Accelerator and the Persistence of Business Cycles." *Econometrica*, vol. 19, pp. 1-17.

[38] Grandmont, J. M. (1985). "On Endogenous Competitive Business Cycles." *Econometrica*, vol. 53, pp. 995-1045.

[39] Greenwood, J.; Z. Hercowitz and P. Krusell (1997). "Long-Run Implications of Investment-Specific Technological Change." *American Economic Review*, vol. 87, pp. 342-362.

[40] Gregory, A. W.; A. C. Head and J. Raynauld (1997). "Measuring World Business Cycles." *International Economic Review*, vol. 38, pp. 677-701.

[41] Guo, J. T. and S. Harrison (2001). "Tax Policy and Stability in a Model with Sector-Specific Externalities." *Review of Economic Dynamics*, vol. 4, pp. 75-89.

[42] Guo, J. T. and K. J. Lansing (2002). "Fiscal Policy, Increasing Returns and Endogenous Fluctuations." *Macroeconomic Dynamics*, vol. 6, pp. 633-664.

[43] Hallegatte, S. and M. Ghil (2007). "Endogenous Business Cycles and the Economic Response to Exogenous Shocks." Fondazione Enrico Mattei, *nota di lavoro* 20.2007.

[44] Hallegatte, S.; M. Ghil; P. Dumas and J. C. Hourcade (2007). "Business Cycles, Bifurcations and Chaos in a Neo-Classical Model with Investment Dynamics." *Journal of Economic Behavior and Organization*, forthcoming.

[45] Hicks, J. R. (1950). *A Contribution to the Theory of the Trade Cycle*. London: Clarendon Press.

[46] Hommes, C. H. (2006). "Heterogeneous Agent Models in Economics and Finance." in L. Tesfatsion and K. L. Judd (eds.), *Handbook of Computational Economics*, vol. 2, pp. 1109-1186.

[47] Ireland, P. N. (2003). "Endogenous Money or Sticky Prices." *Journal of Monetary Economics*, vol. 50, pp. 1623-1648.

[48] Jaimovich, N. (2004). "Firm Dynamics, Markup Variations and the Business Cycle." *University of California working paper*.

[49] Kaldor, N. (1940). "A Model of the Trade Cycle." *Economic Journal*, vol. 50, pp. 78-92.

[50] Kalecki, M. (1935). "A Macrodynamic Theory of Business Cycles" *Econometrica*, vol. 3, pp. 327-344.

[51] King, R. (1991). "Value and Capital in the Equilibrium Business Cycle Program." in L. McKenzie and S. Zamagni, *Value and Capital Fifty Years Later*, London: MacMillan, pp. 279-309.

[52] King, R. G. and S. Rebelo (1999). "Resuscitating Real Business Cycles." in J. Taylor and M. Woodford (eds.), *Handbook of Macroeconomics*, vol. 1B, pp. 928-1002.

[53] King, R. G.; C. Plosser and S. Rebelo (1988). "Production, Growth and Business Cycles: I. The Basic Neoclassical Model." *Journal of Monetary Economics*, vol. 21, pp. 195-232.

[54] Kirman, A. (2004). "The Structure of Economic Interaction: Individual and Collective Rationality." In P. Bourgine and J. P. Nadal (eds.), *Cognitive Economics: an Interdisciplinary Approach*. Berlin: Springer-Verlag, pp. 293-311.

[55] Kose, M. A.; C. Otrok and C. H. Whiteman (2003). "International Business Cycles: World, Region and Country-Specific Factors." *American Economic Review*, vol. 93, pp. 1216-1239.

[56] Kurz, M. (1994). "On the Structure and Diversity of Rational Beliefs." *Economic Theory*, vol. 4, pp. 877-900.

[57] Kurz, M. (1996). "Symposium: Rational Beliefs and Endogenous Uncertainty." (ed.) *Economic Theory*, vol. 8, pp. 383-553.

[58] Kurz, M. (1997). *Endogenous Economic Fluctuations: Studies in the Theory of Rational Belief*, Studies in Economic Theory, number 6, Berlin and New York: Springer-Verlag.

[59] Kurz, M. and M. Motolese (2001). "Endogenous Uncertainty and Market Volatility." *Economic Theory*, vol. 17, pp. 497-544.

[60] Kurz, M.; H. Jin and M. Motolese (2003). "Endogenous Fluctuations and the Role of Monetary Policy." in Aghion, P.; R. Frydman; J. Stiglitz and M. Woodford (eds.) *Knowledge, Information and Expectations in Modern Macroeconomics* (in honor of E. S. Phelps). Princeton, New Jersey: Princeton University Press. pp. 188-227.

[61] Kurz, M.; H. Jin and M. Motolese (2005). "The Role of Expectations in Economic Fluctuations and the Efficacy of Monetary Policy." *Journal of Economic Dynamics and Control*, vol. 29, pp. 2017-2065.

[62] Kydland, F. and E. C. Prescott (1982). "Time to Build and Aggregate Fluctuations." *Econometrica*, vol. 50, pp. 1345-1370.

[63] Lloyd-Braga, T.; C. Nourry and A. Venditti (2007). "Indeterminacy in Dynamic Models: when Diamond meets Ramsey." *Journal of Economic Theory*, vol. 134, pp. 513-536.

[64] Long, J. B. and C. I. Plosser (1983). "Real Business Cycles." *Journal of Political Economy*, vol. 91, pp. 39-69.

[65] Lucas, R. (1976). "Econometric Policy Evaluation: a Critique." *Carnegie-Rochester Conference Series on Public Policy*, vol. 1, Amsterdam: North-Holland, pp. 19-46.

[66] Mankiw, N. G. (1985). "Small Menu Costs and large Business Cycles: a Macroeconomic Model of Monopoly." *Quarterly Journal of Economics*, vol. 100, pp. 529-537.

[67] Mankiw, N. G. (2006). "The Macroeconomist as Scientist and Engineer." *Journal of Economic Perspectives*, vol. 20, pp. 29-46.

[68] McGrattan, E. (1994). "The Macroeconomic Effect of Distortionary Taxation." *Journal of Monetary Economics*, vol. 33, pp. 573-601.

[69] Mejia-Reyes, P. (2004). "Classical Business Cycles in America: Are National Business Cycles Synchronised?" *International Journal of Applied Econometrics and Quantitative Studies*, vol. 1, pp. 75-102.

[70] Mitra, T.; K. Nishimura and G. Sorger (2006). "Optimal Cycles and Chaos." in R.A. Dana, C. Le Van, T. Mitra and K. Nishimura (eds.), *Handbook on Optimal Growth* 1 *(Discrete Time)*, Berlin, Heidelberg: Springer, pp. 141-169.

[71] Nishimura, K. and M. Yano (1995). "Nonlinear Dynamics and Chaos in Optimal Growth: an Example." *Econometrica*, vol. 63, pp. 981-1001.

[72] Nishimura, K.; T. Shigoka and M. Yano (1998). "Interior Optimal Chaos with Arbitrarily Low Discount Rates." *Japanese Economic Review*, vol. 49, pp. 223-233.

[73] Phelps, E. (1968). "Money Wage Dynamics and Labor Market Equilibrium." *Journal of Political Economy*, vol. 76, pp. 678-711.

[74] Raberto, M.; A. Teglio and S. Cincotti (2006). "A Dynamic General Disequilibrium Model of a Sequential Monetary Production Economy." *Chaos, Solitons and Fractals*, vol. 29, pp. 566-577.

[75] Rebelo, S. (2005). "Real Business Cycle Models: Past, Present and Future." *Scandinavian Journal of Economics*, vol. 107, pp. 217-238.

[76] Romer, D. (1996). *Advanced Macroeconomics*. New York: McGraw-Hill.

[77] Rotemberg, J. and M. Woodford (1996). "Imperfect Competition and the Effect of Energy Price Increases on Economic Activity." *Journal of Money, Credit and Banking*, vol. 28, pp. 549-577.

[78] Samuelson, P. (1939). "Interactions between the Multiplier Analysis and the Principle of Acceleration." *Review of Economics and Statistics*, vol. 21, pp. 75-78.

[79] Samuelson, P. and R. M. Solow (1960). "Analytical Aspects of Anti-Inflation Policy." *American Economic Review*, vol. 50, pp. 177-194.

[80] Sargent, T. J. and N. Wallace (1975). ""Rational" Expectations, the Optimal Monetary Instrument, and the Optimal Money Supply Rule." *Journal of Political Economy*, vol. 83, pp. 241-254.

[81] Schmitt-Grohé, S. (2000). "Endogenous Business Cycles and the Dynamics of Output, Hours, and Consumption." *American Economic Review*, vol. 90, pp. 1136-1159.

[82] Smets, F. and R. Wouters (2003). "An Estimated Dynamic Stochastic General Equilibrium Model of the Euro Area." *Journal of the European Economic Association*, vol. 1, pp. 1123-1175.

[83] Solow, R. M. (1956). "A Contribution to the Theory of Economic Growth." *Quarterly Journal of Economics*, vol.70, nº 1, pp.65-94.

[84] Stutzer, M. J. (1980). "Chaotic Dynamics and Bifurcations in a Macro-Model." *Journal of Economic Dynamics and Control*, vol. 2, pp. 353-376.

[85] Taylor, J. B. (1980). "Aggregate Dynamics and Staggered Contracts." *Journal of Political Economy*, vol. 88, pp. 1-23.

[86] Yun, T. (1996). "Nominal Price Rigidity, Money Supply Endogeneity and Business Cycles." *Journal of Monetary Economics*, vol. 37, pp. 345-370.

In: Recessions: Prospects and Developments
Editors: N.M. Pérez and J.A. Ortega, pp. 45-64
ISBN: 978-1-60456-866-0

Chapter 3

EVALUATING THE POTENTIAL FOR A RECESSION IN 2008*

Marc Labonte
Macroeconomic Policy
Government and Finance Division

Abstract

The U.S. economy has faced some bad news lately. The housing boom has come to an abrupt halt, and housing sales and house building have been falling at double digit rates. Problems in housing markets have spread to financial markets, causing a "liquidity crunch" in August 2007, and calm has not been restored since. Financial institutions have written off large losses because of falling asset values, particularly for mortgage-backed securities. Commodity prices have been rising, and the price of crude oil has recently topped $120 per barrel. While each of these factors might not be enough to cause a recession in isolation, their cumulative effect could be great enough to push the economy into recession. In light of this news, it is perhaps unsurprising that consumer confidence is at a five-year low.

In response to these events, Congress has enacted an economic stimulus package (P.L. 110-185) and the Federal Reserve has aggressively cut interest rates and lent directly to the financial system to spur economic growth. Despite these actions, a recent survey of private sector forecasters put the chance of a recession in 2008 at 60%.

A look at the available data suggests that economic growth has slowed considerably, but it is too soon to tell if the economy has entered a recession. Typically, the NBER does not announce that the economy has entered a recession until the recession is well under way, for good reason. Recessions are defined as prolonged and sustained declines in economic activity, so by definition, a persistent downturn cannot be identified until it has persisted. Any decline in economic activity at this point is only nascent. Growth was slow in the last two quarters for which data are available, but remained positive. During the onset of the liquidity crunch, economic growth was an unusually high 4.9% in the third quarter of 2007. Employment declined slightly in the first four months of 2008. The same forecasters who believe there is a one in two chance of recession also predict that growth will average 1.4% in 2008.

Given the lags between policy changes and their effects on the economy, the economy has not yet felt the full impact of the stimulus package and the Federal Reserve's actions.

---

* This report is excerpted from CRS Report RL34484. Dated May 13, 2008

Introduction

The U.S. economy has faced some bad news lately. The housing boom has come to an abrupt halt, and housing sales and house building have been falling at double digit rates. Problems in housing markets have spread to financial markets, causing a "liquidity crunch" in August 2007, and calm has not been restored since. Commodity prices have been rising, and the price of crude oil has recently topped $120 per barrel. In light of this news, it is perhaps unsurprising that consumer confidence is at a five-year low.[1]

In response to these events, Congress has enacted an economic stimulus package (P.L. 110-185) and the Federal Reserve has aggressively cut interest rates and lent directly to the financial system to spur economic growth. Despite these actions, a recent survey of private sector forecasters put the chance of a recession in 2008 at 60%.[2]

A look at the available data suggests economic growth has slowed considerably, but it is too soon to tell if the economy has entered a recession. Recessions are defined as prolonged and sustained declines in economic activity, and any decline in economic activity at this point is only nascent. Growth was slow in the last two quarters for which data is available, but remained positive.[3] During the onset of the liquidity crunch, economic growth was an unusually high 4.9% in the third quarter of 2007. Employment declined slightly in the first four months of 2008. The same forecasters who believe there is a one in two chance of recession also predict that growth will average 1.4% in 2008.

Given the lags between policy changes and their effects on the economy, the full impact of the economic stimulus package and the Federal Reserve's actions has not yet been felt. This report summarizes the available evidence pointing for and against a recession in the near term.

How Recessions Are Defined

Recessions are officially designated by the National Bureau of Economic Research (NBER), a non-profit research organization.[4] According to popular belief, recessions are periods of two or more consecutive quarters of negative economic growth. While historical recessions have often followed this pattern, it is not the official definition. In fact, the 2001 recession did not follow this pattern — economic growth contracted in the first and third quarters of 2001, but not the second. Rather, the NBER defines a recession as a significant decline in economic activity spread across the economy, lasting more than a few months, normally visible in real GDP, real income, employment, industrial production, and wholesale-retail sales.[5]

Gross domestic product (GDP) data is released quarterly and the latter four measures are available monthly. Since recessions are dated on a monthly basis, GDP data does not offer enough precision for the NBER's purposes. Of the four monthly factors, the NBER places particular emphasis on real personal income excluding transfers and on employment, since both measures reflect activity across the entire economy. The committee places less emphasis on the industrial production and real sales series, which mainly cover the manufacturing and goods-producing sectors of the economy.[6]

Typically, the NBER does not announce that the economy has entered a recession until the recession is well under way — for good reason. By definition, a persistent downturn cannot be identified until it has persisted. For example, the recession which began in March

2001 was not announced by the NBER until November 2001. As it turns out, the NBER later identified November as marking the end of the 2001 recession. Thus, it is possible that at some future date, the NBER could identify the economy as currently experiencing a recession.

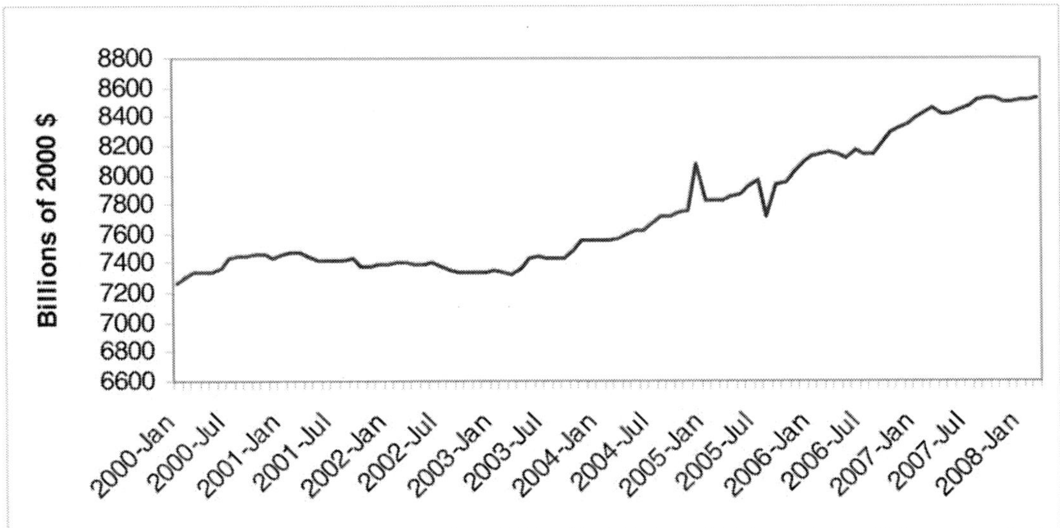

Source: CRS calculations based on data from the Bureau of Economic Activity

Note: Series constructed by subtracting government transfers from personal income and adjusting for inflation by the personal consumption expenditures deflator, as used by the NBER. Monthly data are annualized.

Figure 1. Real Personal Income.

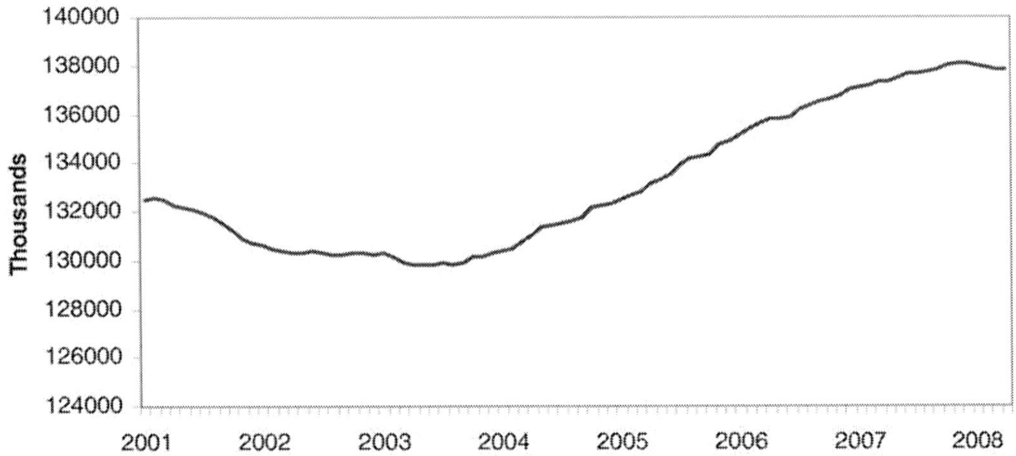

Source: Bureau of Labor Statistics

Note: The figure plots the "payroll" employment series from the Current Employment Statistics, as used by the NBER.

Figure 2. Non-farm Employment.

Figures 1 and 2 show real personal income (less government transfers) and employment, respectively, before, during, and since the 2001 recession. While both figures show a clear and sustained downturn in 2001, neither shows a similar downturn to date. Real personal income has flattened since mid-2007, but has not shown any persistent decline. (It fell, but only modestly, during the 2001 recession.) Employment has declined in the first four months of 2008, but only modestly compared to past recessions.[7] Industrial production has been flat but shown no downward trend since mid-2007. Retail sales fell in February, but rose in January and March 2008. On balance, a recession may have already started, but it is too soon to be sure since data do not exhibit a smooth trend.

What Causes Recessions?

In the long run, economic growth is determined solely by the growth rate of productivity and capital and labor inputs that determine the overall production of goods and services — what is sometimes referred to as the "supply side" of the economy. But in the short run, growth can be influenced by the rate of overall spending, also known as the "demand side" of the economy. The pattern caused by these short-term fluctuations in spending is known as the business cycle. Overall spending includes consumer spending, business spending on capital goods, government spending, and net exports (exports less imports).

Spending and production are equalized by prices. Because prices adjust gradually, spending can temporarily grow faster or slower than the potential growth rate of the supply side of the economy. Recessions are characterized by a situation where spending is not growing fast enough to employ all of the economy's labor and capital resources. Recessions can come to an end because government has used fiscal or monetary policy to boost spending or because spending recovers on its own when prices have gradually adjusted. Then the economy begins a period of expansion. Economic booms eventually give way to "overheating," which is characterized by a situation where spending is growing too fast, and labor, capital, and productivity cannot grow fast enough to keep up. In this scenario, faster economic growth can become "too much of a good thing" because it is unsustainable. Overheating is typified by a rise in inflation — because there is a greater demand for goods than supply of goods, prices begin to rise. Overheating then gives way to recession. While the pattern is predictable, the timing of the pattern is not — some expansions are longer than others.

Although there is no foolproof way to differentiate between changes in growth being caused by cyclical forces and structural forces, movements in the inflation rate offer a good indication. When inflation is rising, growth is probably above its sustainable rate because overall spending is growing too fast, and when inflation is falling, growth is probably below its sustainable rate because overall spending is too sluggish. Inflation is not a perfect indicator of cyclical activity, however, because sudden spikes in the price of specific goods sometimes cause overall inflation to temporarily change. Volatile energy prices are the prime example of when a change in inflation may not be indicative of the stage of the business cycle.

Employment and the Business Cycle

Just as rapid economic growth can be too much of a good thing, so too can rapid increases in employment and decreases in the unemployment rate. As explained above, the economy's potential growth rate is determined by the growth rate of inputs to the production process, such as labor. When employment rises faster (slower) than the labor force grows, the unemployment rate will fall (rise). With enough employment growth, at some point all available labor will be utilized in the production process, and this will happen before the unemployment rate reaches zero. Unemployment never reaches zero because some workers will always be in the process of leaving an old job and finding a new one, and some workers will always be in the wrong place at the wrong time for the skills they have compared to the skills needed for local employment opportunities. The rate of unemployment consistent with employment for all workers who do not fall into these two categories is known as the "natural rate of unemployment" or "full employment" or the "non-accelerating inflation rate of unemployment (NAIRU)."[8]

If overall spending is growing rapidly enough, unemployment can be temporarily pushed below the natural rate. When unemployment is pushed below the natural rate, too many jobs will be chasing too few workers, causing wages to rise faster than productivity. But wages cannot persistently rise faster than productivity because, again, overall spending cannot grow faster than production (assuming labor's share of income remains constant). Wages can temporarily rise faster than productivity, but the result would be rising inflation. In recessions, the process works in reverse. Because spending is insufficient to match potential production, businesses lay off workers. This causes the unemployment rate to rise above the natural rate. As unemployment rises, workers moderate their wage demands in order to find scarce jobs or keep existing jobs. As a result, inflation falls.

What Causes the Business Cycle?

Expectations play an important role in the business cycle, and people's expectations are not always rational. John Maynard Keynes described the cause of the business cycle as "animal spirits," or people's tendency to let emotions, particularly swings from excessive optimism to excessive pessimism, influence their economic actions. For example, businesses make investment decisions based on their projections of future rates of return, which will depend on future sales and so on. These inherently uncertain projections change as current conditions change. If businesses believe economic conditions will be unfavorable in the future, they will not make investments today, reducing the growth rate of GDP from what it otherwise would have been. Likewise, households may postpone purchases of durable goods or housing if economic conditions look unfavorable. People's projections of the future may be overly influenced by the present or recent past.

Even when expectations are rational, expectations can change as unexpected events occur. "Economic shocks" also play a dominant role in the business cycle. A shock refers to any sharp and sudden change in economic circumstances on the demand or supply side of the economy that disrupts the steady flow of economic activity. A well known example is an energy shock: when the price of energy suddenly rises, it disrupts both production, because energy is an important input to the production process, and consumer demand, because energy products account for a sizeable portion of consumer purchases.[9] Other prominent shocks include natural disasters, global events that influence foreign trade, financial market unrest, and so on. A sudden change in expectations that affects consumer or investment spending can also be thought of as a shock to aggregate demand. Since these shocks are typically unpredictable, the business cycle remains unavoidable.

Policy can also play an important role in the timing and shape of the business cycle. The speed at which a recession ends can depend on the amount of monetary and fiscal stimulus. Although overheating may not be directly caused by stimulative policy, sometimes policymakers do not realize the economy is beginning to overheat until it is too late. Expansions often end when, in order to offset the rise in inflation, monetary policy is tightened to reduce overall spending to the point where it is growing at the same pace as overall supply again. In the process of policy-induced deceleration, the economy can easily overshoot and begin to contract. In essence, policymakers trade off a lower rate of economic growth in the short run to achieve a more stable and higher average growth rate over time.

Current Recessionary Pressures

As discussed in the last section, recessions are started by negative economic shocks or the normal boom and bust pattern inherent in the business cycle. Both of these factors may be present currently. The economy has undergone an energy shock in the form of a sudden spike in energy prices. While a boom and bust pattern is only modestly visible in price inflation data, it is starkly present in the housing market. Furthermore, the housing downturn has spilled over into financial markets, and the resulting pullback in credit offers another potential recessionary channel.

Although any one of these factors in isolation might not be powerful enough to cause a recession (depending on their severity), in concert they could. An economy-wide recession would result if spillover effects from the downturn in these three areas caused activity in the rest of the economy to decline as well. In the fourth quarter of 2007, declines in residential investment and inventories dragged down GDP growth, but the other sectors of the economy grew at relatively healthy rates. In the first quarter of 2008, weakness in the economy was more widespread.[10] The following sections will discuss the channels through which these shocks could lead to an economy-wide slowdown for each factor.

Housing Bust

After years of rapid appreciation, national house prices flattened in 2006 and have fallen slightly since.[11] Larger price declines have occurred in several regional markets. There have already been large drops in house sales and residential investment (house building). Since the rise in prices during the preceding housing boom was unusually large, it is difficult to say how deep and long-lasting the housing downturn will be. Given the central role that the housing boom has played in the current economic expansion, many observers fear that a crash in the housing market will lead to an economy-wide recession.[12] They are concerned that the fall in house prices could spill over into a decline in aggregate spending through four channels.

First, builders could respond to lower prices by reducing residential investment, an important component of gross domestic product (GDP). This effect has already been felt, with the rate of residential investment falling by double digits since mid-2006 and reducing overall GDP growth by about one percentage point on average, all else equal. While this drag on growth may persist in coming quarters, most observers agree that it is unlikely to get much larger. This suggests that the drag from the slowdown in house building is too small to cause a recession by itself.

Second, the fall in housing prices could lead to a decline in consumer spending through a negative "wealth effect." Some economists have argued that when house prices were rising, households responded to their greater housing wealth by increasing their consumption spending; were prices to fall, presumably the effect would be reversed. This effect is difficult to measure and faces some theoretical objections. For example, every housing transaction is composed of a buyer and seller. When house prices fall, sellers are made poorer but buyers are made wealthier, in the sense that they are provided an opportunity to devote less of their income to mortgage payments and more to other consumption.

Third, the reset of mortgages to higher payments for many recent buyers has led to a significant increase in the share of households suffering from financial distress, as evidenced by the rise in the mortgage default rate. Resets can occur because borrowers took out adjustable rate mortgages or mortgages with introductory payments that later increase. During the runup in house prices, both types of mortgages increased sharply. For some homeowners, a fall in prices would eliminate the option to refinance to avoid the distress. These homeowners may then be forced to reduce consumption spending in response. A rise in defaults can feed back through and deepen the housing downturn.

Fourth, since mortgages are backed by the value of the underlying house, a fall in prices could feed through to financial sector instability. This channel will be discussed in the next section.

Liquidity Crunch

Since efficient financial intermediation is vital to a healthy economy, if a housing downturn caused widespread harm to the financial sector, the overall economy could suffer.

A change in the value of a house has no direct effect on the value of a loan. But falling prices would be harmful to the financial system if homeowners responded by defaulting on existing loans.[13] For the value of the mortgage to exceed the value of the house, even after prices have fallen, the loan would have to have a high loan-to-value ratio (a loan made fairly recently and probably to a first time homeowner). It should be noted, however, that loan-to-value ratios have risen significantly in the past few years, because homes are being purchased with smaller downpayments and because existing homeowners have borrowed against their equity.

Overall default rates have risen since late 2006 for reasons beyond the traditional causes of unemployment, illness, divorce, and so on. Default rates on subprime loans, which are loans made to borrowers with weak credit profiles, have risen more rapidly. Default rates on all adjustable rate mortgages (prime and subprime) have risen as well, and the problem may worsen in the near future as a significant share of existing mortgages are forecast to adjust to higher interest rates. Falling prices can lead to rising defaults by preventing borrowers from escaping (through refinancing or selling) a mortgage that they cannot afford. Mortgages can either be unaffordable because borrowers could not really afford them in the first place or they can become unaffordable when adjustable mortgages reset to higher payments.[14]

Today, some mortgages are held by depository institutions and some are securitized and sold on the secondary market as mortgage backed securities (MBSs). One rationale for the development of a secondary market was to move non-diversified risk off of bank balance sheets and disperse it throughout financial markets. So far, the increase in default rates has not resulted in any widespread problems for depository institutions. There is a fear, however, that as the mortgages underlying the MBS default, they will be brought back onto the bank's balance sheets, either through guarantees made to MBS investors or structured investment vehicles (SIVs).[15]

Although securitization may have softened the blow of the housing crash for commercial banks, it has caused widespread financial turmoil in secondary markets. Even though subprime MBSs are only a small part of overall financial markets, the repricing of MBSs to reflect the housing downturn has been untidy, leading to bankruptcy for many non-bank mortgage lenders that rely on securitization and for MBS investors. In August 2007, problems with MBSs spilled over into other financial markets, leading to a widespread "liquidity crunch," in which financial intermediation ceased to function smoothly.[16] At this point, it is too soon to tell how quickly financial markets will recover from the liquidity crunch, and if the crunch will have lasting effects on the rest of the economy.

Since the beginning of the liquidity crunch financial institutions, particularly investment banks, have written off large losses as a result of the fall in asset prices. These losses could lead the banks to curtail new lending through a balance sheet effect. When the value of a bank's assets declines, then its capital will also decline if its liabilities remain constant. The bank may then wish to replenish its capital by taking on fewer new loans. If banks make fewer loans, then all bank-financed projects could decline, including business capital investment unrelated to housing. Through this channel, the liquidity crunch could spread to the overall economy.

Energy Shock

Because of the central role energy plays in the functioning of the U.S. economy and its unusual price volatility, changes in energy prices tend to have a greater short-term impact on the economy than changes in the prices of most other goods. Energy "shocks" can have macroeconomic consequences, in terms of higher inflation, higher unemployment, and lower output. Historically, energy price shocks have proven particularly troublesome for the U.S. economy. Sharp spikes in the price of oil have preceded nine of the 10 post-war recessions. But since the current economic expansion began in 2001, energy prices have spiked on several occasions.

Economic theory suggests that economies suffer from recessions due to the presence of "sticky prices." If markets adjusted instantly, then recessions could be avoided: whenever economic conditions changed, price and wage changes would automatically bring the economy back to full employment. In actuality, however, there are menu costs,[17] information costs, uncertainty, and contracts in the U.S. economy that make prices sticky. As a result, adjustment takes time, and unemployment and economic contraction can result in the interim.

When oil prices rise suddenly, it directly raises the energy portion of inflation measures such as the consumer price index (energy prices make up about 9% of the consumer price index.) As a result, the overall inflation rate is temporarily pushed up since other prices do not instantly adjust and fall. If other energy prices rise at the same time, as has often been the case, then the effect on overall inflation will be magnified.

Because energy is an important input in the production process, the price shock raises the cost of production for many industries. Transportation accounts for a majority of oil consumption in the United States, but hydrocarbons are also used for heating and industrial uses, such as the production of plastics. Because other prices do not instantly fall, the overall cost of production rises and producers respond by cutting back production, which causes the contraction in output and employment, all else equal. There may also be adjustment costs to shifting toward less energy intensive methods of production, and these could temporarily have a negative effect on output. Typically, the effect on output occurs over a few quarters.[18]

The effects described thus far can be thought of as occurring on the supply side of the economy. Oil shocks may also affect aggregate demand. When energy prices rise, they involve an income transfer from consumers to producers. Since producers are also consumers, aggregate demand is likely to fall only temporarily as producers adjust their consumption to their now higher incomes. This adjustment is likely to be less or to take longer when the income recipients are foreigners than when they are Americans.

Since the United States is a net importer of oil, the net effect on U.S. aggregate demand depends on how foreign oil producers use their increase in wealth. The adjustment to the wealth transfer from consumer to producer is transmitted through the international balance of payments. How the increase in oil prices affects the current account deficit (a measure that primarily consists of the trade deficit) depends, in turn, on how foreign oil producers decide to use this purchasing power.

If they use it to purchase U.S. goods, then U.S. exports would increase and there would be little effect on the current account deficit. If they use it to purchase U.S. assets — whether corporate stocks, Treasury bonds, or by simply leaving the revenue in a U.S. bank account — then it would represent an inflow of foreign capital to the United States, which would increase the current account deficit. The purchase of U.S. assets would stimulate total demand in the United States through lower interest rates, thereby offsetting the contractionary effects of the larger trade deficit, at least in part and possibly with a lag. Or the foreign oil producers may use their increased wealth to purchase other countries' goods or assets, in which case the adjustment process in the United States could take longer.

A second effect on demand can be expected to occur because the rise in energy prices will probably push up the overall price level because other prices do not fall immediately in the face of a decline in demand. The increase in the price level will reduce the real value of the available amount of money in the hands of buyers, and this reduction in the value of money will also reduce spending. A third effect on demand can occur if the rise in energy prices increases uncertainty and causes buyers to defer purchases. This effect is also likely to be of a short-run nature. The magnitude of all three effects will depend on how much energy prices rise and how long they remain high.

Both the inflation and output effects of energy shocks are temporary: that is, once prices adjust, the economy returns to full employment and its sustainable growth path.[19] This observation yields an important insight: it is not the *level* of energy prices that affects economic growth and inflation, but rather the *change* in energy prices. Thus, if policymakers are concerned about the effect of energy prices on output and inflation, they should focus more on rising energy prices than "high" energy prices, even if the high prices are permanent. The only permanent macroeconomic effect of higher energy prices is their negative effect on the terms of trade. The "terms of trade" is the ratio of export prices to import prices.[20] It means that the United States has to give up more of the goods it produces than previously to obtain a barrel of oil. Permanently higher energy prices lead to a one-time permanent decline in the terms of trade and the standard of living of U.S. consumers, all else equal.

Popular Leading Indicators of Recessions

As discussed below, using policy to avoid a recession requires accurate predictions of where the economy is heading before it has already slowed down. Forecasters are always looking for "leading indicators" — reliable signs of where the economy is headed in the short run. This section focuses on popular leading indicators of recessions. These indicators should not be thought of as the cause of recessions; rather, forecasters attempt to identify predictable patterns within economic data. If the same economic forces that cause a recession first surface in leading indicators, then leading indicators can be watched to spot a recession before it emerges. A measure could also be a leading indicator because it is more readily available than GDP data. GDP data is released quarterly, with a lag of about a month after the quarter has ended, and is subject to significant revisions in later months.

Leading indicators will be successful only if the business cycle features predictable patterns. If every business cycle is unique, then leading indicators based on past experience may have little predictive power going forward. Since the economy is constantly changing and recessions are infrequent, it may be that indicators that were useful a few recessions ago (i.e., a few decades ago) are no longer relevant in today's economy.[21]

The remainder of this section will discuss some of the most famous leading indicators to explain why their predictive power is believed to be high.

Yield Curve Inversion

The yield curve inversion is a well-known recession indicator. A "yield curve" refers to a graph plotting the yield on securities by maturity, from three month to thirty years in the case of U.S. Treasuries. Typically, interest rates are higher on securities with a longer time to maturity. Prior to each of the last six NBER-designated downturns (12/69, 11/73, 01/80, 07/81, 07/90, and 03/01), the yield on all maturities of U.S. Treasury securities fell below the federal funds rate (the rate that the Federal Reserve targets to conduct monetary policy).[22] In the discussion to follow, this will be referred to as an inversion of the yield curve.[23]

It should be noted that the time that elapses between the month the inversion occurs and the subsequent NBER-designated peak in economic activity is not a constant. The number of months prior to the peak that the inversion occurred (and the peak) have been: 20

months/December 1969; 8 months/November 1973; 15 months/January 1980; 9 months/July 1981; 16 months/July 1990; and 9 months/ March 2001.

Although the structure of Treasury interest rates has had a good predictive record, it is not perfect. There have been two economic contractions since the federal funds market was developed in 1954 that were not preceded by an inversion (those beginning in August 1957 and April 1960). In addition, inversions occurred in both June 1966 and August 1998 with no subsequent economic contraction. The 1957, 1960, and 1966 anomalies may be due to the early and limited nature of the federal funds markets and the fact that this rate was not then the main vehicle for carrying out monetary policy. It is now widely accepted that the decline in longer term Treasury yields in the 1998 episode was associated with an international "flight to quality" following the financial crisis in East Asia in the last half of 1997 and the debt default by Russia in the summer of 1998.

Between June 2004 and June 2006, the Federal Reserve executed 17 equal hikes of ¼ percentage point in the federal funds rate, raising the target rate from 1% to a high of 5.25%. The yields on short maturity Treasury securities have risen in harmony with the federal funds target; the yields on longer term Treasuries have not. This has resulted in a flattening of the yield curve. By late July 2006, the yields on all Treasury securities were below the target on federal funds, where they remained until late 2007, when Fed easing brought the federal funds rate below the 30 year Treasury yield.

To understand why a yield curve inversion might precede a recession, it may first be useful to explain why the yield curve is usually upward sloping. Investors are only willing to take on more risk if they receive a higher rate of return. In this case, the greater riskiness of longer term Treasuries comes not from default risk, but from interest-rate risk. The price of a bond fluctuates inversely with changes in interest rates, and bonds with a greater maturity length will change in value more than short-term bonds for a given change in interest rates. Thus, even if investors expected interest rates to be constant over the next five years, a five-year bond would have to offer a higher rate of return than a one-year bond to compensate for interest rate risk in order for investors to be indifferent between the two, and this results in an upward sloping yield curve.

Next, consider what could cause a yield curve inversion. An inversion usually occurs as a result of a rising federal funds rate, which is consistent with a tightening of monetary policy. The Federal Reserve reduces the supply of federal funds, pushing up the federal funds rate. With fewer reserves, banks are forced to reduce loans and sell other assets, leading to a reduction in the growth of money and credit and, ultimately, a reduced rate of total spending. If this reduction is large enough, it can cause an economic contraction.[24] (An additional incentive for banks to contract credit following an inversion is that the rate they must now pay to borrow reserves is above what they can earn using those reserves for the acquisition of very safe assets.) Borrowing for, say, five years could be financed by issuing a five year note or by issuing a one year note and rolling it over into a new note each time it matures. As a result, there is a relationship between interest rates at different maturities. If long-term rates are partly determined by the average of present and future short-term rates, then the yield curve would become inverted if short-term rates today were higher than short-term rates expected in the future. This would occur when the federal funds rate was rising if investors expected it to fall in the future. For example, if they thought that the higher rate was going to reduce GDP growth, they might expect that the Fed would be forced to reduce the target rates in the future to increase GDP growth.

Why is there a time lag between the yield curve inversion and the recession? In this case, the delay is because of the lag between the change in Fed policy and the slowdown in economic activity that a tightening of credit conditions eventually causes. As economists are prone to argue, the time that elapses from a decrease in the growth of money and credit to a decrease in the growth of money spending is not uniform (mainly because economic conditions differ when monetary policy is tightened). It can be both long and of a variable length. This accounts for the variable lag reported above between the month the inversion occurs and the month in which the economy reaches a business cycle peak. With a long and variable lag and cases of "false positives," such as 1998, some skeptics have questioned whether the yield curve is really a useful recession predictor.

Credit Spreads

Forecasters have also focused on the "credit spread" as a business cycle predictor. The credit spread refers to the difference in yield on two assets that have the same characteristics except that one is riskier than the other. Many different assets have been used to measure credit spreads, including the spread between Treasury bills and commercial paper and between highly rated and lower rated bonds.

Credit spreads are seen as a measure of investors' perception and tolerance of risk — when spreads are higher, investors require a higher rate of return to be willing to take on risk. When the economy slows down, more firms fail and investors become more fearful of risk. The financial turmoil that has gripped markets since August 2007 has led to a sharp increase in credit spreads, with Treasury yields falling sharply while other asset yields have risen.[25]

But just as financial market downturns do not always translate into economic downturns, a rise in credit spreads does not always accurately predict a recession. For example, financial turmoil in 1998 led to a sharp rise in credit spreads, but did not result in a recession. Economists Estrella and Mishkin found the commercial paper-Treasury bill spread to be a statistically significant recession predictor only up to two quarters forward, and it did not perform well in out-of-sample forecasts.[26]

Stock Prices

Economic theory states that stock prices are determined by the present discounted value of future earnings. In a recession, corporate earnings would be expected to fall for the market as a whole, and this would reduce stock prices. If the slowdown were anticipated by investors, the fall in prices would happen before the economy began to slow. If the combined wisdom of the marketplace is accurate, stock prices could potentially offer valuable information about the future path of the economy. Even if investors cannot accurately forecast future economic growth, movements in stock prices may provide useful "real time" information about the current economy given that economic data is released with a lag, and recessions are not declared until after the fact.

As discussed in the next section, stock prices are seen as providing useful enough information that they are one of the Conference Board's leading indicators. Moreover, stock prices fell in the months before the 2001 recession. But econometric analysis has mostly found that stock prices do not predict economic growth.[27] One exception is an article by Estrella and Mishkin that found stock prices to be a statistically significant recession predictor up to four quarters forward.[28] Evidence presented by Hamilton and Lin suggests that while recessions and bear markets go hand in hand, recessions have often started before the decline in the stock market.[29]

Index of Leading Indicators

It may be that no single measure can reliably predict a recession, so some forecasters have attempted to evaluate several measures simultaneously. For example, the Conference Board, a private firm, compiles a well-known composite index of leading indicators, and tracks the index on a monthly basis. Its index is composed of the following measures:

1. Average weekly hours, manufacturing
2. Average weekly initial claims for unemployment insurance
3. Manufacturers' new orders, consumer goods and materials
4. Vendor performance, slower deliveries diffusion index
5. Manufacturers' new orders, nondefense capital goods
6. Building permits, new private housing units
7. Stock prices, 500 common stocks
8. Money supply, M2
9. Interest rate spread, 10-year Treasury bonds less federal funds
10. Index of consumer expectations

In recent months, the index has shown a downward trend. The largest drag on the index recently has been building permits, as a result of the housing downturn.

Including so many different measures in an index could lead to a problem of "over-identification," where variables are included that just coincidentally moved in concert with the economy in the past, without any structural relationship. If the past correlation was coincidental, it is unlikely to result in accurate predictions in the future.

Of course, some indicators in the composite may be more important than others. Weekly manufacturing hours and the money stock have the largest shares in the index. The index is supposed to provide predictions about all stages of the business cycle, whereas some indicators may be more useful for predicting a downturn than others. According to forecaster Edward Leamer, the interest rate spread, unemployment claims, and building permits, in that order, are the best predictors of when a recession will start.[30] Filardo shows that while the composite of leading indicators has predicted most past recessions successfully, its usefulness is limited by the fact that the lead time between the prediction and the onset of the recession is highly variable, and the index has at times predicted false positives (i.e., predicted a recession when no recession occurred).[31]

Policy Responses

Just as an economic slowdown is caused by market forces, market adjustment will also cause economic activity to eventually recover on its own. But policymakers may prefer to use stimulative policy to attempt to hasten that adjustment process, in order to avoid, or at least ameliorate, the detrimental effects of cyclical unemployment. By definition, a stimulus proposal can be judged by its effectiveness at boosting total spending in the economy. Total spending includes personal consumption, business investment in plant and equipment, residential investment, net exports (exports less imports), and government spending. Stimulus could be aimed at boosting spending in any of these categories.

Fiscal Stimulus

Fiscal stimulus can take the form of higher government spending (direct spending or transfer payments) or tax reductions, but either way it can boost spending only through a larger budget deficit. A deficit-financed increase in government spending directly boosts spending by borrowing to finance higher government spending or transfer payments to households. A deficit-financed tax cut indirectly boosts spending if the recipient uses the tax cut to increase his spending. If an increase in spending or a tax cut is financed through a decrease in other spending or increase in other taxes, the economy would not be stimulated since the deficit-increasing and deficit-decreasing provisions would cancel each other out.

Since total spending can be boosted only temporarily, stimulus has no long-term benefits, and may have long-term costs. Most notably, the increase in the budget deficit "crowds out" private investment spending because both must be financed out of the same finite pool of national saving, with the greater demand for saving pushing up interest rates.[32] To the extent that private investment is crowded out by a larger deficit, it would reduce the future size of the economy since the economy would operate with a smaller capital stock in the long run. In recent years, the U.S. economy has become highly dependent on foreign capital to finance business investment and budget deficits.[33] Since foreign capital can come to the United States only in the form of a trade deficit, a higher budget deficit could result in a higher trade deficit, in which case the higher trade deficit could dissipate the boost in spending. Indeed, conventional economic theory predicts that fiscal policy has no stimulative effect in an economy with perfectly mobile capital flows.[34] Some economists argue that these costs outweigh the benefits of fiscal stimulus.

The most important determinant of a stimulus' macroeconomic effect is its size. The recently adopted stimulus package (P.L. 110-185) increases the budget deficit by about 1% of gross domestic product (GDP). The major provisions of the package were tax rebates for individuals and investment tax incentives for corporations, which would be expected to boost consumption and capital investment, respectively.[35] In a healthy year, GDP grows about 3%. In the moderate recessions that the U.S. experienced in 1990-1991 and 2001, GDP contracted in some quarters by annualized rates of 0.5% to 3%. (The U.S. economy has not experienced contraction in a full calendar year since 1991.) Thus, a swing from expansion to recession would result in a change in GDP growth equal to at least 3.5 percentage points. A stimulus package of 1% of GDP could be expected to increase total spending by about 1% for the year (with the effect concentrated in the quarters that the stimulus was delivered).[36] To the extent that spending begets new spending, there could be a multiplier effect that makes the total increase in spending larger than the increase in the deficit. Offsetting the multiplier effect, the increase in spending could be neutralized if it results in crowding out of investment spending, a larger trade deficit, or higher inflation. The extent to which the increase in spending would be offset by these three factors depends on how quickly the economy is growing at the time of the stimulus — an increase in the budget deficit would lead to less of an increase in spending if the economy were growing faster.

The effectiveness of the stimulus package in the current environment may also depend on the nature of the slowdown. If the fundamental problem retarding economic growth is a credit crunch, caused by banks' desire to repair their balance sheets, it is unclear how much a general boost to consumer spending and tax incentives for firms to invest can solve the problem.

In judging the need for fiscal stimulus, policymakers might also consider that stimulus is already being delivered, in addition to the stimulus package passed in February, from two other sources. First, the federal budget has *automatic stabilizers* that cause the budget deficit to automatically increase (and thereby stimulate the economy) during a downturn in the absence of policy changes. When the economy slows, spending on entitlement programs such as unemployment compensation benefits automatically increases as program participation rates rise and the growth in tax revenues automatically declines as the recession causes the growth in taxable income to decline. In addition to the stimulus package, the Congressional Budget Office projected in March 2008 that under current policy, the budget deficit would increase by another $42 billion in 2008 compared to 2007.[37]

Second, the Federal Reserve has already delivered a large monetary stimulus. Its actions will be discussed in the next section.

Monetary Policy

The Federal Reserve can use expansionary monetary policy to boost spending in the economy by lowering the overnight interest rate, called the federal funds rate. The Fed alters interest rates by adding or withdrawing reserves from the banking system. Lower interest rates increase interest-sensitive spending, which includes physical investment (i.e., plant and equipment) by firms, residential investment (housing construction), and consumer durable spending (e.g., automobiles and appliances) by households. In addition, lower interest rates would stimulate the economy by reducing the value of the dollar, all else equal, which would lead to higher exports and lower imports. Changes in the federal funds rate lead to changes in spending with a lag.[38]

Beginning in September 2007, before data were publicly available to demonstrate that economic growth had slowed, the Fed began lowering the federal funds rate. Since then it has lowered the rate several times. The Fed has also greatly increased its direct lending to the financial sector, through the discount window and a series of new lending initiatives, including lending to non-depository institutions for the first time. In March 2008, it financed the purchase of $30 billion of assets from the investment bank Bear Stearns to prevent it from filing for bankruptcy. The assistance was unprecedented for its size, nature, and recipient (Bear Stearns was not a member of the Federal Reserve system).[39]

Some critics have argued that financial institutions will be relatively unresponsive to interest rate cuts until they have strengthened their balance sheets. Thus they argue that the Fed's moves are well-intentioned, but will prove ineffective. Others argue that the Fed has neglected the risk that excessive monetary expansion will result in a problem of rising inflation. They argue allowing market forces to adjust would be better for the economy than rate cuts in the long run, even if it deepened the downturn in the short run. Since monetary policy affects the economy with a lag, it is too soon to say whether the Fed or its critics are correct.

Are Recessions Unavoidable?

If recessions are usually caused by declines in aggregate spending, and the government can alter aggregate spending through changes in monetary and fiscal policy, then why is it that the government cannot use policy to prevent recessions from occurring in the first place? While recessions should theoretically be avoidable, there are several real world problems that keep stabilization from working with perfect efficiency in practice.

First, many of the economic shocks that cause recessions are unforeseeable. By the time policymakers can react to the shocks, it may be too late to avoid a recession. As their name suggests, economic shocks tend to be sudden and unexpected. Few energy analysts predicted that the price of oil would rise from less than $20 per barrel in 2001 to about six times as high today; if the rise in price could not be predicted, then neither could its effects on the economy.

Second, there is a time lag between a change to monetary or fiscal policy and its effect on the economy because individual behavior adjusts to interest rate or tax changes slowly. It will take time for firms to boost investment in response to lower interest rates and the tax incentives included in the stimulus package. Also, although the stimulus bill became law in February 2008, consumers did not begin receiving their "rebate" checks until May. Because of lags, an optimal policy would need to be able to respond to a change in economic conditions before it occurred. For example, if the economy were going to fall below full employment next year, policy would need to be changed this year to prevent it.

Third, for stabilization policy to be effective given lags, policymakers must have accurate economic forecasts. Yet even short-term economic forecasting —particularly in the case of turning points in the business cycle — is notoriously inaccurate. In January 2001, the Congressional Budget Office, the Office of Management and Budget, the Federal Reserve, and virtually all major private forecasts predicted growth between 2.0% and 3.1% for the year.[40] In reality, the economy entered a recession two months later, and grew by 0.8% for the year. Given the important role of unpredictable shocks in the business cycle, perhaps this should not be a surprise.

Fourth, since forecasts are not always accurate, our understanding of the economy is limited, and the economy does not always respond to policy changes as expected, policy changes do not always prove to be optimal in hindsight. For example, if the natural rate of unemployment (NAIRU) rises and policymakers do not realize it, they may think that expansionary policy is needed to reduce unemployment. Economists believe that this is one reason inflation rose in the 1970s.

Fifth, in the case of monetary policy, changes in short-term interest rates do not lead to one-for-one changes in long-term interest rates. Long-term interest rates are determined by supply and demand, and many factors enter that equation besides short-term interest rates. Yet many types of spending may be more sensitive to long-term rates, reducing monetary policy's effectiveness. One reason the housing boom continued after 2004 was that mortgage rates increased far less than the federal funds rate.

Sixth, since policy changes do not lead to large and rapid changes in economic activity for the reasons listed above, it may take extremely large policy changes to forestall a recession. Yet policy changes of that magnitude could be destabilizing in their own right. Extremely large swings in interest rates could impede the smooth functioning of the financial system and lead to large swings in the value of the dollar. Large increases in the budget deficit could hamper the government's future budgetary flexibility. Uncertainty is an argument in favor of more modest policy changes.

Finally, policy's influence on the economy is blunted by the open nature of the U.S. economy in an era of increasing globalization. As discussed above, the expansionary effects of increases in the budget deficit have been largely offset by increases in the trade deficit in recent years. Likewise, the contractionary effects of higher short-term interest rates have not led to significantly higher long-term rates because of the ready supply of foreign capital. Nevertheless, higher short-term interest rates would still have a contractionary effect on the economy through the larger trade deficit that accompanies foreign capital inflows. But if foreign capital flows kept long-term interest rates (such as mortgage rates) from rising in response to contractionary monetary policy, capital mobility may have rendered monetary policy unable to effectively counteract the housing bubble. An open economy is also one that is more influenced by developments abroad — as the economy's openness has increased over time, foreign economic shocks (positive or negative) have had a larger effect on the United States, and domestic events, including policy changes, have had a smaller effect.

References

[1] Conference Board, "The Conference Board Consumer Confidence Index Declines Almost 12 Points," press release, March 25, 2008.

[2] Blue Chip, *Economic Indicators*, vol. 33, no. 5, May 2008.

[3] It is noteworthy that final sales declined in the first quarter of 2008. In other words, GDP growth was positive only because firms added to inventories.

[4] For more information, see CRS Report RS22793, *What is a Recession, Who Decides When It Starts, and When Do They Decide?*, by Brian W. Cashell.

[5] National Bureau of Economic Research, "The NBER's Business Cycle Dating Procedure," Oct 21, 2003, p. 2.

[6] Ibid.

[7] There are two major official employment series kept by the Bureau of Labor Statistics, the Current Employment Series (known as the "payroll" series) and the Current Population Series (known as the "household" series). The NBER, and most economists, favor the payroll series because it has a larger and more robust sample. For that reason, the payroll series is discussed in the main text and shown in **Figure 2**. In 2008, the two series have moved together. The unemployment rate is calculated from the household series, and has also shown a slight deterioration in the second half of 2007.

[8] For more information, see CRS Report RL30391, *Inflation and Unemployment: What Is the Connection?*, by Brian Cashell.

[9] For more information, see CRS Report RL31608, *The Effects of Oil Shocks on the Economy: A Review of the Empirical Evidence*, by Marc Labonte.

[10] Output data by industry are released with a considerable lag. The most recent industry data available show that 80% of the slowdown in growth in 2007 was caused by a decline in output in the financial sector and construction, and a slowdown in growth in real estate/rental housing and mining. While growth slowed somewhat across many industries, these data suggest that problems in housing and the financial sector were still mostly contained in those industries in 2007. Source: Bureau of Economic Analysis, "Advance GDP-by-Industry Statistics," press release BEA 08-17, April 29, 2008.

[11] Based on government data from the Office of Federal Housing Oversight for resales of owner-occupied homes with conforming mortgages. Private sector data sources show a sharper decline in house prices.

[12] For in-depth analysis, see CRS Report RL34244, *Would a Housing Crash Cause a Recession?*, by Marc Labonte.

[13] Lower housing sales would require financial institutions to shift some of their activity from mortgage lending to other types of lending or investments. While this would not necessarily affect the overall profitability of the financial sector, some institutions might find the shift in lending difficult, particularly if they are small and heavily reliant on mortgage lending.

[14] For information on mortgage resets, see CRS Report RL33775, *Alternative Mortgages*, by Edward Murphy.

[15] SIVs are off-balance sheet entities established (but not owned) by commercial banks. An SIV finances the purchase of long-term MBS by selling short-term notes and commercial paper. The spread between the long- and short-term rates is profit. For the concept to work, the SIV must be able to borrow cheaply — a triple-A rating is a basic requirement. To secure that rating, the SIV generally agrees to maintain certain levels of collateral and the sponsoring banks often commit themselves to providing lines of credit if the SIV becomes unable to raise funds in the market.

[16] See CRS Report RL34182, *Financial Crisis? The Liquidity Crunch of August 2007*, by Darryl Getter, Mark Jickling, Marc Labonte, and Edward Murphy.

[17] Products with high "menu costs" are those which are costly to re-price, and therefore have sticky prices. Restaurant menus, periodicals, and catalog items are examples of products with high menu costs.

[18] If rising energy prices affect the economy through this transmission mechanism, then falling energy prices should have the opposite effect on the economy: they should temporarily lower inflation and raise output, all else equal.

[19] This point is not always explicitly made in the time series analyses reviewed below, which tend to end their estimates at the last time lag that yields statistically significant results or arbitrarily cut off the estimates after a few lags to meet a statistical criterion concerning the limit on the number of variables allowed.

[20] See CRS Report RL32591, *U.S. Terms of Trade: Significance, Trends, and Policy*, by Craig K. Elwell.

[21] A further objection to leading indicators is that they fall foul of the "Lucas critique." Economist Robert Lucas argued that one cannot assume that past relationships between

economic variables will remain stable in the future because economic actors learn about past relationships and adjust their behavior accordingly. For example, once there is a consensus that a specific economic variable is a leading indicator of a recession, economic actors are likely to react to changes in that indicator in a way that they did not previously.

[22] For analytical purposes, only the yields on U.S. Treasury securities are used in order to hold the risk factor constant. The yield on private sector securities can vary across time because investors change their evaluation of their riskiness. Unlike private sector securities, Treasury securities have virtually zero default risk.

[23] In this report, inversion does not necessarily mean that the yield on all shorter term Treasury securities was above those on longer term debt. It only means that the federal funds rate was above the yield on all marketable Treasury securities.

[24] A rising federal funds rate is also consistent with an increased demand for those funds, the sign of a vigorous economic expansion. By letting the rate rise, the Fed may also be tightening money and credit growth relative to what would be the case if it had held the rate constant. However, this tightening will be less than would be the case if it actually reduced the supply of those funds.

[25] Stock and Watson found that the commercial paper-U.S. Treasury spread did not predict the 2001 recession, but the junk bond yield spread did. James Stock and Mark Watson, "How Did the Leading Indicator Forecasts Perform During the 2001 Recession?", Federal Reserve Bank of Richmond, *Economic Quarterly*, vol. 89, no. 3, Summer 2003.

[26] Arturo Estrella and Frederic Mishkin, "Predicting U.S. Recessions: Financial Variables as Leading Indicators," National Bureau of Economic Research, working paper 5379, December 1995. A test of the usefulness of an indicator is whether the relationship fitted to past data holds for future ("out of sample") data.

[27] For a review, see James Stock and Mark Watson, "Forecasting Output and Inflation: The Role of Asset Prices," *Journal of Economic Literature*, vol. XLI, no. 3, September 2003.

[28] Arturo Estrella and Frederic Mishkin, "Predicting U.S. Recessions: Financial Variables as Leading Indicators," National Bureau of Economic Research, working paper 5379, December 1995.

[29] James Hamilton and Gang Lin, "Stock Market Volatility and the Business Cycle," *Journal of Econometric Forecasting*, v. 11, no. 5, September 1996, p. 573.

[30] Edward Leamer, "Is a Recession Ahead? The Models Say Yes, but the Mind Says No," *Economists' Voice*, January 2007. According to a model based on those three measures, there was a 100% chance of recession in the next twelve months from October 2006 to the article's publication in January 2007.

[31] Andrew Filardo, "How Reliable Are Recession Prediction Models?", Federal Reserve Bank of Kansas City, *Economic Review*, vol. 84, no. 2, 1999:Q2, p. 35.

[32] Crowding out is likely to be less of a concern if the economy enters a recession since recessions are typically characterized by falling business investment.

[33] If foreign borrowing prevents crowding out, the future size of the economy will not decrease but capital income will accrue to foreigners instead of Americans.

[34] For more information, see CRS Report RS21409, *The Budget Deficit and the Trade Deficit: What Is Their Relationship?*, by Marc Labonte and Gail E. Makinen.

[35] For details of the stimulus package, see CRS Report RL34349, *Economic Slowdown: Issues and Policies*, by Jane G. Gravelle, Thomas L. Hungerford, Marc Labonte, N. Eric Weiss, and Julie M. Whittaker.

[36] See, for example, "Options for Responding to Short-term Economic Weakness," Testimony of CBO Director Peter Orszag before the Committee on Finance, January 22, 2008.

[37] Note also that, in January 2008, CBO estimated that if supplemental military spending to maintain current troop levels overseas and an alternative minimum tax patch are enacted, and expiring tax provisions are extended, the 2008 deficit could increase by another $42 billion compared to 2007.

[38] For more information, see CRS Report RL30354, *Monetary Policy and the Federal Reserve*, by Marc Labonte and Gail E. Makinen.

[39] For more information, see CRS Report RL34427, *Financial Turmoil: Federal Reserve Policy Responses*, by Marc Labonte.

[40] Blue Chip, *Economic Indicators*, January 2001.

In: Recessions: Prospects and Developments
Editors: N.M. Prez and J.A. Ortega, pp. 65-97
ISBN 978-1-60456-866-0

Chapter 4

The Recessionary Impact of Stabilizing Inflation

*Federico Ravenna**
Department of Economics, University of California,
Santa Cruz, CA 95064

Abstract

Efforts to reduce the inflation volatility caused by inflationary shocks have been accompanied in many countries by higher output gap volatility and prolonged recessions. The empirical relationship known as the Phillips curve summarizes the trade-off between stabilizing inflation and stabilizing the output gap faced by the monetary authority. If the Phillips curve is not a structural feature of the economy, but only a reduced-form relationship, the policymaker can in principle influence the recessionary impact of inflation stabilization. This chapter examines the impact of the Canadian inflation targeting policy adopted in 1991 on the inflation-output gap trade-off, and the role it played in the ensuing recession. We document that the empirical relationship between the output gap and the inflation rate in Canada changed after the shift to the inflation targeting regime, and show that the shift in the inflation process and in the inflation-output trade-off can be explained as the result of the inflation targeting monetary policy. Using a sticky price-sticky wage model and data on output, inflation, exchange and interest rates, we build the historical series of exogenous shocks that affected the economy since 1991, and compare the Phillips curve relationship and inflation's time series properties under the inflation targeting regime with its counterfactual under the previous monetary policy. The results show that: (i) the shifts in the inflation dynamics and inflation-output gap trade-off since 1991 would not have happened under the pre-1991 monetary policy; (ii) the disinflation in the early 1990s occurred at the cost of a significant output loss. Therefore, while inflation targeting allowed the policymaker to lower the recessionary impact of inflation stabilization on average, conditional on the vector of shocks that affected the economy it was among the causes of the 1992-1994 recession.

*E-mail address: fravenna@ucsc.edu

1. Introduction

It is the experience of monetary policymakers worldwide that efforts to lower inflation volatility come at a cost in terms of output gap volatility. As a consequence, the severity of recessions - defined in this chapter as periods when output is below potential output - increases the more aggressively policymakers respond to inflationary shocks.

The trade-off faced by the monetary authority between stabilizing inflation and stabilizing the output gap is summarized by the Phillips curve. The Phillips curve provides an estimate of the potential output loss necessary to bring inflation down to the desired monetary authority's target whenever inflation overshoots this set goal. An optimizing policymaker would desire a better inflation-output gap trade-off. The advantage of a flatter Phillips curve is smaller output gap volatility for given inflation volatility - also implying, on average, that milder recessions are needed to keep inflation from overshooting the target over the course of the business cycle.

Traditionally, economics names as 'Phillips curve' the empirical relationship between inflation, output gap, and lags of inflation. This relationship is often referred to as the 'accelerationist' or 'backward-looking' Phillips curve. Macroeconomists are divided over its interpretation - and have been in disagreement for over 25 years. Part of the literature regards it as a structural feature of the economy, therefore representing a given, unchangeable constraint for the policymaker (Fischer, 1977, Taylor, 1979, Rudd and Whelan, 2005). Many researchers, and policymakers, consider instead the backward-looking Phillips curve (and the persistence it implies in inflation dynamics) as simply a reduced-form, statistical relationship (Lucas and Sargent, 1978, Gali and Gertler, 1999).

If this were the case, the policymaker could in principle influence the recessionary impact of inflation stabilization. A large portion of monetary policy decisions represents the monetary authority's systematic reaction to the (current or forecasted) state of the economy. Moreover, the private sector holds expectations about the behaviour of the monetary authority in response to shocks, and takes these expectations into account when deciding the optimal plan. Therefore the inflation - output gap trade-off and the inflation persistence *as measured ex-post* by a reduced-form, backward-looking Phillips curve will change when the monetary authority modifies its behaviour.

To examine the issue, this chapter discusses the impact of the Canadian inflation targeting policy adopted in 1991 on the inflation - output gap trade-off, and the role it played in the following recession over the 1992-1994 period.

I first document that the empirical relationship between the output gap and the inflation rate in Canada changed after the shift to the inflation targeting regime. At the same time, the inflation dynamics changed from a near-unit root to a stationary regime. I then show that the shift in the inflation process and in the inflation - output gap trade-off can be explained as the result of the inflation targeting monetary policy, and argue that inflation persistence and the backward-looking Phillips curve are not structural features of the Canadian economy, but simply useful reduced-form regularities contingent on the monetary policy regime[1].

The approach I take in this chapter is to build from the data a counterfactual history of the Canadian economy since the adoption of inflation targeting, consistent with a structural

[1]There is a vast literature on the impact of inflation targeting policies. For cross-country evidence see Bernanke et al. (1999), Ball and Sheridan (2005), Levin, Natalucci and Piger (2004).

stochastic general equilibrium model of the economy. In this way I can simulate how the economy would have behaved under an alternative monetary policy. This approach is akin to the business cycle accounting methodology in Chari, Kehoe, McGrattan (2006). I build a quarterly model of the Canadian economy where staggered wage and price adjustment implies a trade-off between inflation and output gap. I use data on output, inflation, exchange and interest rates to back out the historical series of exogenous shocks that affected the Canadian economy since the adoption of inflation targeting, conditional on the model being an accurate description of the economy. I then compare the Phillips curve relationship and inflation's time series properties under the monetary policy that was actually implemented with its counterfactual under alternative monetary policies, assuming the economy is buffeted by the same shocks as the Canadian economy in the sample period.

The estimates show that the inflation targeting regime was responsible for changing the Canadian inflation process from a near random walk to a stationary process, and accounted for a structural break in the output gap-inflation trade-off as measured by a backward-looking Phillips curve equation. The chapter also shows that the disinflation in the early 1990s occurred at the cost of a significant output loss. Therefore, while inflation targeting allowed the policymaker to lower the recessionary impact of inflation stabilization on average, conditional on the vector of shocks that affected the economy it was among the causes of the 1992-1994 recession.

Section 2 provides empirical evidence of shifts in the Canadian Phillips curve and inflation process after the introduction of the inflation targeting regime. Section 3 builds a model of the Canadian economy. Section 4 describes the method used to evaluate the effect of shifts in the monetary policy rule using the structural model and data on the Canadian economy. In section 5 I build counterfactual histories to evaluate the impact of the inflation targeting regime on the Phillips curve, and the role played by inflation targeting in the 1992-1994 recession. Section 6 concludes.

2. Regime Shifts in Canadian Inflation Dynamics

In February 1991 the Bank of Canada and the federal government jointly announced inflation reduction guidelines, setting the goal of monetary policy to reduce CPI inflation to a 1 to 3 percent range by the end of 1995. The inflation targeting policy agreement was further extended to 1998, and at regular intervals henceforth (see Mishkin and Posen, 1997, for a detailed account).

There are at least three reason why the Canadian inflation targeting policy, widely considered very successful, warrants in-depth examination. First, the introduction of Canada's inflation targeting policy has many features of a sudden, credible monetary regime shift. The announcement of the central bank's commitment to inflation targeting was carefully planned to attract public attention. It shared the support of the government. A key feature of the inflation targeting policy has always been a strong commitment to transparency and the communication of monetary policy strategy to the public. Yet there had been no advance notice of the policy shift. Before the announcement of specific inflation targets, the three-year campaign by the Bank of Canada to promote price stability as the long term objective of monetary policy had in fact made little headway against the momentum in inflation expectations that had built up. In the fourth quarter of 1990 inflation was still at 4.2%,

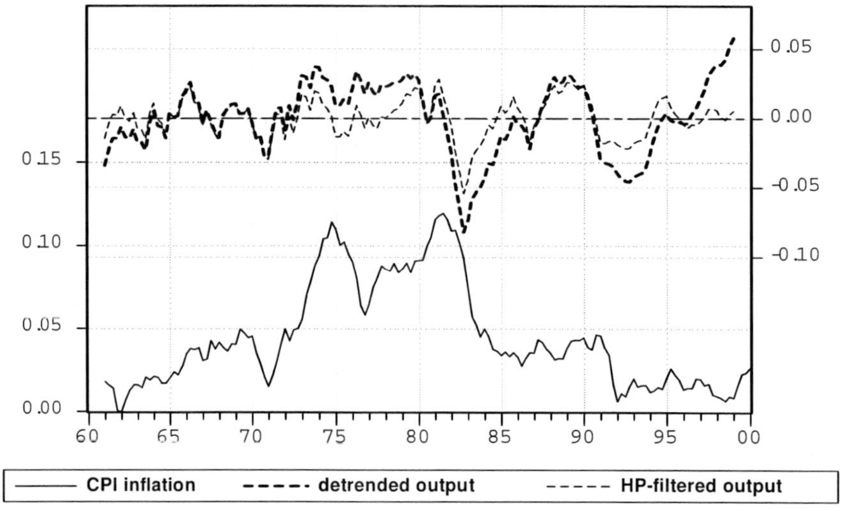

Figure 1. Canadian CPI inflation and real GDP, 1960:1 2000:1.

versus a high of 5.5% early in 1989. Figure 1 shows the clear drop in the mean inflation rate after 1991. Second, the Canadian inflation stabilization occurred at a time when the US monetary policy was very careful to avoid inflationary episodes during the long expansion of the 1990s. It is fair to ask whether Canada simply 'imported' monetary discipline via the commercial and financial linkages with the US. Third, there is very clear-cut empirical evidence, discussed in the next section, of a regime shift in the inflation process and in reduced-form models of inflation after the inflation targeting policy was adopted.

2.1. The Backward-Looking Phillips Curve

The transition to a stable inflation environment may be accompanied by parameter instability in reduced form models of inflation. Structural models, which involve only 'deep' parameters defining preferences and technology, do not suffer from this drawback. An example of a structural model for inflation dynamics which has gained wide popularity in the last decade is the New Keynesian forward-looking Phillips curve (Gali and Gertler, 1999):

$$\pi_t = \beta E_t \{\pi_{t+1}\} + \lambda(y_t - y_t^*) \tag{1}$$

where π is inflation, y is output, y^* is potential output and $(y - y^*)$ is the output gap. Backward looking formulations of the Phillips curve, such as:

$$\pi_t = \sum_{i=1}^{k} a_i \pi_{t-i} + \lambda(y_t - y_t^*) \tag{2}$$

assume that inflation expectations are formed according to some variety of the adaptive expectations model:

$$\pi_t^e = \sum_{i=1}^{k} a_i \pi_{t-i} \tag{3}$$

Alternatively, rational expectations models with a significant degree of endogenous persistence, adjustment costs and time-to-build constraints may imply that eq. (2) is a good approximation to the structural Phillips curve, while expected inflation plays a marginal role. If it were simply a reduced form expression, the backward looking Phillips curve should not be insensitive to shifts in the monetary policy rule, unless private agents actually form expectations according to eq. (3), or unless the autoregressive reduced-form representation for expectation formation is fairly robust to changes in the conduct of monetary policy (Estrella and Fuhrer, 2000).

I estimate the backward looking Phillips curve :

$$\pi_t^q = a_0 + a_1\pi_{t-1}^q + a_2\pi_{t-2}^q + a_3\pi_{t-3}^q + a_4\pi_{t-4}^q + a_5(y - y^*)_{t-1} + \epsilon_t \qquad (4)$$

on Canadian quarterly data of the CPI inflation net of indirect taxes and the output gap $(y - y^*)$. Note that while estimates of eq. (1) might be less accurate, nonetheless they are expected to be stable across monetary policy regimes. In the case the backward-looking Phillips curve represents a reduced-form approach to the modeling of the inflation process, the parameters are not independent of the way the expectation formation process varies across monetary regimes.

2.2. Evidence of Structural Breaks in Reduced-Form Inflation Models

2.2.1. Structural Breaks: Quarterly Data

Figure 1 shows the CPI inflation together with two widely used statistical measure of deviations from potential output, obtained by fitting to Canadian real GDP a linear and quadratic trend, and the Hodrick-Prescott smoothed trend[2]. The high inflation period of the '70s, and the slowdown in the price level growth in the second half of the eighties, common to many OECD countries, is very clear. The graphs shows that inflation was stable in the second half of the eighties, and that since the beginning of 1991, when inflation targeting was introduced, inflation has stabilized around a lower mean level. Hostland's (1995) narrative of Canadian inflation describes the period from 1954 to 1970 as one of low and stable inflation, followed by inflationary episodes corresponding to the two oil shocks, and then by a sharp decline of inflation in two steps, during the recessions of early 1980s and early 1990s.

I examine the timing of structural breaks in the estimated equations (4) using a sequential Chow breakpoint test. The data are partitioned in two subsets, and the statistical distance between the parameters of the restricted (whole sample) and unrestricted regression is measured by an F-statistic. The test provides strong evidence of parameter instability in the Phillips curve. Figure 2 shows that the relationships breaks down (at a 5% confidence level) after the first oil shock, as expected, and subsequently only in the early part of 1991, when explicit inflation targeting begins. Note that the test does not detect a structural break around 1983 (at the 5% confidence level), the start of a low and stable inflation period. Similar result obtain using the core CPI inflation rate (the operational target of the Bank of

[2]I report results for a Phillips curve estimated using detrended output, but analogous results are obtained using Hodrick-Prescott filtered output data. Hostland (1995) presents additional evidence on the structural breaks in the Canadian Phillips curve.

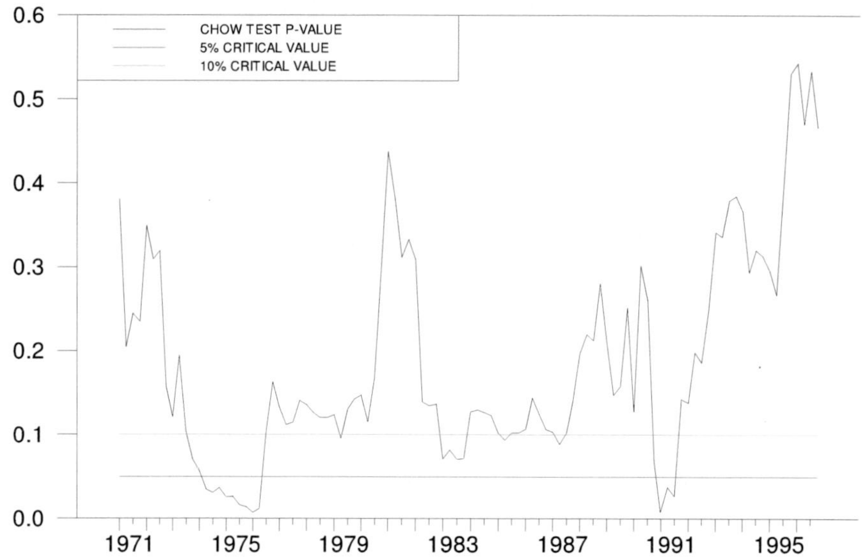

Figure 2. Phillips curve: Sequential Chow Breakpoint test (p-value of structural break).

Canada), and running the test allowing for an interval of 2 to 6 quarters between the two subsamples.

2.2.2. Structural Breaks in the Post-1984 Period: Monthly Data

Monthly data allow a number of observations large enough to focus on the post-1984 sample, covering both a period of low and stable inflation, and the period when inflation stabilization was explicitly the goal of monetary policy. I estimate the Phillips curve using thirteen lags of month to month inflation and the two-quarters lagged output gap:

$$\pi_t^m = a_0 + a_1\pi_{t-1}^m + a_2\pi_{t-2}^m ... + a_{13}\pi_{t-13}^m + a_{14}(y - y^*)_{t-6} + \epsilon_t$$

The sequential Chow Breakpoint test (Fig. 3) clearly indicates a structural break around the time of monetary policy shift to inflation targeting. The forecasting performance of the equation estimated up to mid 1990 as measured by computing the recursive root mean square error and the recursive Chow forecast test also decreases dramatically after 1991.

As Hostland (1995) and Ricketts and Rose (1995) point out, the structural break might correspond to a switch to an inflation regime with the same dynamics but a different long run mean. In fact tests for instability in the conditional mean based on OLS recursive residuals, like the cumulative sum of squared residuals (CUSUM) test, indicate a breakpoint around the beginning of 1991. Figure 4 shows that the break is not only due to a shift in the intercept of the regression. The recursive OLS estimates show instability in the output gap and inflation lags coefficients as well (the result is not especially clear-cut because after 1991 OLS regression coefficient will average between the values appropriate for the pre-1991 regime and those appropriate for the inflation-targeting regime.). Table 1 compares selected coefficients of the Phillips curve equation estimates in the pre- and post-inflation targeting regime.

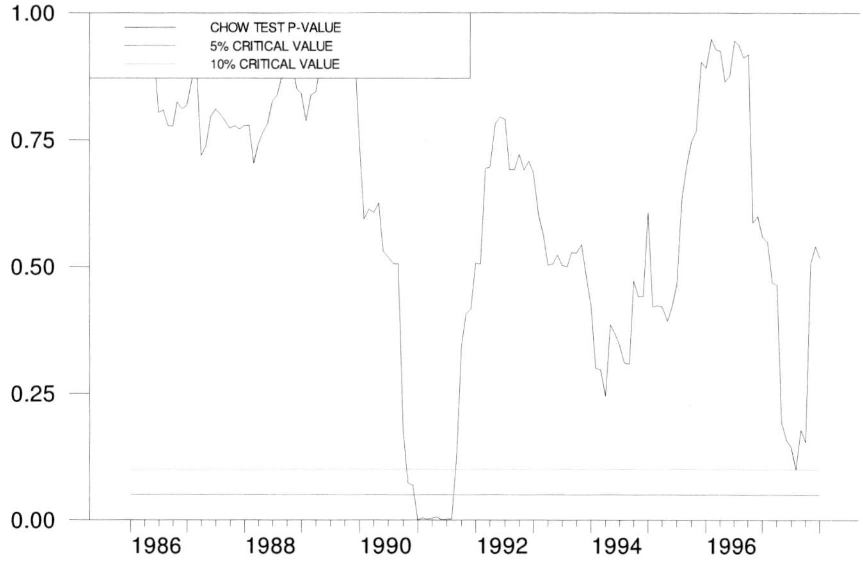

Figure 3. Phillips curve - Sequential Chow test, monthly data (p-value of break).

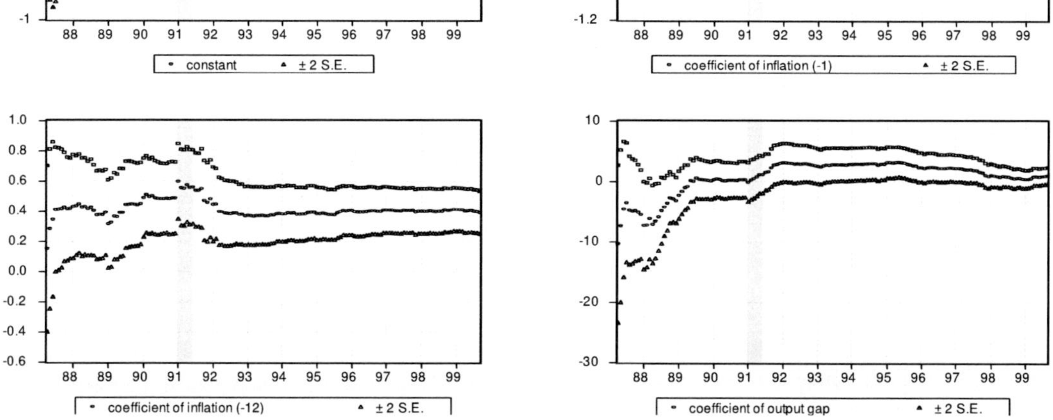

Figure 4. Phillips curve, monthly data - Recursive OLS estimate.

Table 1. Estimates of Phillips curve

	1984:1 1991:1	1991:2 2000:4
a_0	0.25	0.19
	(0.20)	(0.04)
a_1	0.09	0.02
	(0.14)	(0.09)
a_{14}	0.42	0.15
	(1.61)	(0.66)
$R-squared$	0.43	0.24
$Adj.R-squared$	0.28	0.12
$Durbin-Watson$	2.07	2

The R^2 of the monthly Phillips curve drops from 0.43 to 0.24 after the switch to inflation targeting. While the constant in the regression changes between the two samples, so does the coefficient on the output gap. Although the estimate is not accurate, it indicates a flattening of the Phillips curve. Hostland (1995) comments that the shift from a period of large relative price movements in the seventies, when monetary policy has been largely accommodating, to a period in which monetary policy has been committed to stabilizing inflation, leads to a breakdown of traditional reduced form inflation equations. What is remarkable though is that structural instability is detected over a period of low and stable inflation, from 1984 to 2000, and that the reduced form equation is unstable starting from the period when monetary policy is explicitly defined with reference to an inflation target. Credibility of the inflation targeting regime may have radically changed the way the private sectors forms expectations over the course of monetary policy.

2.3. Changes in the Time Series Properties of Canadian Inflation

The time series properties of the inflation rate can be summarized by its autocorrelation and partial autocorrelation functions. It is possible that shifts in the inflation regime happened between stationary autoregressive processes, involving a shift in the steady state inflation or in the dynamics of the autoregression. Ricketts and Rose (1995) find instead that a Markov switching process composed of a stationary and a random walk process better describes Canadian postwar inflation when compared to a process allowing shifts between two stationary regimes. Changes in the time series property of inflation in many OECD economies over the last 20 years have been the subject of an important debate (see Levin and Piger, 2002, Pivetta and Reis, 2007).

To check for non-stationarity in the inflation time series, I perform an augmented Dickey-Fuller test on the quarterly CPI series (excluding the impact of indirect taxes) on the sub-samples preceding and following 1991. The results are reported in Table 2.

Table 2.

ADF test (4 lags) on CPI excluding indirect taxes	
1961:1 1990:4	−1.89
1991:1 2000:1	−4.066***
	*** = 1% p-value

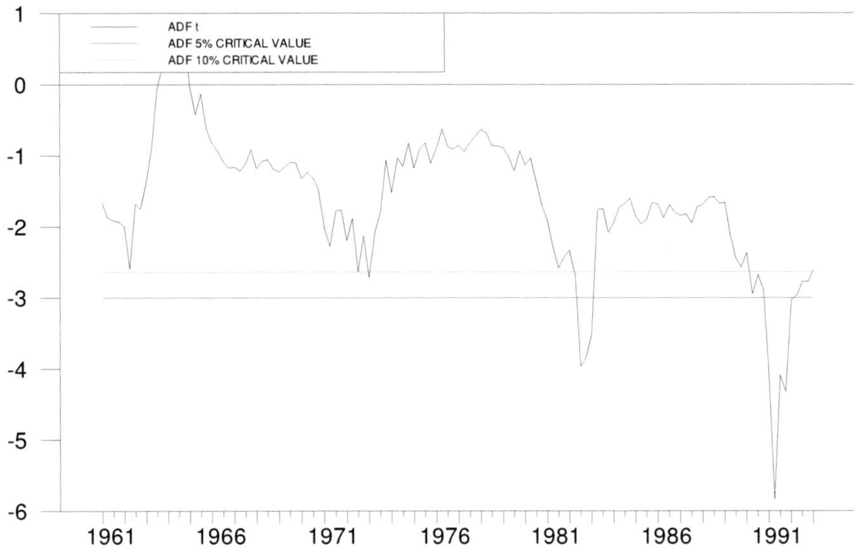

Figure 5. Rolling sample ADF tests on quarterly inflation, n = 9 years - 4 lags included.

The ADF statistic indicate strong rejection of the null hypothesis of a unit root in the post-1991 sample. This test is open to the criticism of including the two oil shocks periods. Therefore it will be biased if it mixes a regime where supply shocks - and therefore inflation - have been persistent, regardless of the stance of monetary policy (Hamilton, 1983), with a stable regime. To check the robustness of the result, I perform a sequence of ADF tests on rolling samples of the inflation series. The results are presented in Figures 5, 6. The value of the t statistics plotted at year t corresponds to the ADF test on the sample starting at year t and ending at year $t + n$. The t statistics allows rejection of the unit root at a 5% confidence level for most of the samples starting post-1991, the time of the shift to inflation targeting. The t statistic briefly allows rejection of the unit root hypothesis around 1984. The existence of shifts in the mean bias the test towards rejection of the alternative hypothesis of stationarity, since they involve an abrupt and permanent shift between different mean levels.

To gain robustness in the results, I perform ADF tests on monthly data rolling samples. The test result plot, with analogous interpretation as the previous one, is reported in figure 7. Starting from 1991, the tests indicate that a unit root for inflation can be rejected at a 10% confidence level for nearly all 5-years samples, while the opposite is true for samples

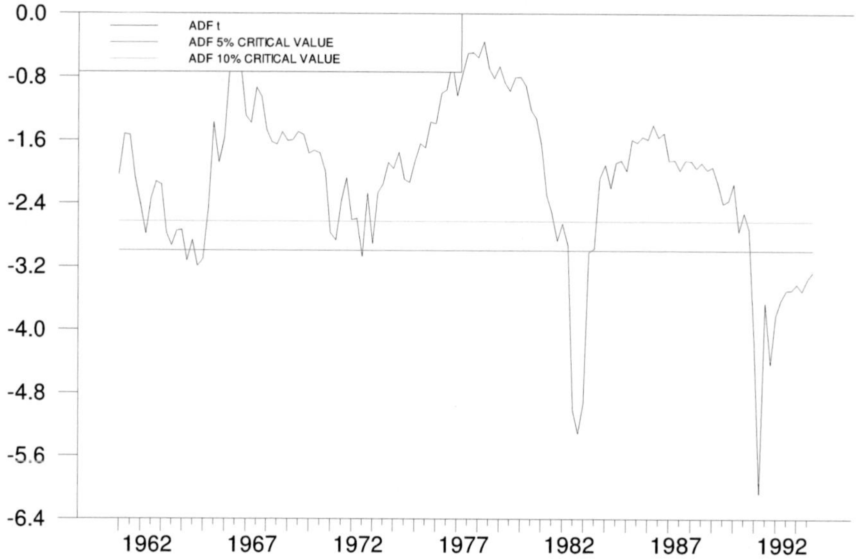

Figure 6. Rolling sample ADF tests on quarterly inflation, n = 7 years - 2 lags included.

starting before inflation targeting was implemented[3]. Similar results obtain with different sample windows[4].

3. A Model of the Canadian Economy

To build historical counterfactuals which account for the shift in expectations following adoption of inflation targeting, and thus overcome the Lucas critique, a structural model of the economy is needed. In this section I build an optimizing model of the Canadian economy, in the spirit of the New Keynesian open economy literature (Obstfeld and Rogoff, 2000). In the next section I describe in detail the strategy to build counterfactuals consistent with the structural model.

The Canadian economy is modeled as a small open economy, following Mendoza (1991), Schmitt-Grohe (1998), Schmitt-Grohe and Uribe (2001). The small open economy framework is similar to recent optimizing models with money where nominal price inertia is introduced using the Calvo (1983) price-setting model. In contrast to large part of

[3]Perron (1989, 1990) demonstrated that Dickey-Fuller tests may have little power when the true generating process is stationary around a broken linear trend. Conversely, Leybourne et al (1998) showed that when the true generating process is difference stationary, but with a break, routine application of Dickey-Fuller tests can yield spurious rejections of the unit root null hypothesis. Rolling and sequential tests like the one proposed by Banerjee et al. (1992) or Perron (1997) do not help to discriminate when the null hypothesis is that a unit root is present only in part of the sample. They are tests built to discriminate the stationarity or non-stationarity of a series, and to allow for the presence of a break (in trend or intercept) at an unknown point in time. As such, they are built under the null that a unit root exists in the whole sample.

[4]It is worthwile to note that all tests based on the assumption on stationarity would detect a break at the same period, though would not imply that inflation dynamics has shifted from non-stationary to stationary. A CUSUM test would report an abrupt and permanent shift in the conditional mean in 1991. Sample autocorrelations would show a marked decrease in persistence for the two subsamples

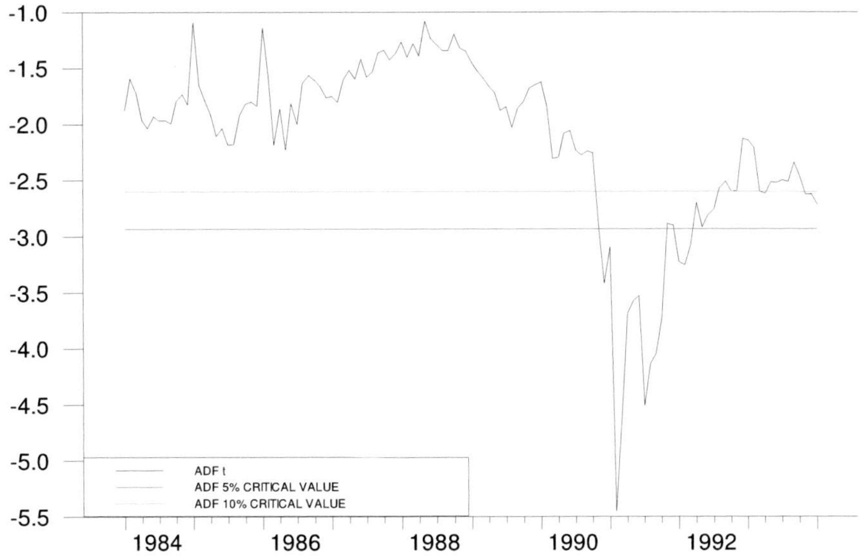

Figure 7. Rolling sample ADF tests on monthly inflation, n = 5 years - 12 lags included.

this literature, nominal wages are set in staggered contracts, along the lines of Erceg, Henderson and Levin (1999) and Kollmann (2001). The introduction of nominal wage rigidity is relevant for two reasons. First, staggered wages generate more realistically persistent effects of monetary shocks on output, when compared to staggered price adjustment models (Andersen, 1998, Edge, 2002). Second, evidence on staggered wage setting is at least as persuasive as evidence on staggered price setting (Backus, 1984, Amato and Laubach, 1999, Sbordone, 2002).

The model. The domestic economy trades all domestically produced goods with the rest of the world (the foreign sector). Firms in the home (H) and foreign (F) country set prices in their respective currency and do not discriminate between the domestic and foreign markets, so that the law of one price holds for each traded good. Domestic producers are monopolistically competitive, and optimally reset prices according to the Calvo (1983) price-setting model. This behaviour implies that domestic price inflation depends on the markup firms charge over the marginal cost of producing the good. Households sell to domestic firms a differentiated labor service in a monopolistically competitive labor market. Since they can renegotiate their nominal wage at random intervals, wage inflation is linked to the gap between the real wage and the marginal rate of substitution of consumption for leisure. The combination of sticky price and wage adjustment implies that inflation is not only proportional to the markup in the goods sector, but also to the markup household charge over the Pareto-optimal wage when selling their labor services. As a consequence, the central bank will face a trade-off between stabilizing the output gap and inflation. I assume that domestic asset markets are complete. Foreign asset markets, however, are not complete: the only foreign asset traded on the international capital market is a foreign currency denominated bond yielding a nominal riskless return.

3.1. Nominal Rigidities and the Dynamics of the Economy

This section describes the modeling of nominal rigidities in the small open economy, which generates the inflation-output gap trade-off. Following is the complete log-linear approximation to the model first order and market clearing conditions. The equilibrium conditions are fully derived in Ravenna (2007). The model parametrization is described in the Appendix.

3.1.1. Firms and Price Setting

The home production sector is made up of a continuum of firms indexed on the unit interval. Each firm produces one type of consumption good only, and faces a downward sloping demand for its product. I assume as in Calvo (1983) that producers are only allowed to reset in any given period the price of the good i they produce ($P_H(i)$) with probability $(1-\theta_p)$, and otherwise cannot adjust the price charged. Since the probability of resetting the price is equal across firms in every period t , a constant fraction $(1-\theta_p)$ of firms can optimally choose the price in each period. The expected time a price remains fixed is $\frac{1}{1-\theta_p}$. Let MC^N indicate nominal marginal cost, and $C^W(i)$ the world demand for good i. Whenever a firm gets the opportunity to change the price charged to consumers, it will choose the price $\tilde{P}_{H,t}(i)$ that maximizes the expected discounted profit stream:

$$E_{(t)}\left\{\sum_{s=0}^{\infty}(\theta_p^s\beta^s)\Lambda_s\left[\tilde{P}_{H,t}(i)-MC_{t+s}^N\right]C_{t+s}^W(i)\right\}$$

subject to the demand function for good i. Real profits are discounted by the (symmetric equilibrium) marginal utility of goods (MUC) consumed at time $t+s$ in terms of goods consumed at time t: $\Lambda_s=\frac{P_t}{P_{t+s}}\frac{MUC_{t+s}}{MUC_t}$.

The optimal price is set so that discounted real marginal revenues equal discounted real marginal cost, in expected value:

$$E_{(t)}\left\{\sum_{s=0}^{\infty}(\theta_p^s\beta^s)\Lambda_s\left[\frac{\vartheta-1}{\vartheta}\frac{\tilde{P}_{H,t}(i)}{P_{H,t+s}}\right]C_{t+s}^W(i)\right\}=E_{(t)}\left\{\sum_{s=0}^{\infty}(\theta_p^s\beta^s)\Lambda_s\left[MC_{t+s}\right]C_{t+s}^W(i)\right\} \tag{5}$$

where $P_{H,t}$ is the price index for home produced goods, and MC is the real marginal cost. If prices are flexible ($\theta_p=0$) the pricing equation implies in a symmetric equilibrium the static monopolistic competition optimal pricing rule of applying a constant markup over nominal marginal cost:

$$P_{H,t}(i)=P_{H,t}=\frac{\vartheta}{\vartheta-1}MC_t^N$$

In real terms, the same equation implies that at optimum real marginal costs are constant: $MC_t=\frac{\vartheta-1}{\vartheta}$. In the flexible price equilibrium labor is paid a real wage $W_t/P_{H,t}$ equal only to a fraction of its marginal product MPL:

$$\frac{\vartheta-1}{\vartheta}MPL_t=W_t/P_{H,t} \tag{6}$$

3.1.2. Labor Supply and Wage Setting

The economy is populated by a continuum of infinitely lived households (indexed by $j \in [0,1]$) each endowed with an ownership share of the firms in the goods producing sector. Households yield utility from real money balances M/P, a consumption aggregate of foreign and home produced goods C, and leisure. The household chooses an optimal plan maximizing the utility functional:

$$U^j = E_{(0)} \sum_{t=0}^{\infty} \beta^t U_t^j (C_t^j, N_t^j, \frac{M_t^j}{P_t}, D_t)$$

where D_t is an aggregate preferences shifter. I assume habit persistent preferences as in Boldrin et al. (2001). Households set nominal wage W in contracts which can be renegotiated only with probability $(1-\theta_w)$. Since for domestic firms different households' labor services are imperfect substitutes, each household j faces a downward sloping demand function for its type of labor:

$$N_t^j = (\frac{W_t^j}{W_t})^{-\phi} N_t \tag{7}$$

where $N_t = \int_0^1 N_t(i)di$ is an index of aggregate employment. Because the contracted wage is higher than in a labor market where workers have no monopoly power, they are willing to satisfy an increase in labor demand (in a neighborhood around the steady state) even if they cannot immediately reset the wage. The wage setting problem is analogous to the firms' staggered price setting problem. In any period t in which household j is able to reset its wage, the household will maximize its utility functional with respect to the nominal wage $\tilde{W}_t^j$, subject to a sequence of budget constraints and the labor demand function (eq. 7) at time $t+s$. The first order condition for a wage setting household j is:

$$E_{(t)} \left\{ \sum_{s=0}^{\infty} (\theta_w^s \beta^s) \left[\frac{\phi - 1}{\phi} MUC_{t+s}^j \frac{\tilde{W}_t^j}{P_{t+s}} \right] N_{t+s}^j \right\} = -E_{(t)} \left\{ \sum_{s=0}^{\infty} (\theta_w^s \beta^s) \left[MUN_{t+s}^j \right] N_{t+s}^j \right\} \tag{8}$$

where $MUN_{t+s}^j = \frac{\partial U_{t+s}^j}{\partial N_{t+s}^j}$ and $MUC_{t+s}^j = \frac{\partial U_{t+s}^j}{\partial C_{t+s}^j}$. The optimal wage is set so that the discounted marginal utility of the income provided by selling labor is equal to the discounted marginal disutility of labor, in expected value terms. In a flexible wage environment $(\theta_w = 0)$, the wage setting equation implies the static monopolistic competition optimal wage setting rule of asking for a constant markup over the marginal rate of substitution between labor and consumption ($MRSC$):

$$\frac{\tilde{W}_t^j}{P_t} = \frac{\phi}{\phi - 1} \left[-\frac{U_{n,t}^{j'}}{U_{c,t}^{j'}} \right] = \frac{\phi}{\phi - 1} MRSC_t^j$$

The marginal utility of the consumption aggregate and the marginal utility of the domestic-good consumption bundle are related by the equation: $MUC_{t+s}^J = MUC_{H,t+s}^j \frac{P_{t+s}}{P_{H,t+s}}$. Therefore we can write:

$$\frac{W_t^j}{P_{H,t}} = \frac{\phi}{\phi - 1} MRSC_{H,t}^j \tag{9}$$

where $MRSC^{j}_{H,t}$ is the marginal rate of substitution between labor and the domestic-good consumption bundle.

3.2. Rational Expectations Equilibrium

The model has six exogenous variables: the technology shock A_t , the preference shifter D_t , the foreign aggregate consumption C^*_t (affecting the domestic economy exports), the price of imports $P^*_{F,t}$, the foreign nominal interest rate I^*_t, the monetary policy shock $\epsilon_{M,t}$. Given a stochastic process for the exogenous variables, an equilibrium can be defined as a stochastic process for the endogenous variables that satisfies the market clearing and optimality conditions. Following the approach widely used in business cycle research (King and Rebelo, 1998), I obtain an approximate solution by taking a linear approximation around a deterministic steady state, which can be solved using the method described in Blanchard and Kahn (1980).

The log-linearized aggregate law of motion of the economy is given by the IS and inflation equations, discussed in detail in the next section, and the following additional equations, where lower case letters indicate log-deviations from the steady state:

1. the consumption index aggregating home (c_H) and foreign (c_F) good consumption baskets:
$$c_t = (1-\gamma)c_{H,t} + \gamma c_{F,t}$$
2. the definition of the marginal utility of consumption with habit-persistent preferences:
$$muc_t = \frac{1}{1-b\beta}d_t - \frac{b\beta}{1-b\beta}E_t d_{t+1} - \left[\frac{b^2\beta+1}{\kappa}\right]c_t + \frac{b}{\kappa}c_{t-1} + \frac{b\beta}{\kappa}E_t c_{t+1}$$
3. the intra-temporal choice between home and foreign goods, as a function of the terms of trade s :
$$c_{H,t} - c_{F,t} = \rho s_t$$
4. the Euler equation linking the real interest rate r to the current and expected marginal utility of consumption:
$$muc_t = r_t + E_t muc_{t+1}$$
5. the uncovered interest parity condition between the nominal return on domestic and foreign bonds, and expected exchange rate depreciation:
$$i_t = i^*_t + E_t \Delta e_{t+1}$$
6. the relationship between the premium paid on foreign borrowing ($i^*_t - \widetilde{i}^*_t$), and the net foreign assets b_t :
$$i^*_t = \widetilde{i}^*_t - \widetilde{\eta} Y b_t$$
7. the production function:
$$y_t = a_t + n_t$$

8. the definition of real marginal costs:

$$mc_t = (w_t - p_{H,t}) + n_t - y_t$$

9. the resource constraint, where $c^*_{H,t}$ are exports of home-produced good:

$$y_t = \frac{C_H}{Y} c_{H,t} + \frac{C^*_H}{Y} c^*_{H,t}$$

10. the foreign asset accumulation equation:

$$b_t = \frac{(1+i^*)(\Delta e)}{(1+\pi_H)} \left[b_{t-1} + i^*_{t-1}\frac{B}{Y} - \pi_{H,t}\frac{B}{Y} + \frac{B}{Y}(\Delta e_t) \right] + \frac{C^*_H}{Y} c^*_{H,t} - \frac{SC_F}{Y}(s_t + c_{F,t})$$

11. the definition of terms of trade depreciation, where $p^*_{F,t}$ is the exogenously given price of foreign goods in terms of foreign currency:

$$s_t - s_{t-1} = \Delta e_t + p^*_{F,t} - p^*_{F,t-1} - \pi_{H,t}$$

12. the Fisher equation:

$$r_t = i_t - E_t \pi_{t+1}$$

13. the relationship between domestic (π_H) and CPI (π) inflation:

$$\pi_t = \pi_{H,t} + \gamma(s_t - s_{t-1})$$

14. the monetary policy rule, which includes an exogenous i.i.d. policy shock ε_i:

$$i_t = (1-\chi)[\omega_p E_t \pi_{t+1} + \omega_y y_t + \omega_e e_t) + \chi i_{t-1} + \varepsilon_{i,t}$$

15. the foreign demand for home goods, as a function of the terms of trade and the exogenously given total foreign consumption c^*:

$$c^*_{H,t} = \rho s_t + c^*_t$$

16. the exogenous stochastic processes for the preference shifter, the technology shock, the world interest rate, the imports' price and the aggregate foreign consumption demand:

$$\begin{aligned}
d_t &= \rho_d d_{t-1} + \varepsilon_{d,t} \\
a_t &= \rho_a a_{t-1} + \varepsilon_{a,t} \\
&\quad Foreign\ Variables \\
\tilde{i}^*_t &= \rho \tilde{i}^*_{t-1} + \varepsilon_{i^*,t} \\
p^*_{F,t} &= \rho_p p^*_{F,t-1} + \varepsilon_{p,t} \\
c^*_t &= \rho_c c^*_{t-1} + \varepsilon_{c,t}
\end{aligned}$$

3.3. Wage and Price Inflation: the Phillips Curve

Linearizing the model we can obtain equations for the IS (Euler equation) and Phillips curves that offer insight into the working of monetary policy in the present framework. If household preferences are not habit -persistent ($b = 0$), household's first order conditions imply a dynamic IS equation:

$$c_t = E_{(t)}c_{t+1} - (i_t - E_{(t)}\pi_{t+1}) - (E_{(t)}d_{t+1} - d_t)$$

or, since $\pi_t = \pi_{H,t} + \gamma(s_t - s_{t-1})$:

$$c_t = E_{(t)}c_{t+1} - (i_t - E_{(t)}\pi_{H,t+1}) + \gamma(E_{(t)}s_{t+1} - s_t) - (E_{(t)}d_{t+1} - d_t)$$

The expected change in consumption demand depends positively on the incentive to save (the real interest rate on domestic goods consumption) and negatively on the expected change in the terms of trade. If households did not yield utility from foreign goods ($\gamma = 0$), an expected devaluation would not raise current consumption relative to future consumption. A preference shock d_t , increasing the marginal utility of consumption at every level of c_t , raises current consumption.

The domestic goods inflation equation is analogous to the one derived in the standard Calvo-type closed economy (Gali and Gertler, 1999):

$$\pi_{H,t} = \lambda_1 mc_t + \beta E_{(t)}\pi_{H,t+1} = \lambda_1[(w_t - p_{H,t}) - mpl_t] + \beta E_{(t)}\pi_{H,t+1} \qquad (10)$$

where $\lambda_1 = (1 - \theta_p)(1 - \beta\theta_p)/\theta_p$. Because of the nominal wage stickiness, the dynamics of the economy turns out to be very different from the standard New Keynesian framework. The wage inflation ξ_t depends on the deviation of the real wage from households' marginal rate of substitution between (home good) consumption and leisure, which can be positive because of the staggered wage contracting:

$$\xi_t = \lambda_2[mrs_{H,t} - (w_t - p_{H,t})] + \beta E_{(t)}\xi_{t+1} = \lambda_2[mrs_t - (w_t - p_t)] + \beta E_{(t)}\xi_{t+1} \qquad (11)$$

where $\lambda_2 = (1 - \theta_w)(1 - \beta\theta_w)/[\theta_w(1 + \phi\eta)]$. To see how staggered wage adjustment affects the working of the model, it is instructive to abstract from movements in the terms of trade. Let us assume that the economy is closed, i.e. $\gamma = 0$ and net exports are zero in every period. Then domestic and CPI inflation will be equal. Define $\tilde{y}_t$ as the level of output that would obtain in a flexible price - flexible wage environment, so that $(y_t - \tilde{y}_t)$ is the output gap. If wage contracts were not staggered, it is easy to show that the output gap is proportional to the real marginal cost:

$$y_t - \tilde{y}_t = \left(\frac{1}{1+\eta}\right) mc_t = \left(\frac{1}{1+\eta}\right) [(w_t - p_t) - mpl_t] \qquad (12)$$

Combining eq. (10) and (12) results in the New Keynesian Phillips curve. But if wages are sticky, it can be proved that equating the real wage to the marginal product of labor (in log-deviations) is not any more neither a sufficient nor a necessary condition for a zero output gap. In fact the real wage can deviate from the households' marginal rate of substitution, as eq. (11) makes clear. In this setup, the output gap can be written as:

$$\begin{aligned} y_t - \tilde{y}_t &= \left(\frac{1}{1+\eta}\right)\{mc_t - [(w_t - p_t) - mrs_t]\\ &= \left(\frac{1}{1+\eta}\right)\{[(w_t - p_t) - mpl_t] - [(w_t - p_t) - mrs_t]\} \end{aligned} \tag{13}$$

Eq. (13) shows that the condition for zero output gap really is $mpl_t = mrs_t$. If wages are not sticky, as is the case in the model where eq. (12) is derived, households' optimality conditions require that $(w_t - p_t) = mrs_t$ in every period t . Substituting this relation in eq. (12) shows that even when wages are flexible the relevant condition for zero output gap is the equality of marginal rate of substitution and marginal product of labor. Another way of looking at eq. (13) is that when wages are not flexible, zero real marginal cost are not enough to guarantee a zero output gap. On the other hand, the real marginal cost may be zero, but eq. (13) and (11) imply that if wage inflation is positive, so will be the output gap. With some algebra, we can obtain the relevant Phillips curve for the staggered wages economy from eq. (10):

$$\pi_{H,t} = \lambda_3(y_t - \tilde{y}_t) + \beta E_{(t)}\pi_{H,t+1} + \lambda_1[(w_t - p_t) - mrs_t] \tag{14}$$

where $\lambda_3 = (1+\eta)\lambda_1$ in a closed economy, and is equal to a more cumbersome function of the structural parameters in the open economy where $b = 0$. As is now clear, the last term would disappear in a flexible wage environment. Then a monetary policy committing to stabilizing inflation or the output gap would ensure that both goals are met. Erceg et al. (1999) show that this result does not hold when wage adjustment is sluggish: the central bank would face a meaningful trade-off between stabilizing inflation and the output gap. Disinflation is now costly even under a credible monetary policy. Other authors (Clarida, Gali, Gertler, 1999) restored the output-inflation trade-off by assuming the existence of an exogenous shock affecting inflation. While adding a second nominal rigidity to the New Keynesian framework generates a meaningful stabilization trade-off, eq. (10) shows that the inflation rate is *not* constrained to follow a persistent process.

4. A Method to Build Counterfactual Histories

The first step in using a structural model to build a counterfactual history of the Canadian economy is to recover the series of unobserved exogenous disturbances. The objective of the exercise is not to test a model, but to build counterfactual histories taking as given the model structural description of the economy (Rotemberg and Woodford, 1998, 1999, take a similar approach). Therefore the historic series of stochastic disturbances must be built in such a way that if they were fed to the model, it would return the historic series of the observable variables. In other words, when building the series of the stochastic disturbances we need to make sure we recover the historical shocks under the restriction that the economy has worked in the way described by the structural model. I will call these series the 'model-consistent' disturbances.

4.1. Model Consistent Disturbances: The One-Shock Case

4.1.1. The Consistency Issue

Assume a standard RBC model with only one exogenous variable, say the technology shock, and one state variable, say capital. A common way of recovering the technology shock is by estimating the (log-linearized) production function:

$$y_t = \alpha k_t + (1 - \alpha) n_t + a_t \tag{15}$$

Given series for the capital stock, output and employment, the parameter α can be estimated, and the series for the technology disturbance a_t easily recovered. But the estimated equation and shock series cannot be used to answer the question: what would output have been in the sample period if the parameter α had taken a different value. In fact theory predicts that a different value of α would imply a different optimal mix of capital and labor. There is no guarantee that the series for capital and labor would have turned out to be the same in the counterfactual economy.

What is needed to answer the question is a full model of the economy. The model can be written in the form:

$$\begin{aligned} k_{t+1} &= a_1 k_t + a_2 z_t && (16) \\ y_t &= b_1 k_t + b_2 z_t && (17) \\ c_t &= c_1 k_t + c_2 z_t && (18) \\ &\ldots \end{aligned}$$

Once the historical series of the technology shock is available, a counterfactual history with a different value for α can be built by solving again the model with the new parameter, and feeding back the historical series of shocks. Thus we take into account how the law of motion of the economy would have changed under different parametrization. Of course, a different model will yield a different counterfactual history.

Using the above law of motion when simulating the economy implies assuming that capital, employment, consumption etc. are chosen according to appropriate maximizing behaviour, and to rational expectations. To be consistent with this assumption, the historical shock series should be built taking into account the same restrictions on the variables.

Is there any hope that the series z_t built from eq. (15) when used in simulating the economy according to the model law of motion described by eq. (16), (17), (18), will give back the historical series for output? This will not happen, as the law of motion is built, among others, under the assumptions of maximizing behaviour and rational expectations, which might not hold for the historical series of capital and employment, even if the production function estimated equation were correct. Unless the economy is perfectly described by the model, the evolution of capital implied by the state variable law of motion will not match the data[5].

[5]This is not a claim that the shock recovered from eq. (15) is not consistent with the theory. In fact the model solution has to be consistent with the production function in eq. (15). But a general equilibrium model of the economy also implies a specific law of motion for capital and labor, which may not match the data.

The only model-consistent representation of z_t will come from inverting eq. (17), and using the law of motion of the state variable, given a value for k_0 (King and Rebelo, 1998, apply this method to build a technology shock series for the US). This does not mean that the recovered technology shock will be the correct one. But it will have the property that, under the assumption that the economy works accordingly to the model, is the only shock series that when fed into the estimated law of motion for the economy will make the simulated output series equal to the historical one.

4.1.2. The Singularity Issue

Let us now abstract from the consistency issue that must be faced when building a counterfactual history. There is another issue (emphasized by Ingram et al., 1994) that must be tackled even if we only seek to build the historical technology shock series per se. The standard RBC model predicts that the marginal product of labor is equalized to households' marginal rate of substitution between consumption and leisure:

$$mrs_t = a_t + \alpha(k_t - n_t) \tag{19}$$

As eq. (15), this first order condition can be estimated and used to recover the technology shock a_t. Obviously, the recovered series will differ from the one implied by eq. (15). This is due to the fact that the RBC model is singular: it predicts that various linear combinations of the observable variables are deterministic. Since this is not the case in the data, it is easy to see that in general a single shock model implies a number of inconsistent representations for the unobservable shock in terms of observable variables (Ingram et al., 1994). In fact, any of the equations describing the solution of the RBC model will imply different, inconsistent representations of the technology shock. Therefore in a single shock model it is only possible to recover the historical series of the shock so that one of the observable variables will perfectly fit the historic path. Choosing to fit a different variables yields a different historical shock series. Some authors (Hall, 1996, McGrattan et al., 1997) augment the Blanchard-Kahn solution with measurement errors to avoid the singularity problem, which would prevent maximum likelihood estimation of the system.

4.2. Multiple-shock Models

The solution to multiple-shock rational expectations model, like the sticky price - sticky wage model built in the previous section, is written in general as:

$$\begin{aligned} k_{t+1} &= \Gamma k_t + \varepsilon_{t+1} \\ f_t &= \Pi k_t \end{aligned} \tag{20}$$

where k_t is the vector of endogenous and exogenous state variables, ε_t is the vector of stochastic shocks, f_t is the vector of the endogenous control variables, of which a subset is observable. By inverting the matrices in the system (20) it is possible to build the

Therefore, if the historical shock series has to be used to build a counterfactual history (and this necessarily involves using the general equilibrium model), the only consistent way to build it is to use the full model.

model-consistent vector of historical stochastic disturbances, given the historical path of the observable variables and an initial condition (see Ingram et al., 1994, Blankenau et al., 2001, Parkin, 1988, for an application of this method).

I apply this methodology to build the disturbances vector for the Canadian economy since 1991 consistent with the quarterly structural model described in the previous section. Because of the singularity issue I can only fit as many observables as the number of exogenous shocks.

5. The Impact of Inflation Targeting on the Phillips Curve: Counterfactual Experiment for the Canadian Economy

To build counterfactual histories of the Canadian economy I use a version of the model where the exogenous disturbance vector includes five variables - the export demand shock is constrained to be zero in every period. The disturbance vector is built using a vector of observables which includes output, inflation, nominal interest rate, terms of trade and nominal exchange rate. The historical disturbance vector is model-consistent in the sense advocated by Rotemberg and Woodford (1999): under the true, estimated monetary rule the model-simulated path for the observables is identical to their historical path. The counterfactuals rest on two assumptions, which let them overcome the Lucas critique. First, the rational expectation hypothesis imposes model-consistency on all expectations, including the inflation expectations formed by the central bank which serves as its policy feedback variable. Seconds, the monetary policy rule is perfectly credible.

5.1. Data

All data are taken from the CANSIM database of Statistics Canada, sampled at quarterly frequency, and run from the first quarter of 1991 to the first quarter of 2000. Output, used to fit the variable y_t , is detrended real per capita GDP[6]. Inflation, used to fit the variable π_t, is the CPI inflation net of indirect taxes. This choice is not only motivated by the fact that the central bank targets this measure of inflation, but also by the observation that the GDP deflator does not take into account movements in the terms of trade that directly affect the purchasing power of households in the model. Experiments with core CPI yield very similar results. I consider as the steady state inflation rate $\Pi_{SS} = 2\%$, the central bank long-run inflation target. The nominal interest rate i_t is the overnight rate, although nearly identical results are obtained with the 3-month T-bill rate. The terms of trade series for s_t is built from the Laspeyres index for import and export prices to the US (accounting for over 85% of total Canadian international trade). Finally, the foreign exchange rate variable e_t is the Canadian / US nominal exchange rate, detrended to take into account historical differences in the two countries' steady state inflation rates.

[6]Detrended output and its model counterpart y_t are *not* equal to the theoretical output gap. In a flexible price model, for example, a permanent technology shock implies a zero output gap in all periods, but a permanent deviation of output from its previous steady state. On the other hand, central banks' measures of the output gap are invariably built as deviations from a (stochastic) trend, such as the HP-filtered output. This justifies the inclusion of y_t rather than the theoretical outout gap in the monetary polkicy rule. The empirical results are very similar when HP-filtered or detrended data are used to fit the y_t variable.

5.1.1. Monetary Policy Rule

The monetary authority is assumed to move the policy instrument i_t according to the (log-linear) policy rule equation:

$$i_t = (1 - \chi)[\omega_\pi E_{(t)}\pi_{t+1} + \omega_y y_t + \omega_E \Delta e_t] + \chi i_{t-1} + \epsilon_{M,t} \tag{21}$$

where i_t and π_t denote absolute deviations from the steady state level. If the central bank targets inflation, the policy rule takes the form:

$$i_t = (1 - \chi)[\omega_\pi E_{(t)}\pi_{t+1}] + \chi i_{t-1} + \epsilon_{M,t}$$

While output is not a feedback variable in the inflation targeting rule, the central bank has considerable leeway in choosing how monetary policy should affect output dynamics. It can choose the degree of interest rate smoothing χ , the policy feedback parameter ω_π , and the inflation forecast targeting horizon. Most central banks targeting inflation choose a forecasting horizon of one to two years, to take into account the transmission lag of monetary policy.

The Bank of Canada targets the forecast of CPI inflation, with a measure of core inflation being the operational target. I estimate eq. (21) in the way advocated by Clarida et al. (1998, 2000) using a GMM estimator, for the periods pre- and post-1991. I obtain estimates in line with the policy reaction functions of other OECD central banks[7]:

$$1961 - 1990 \quad : \quad i_t = (1 - 0.86)[0.8E_{(t)}\pi_{t+1} + 1.01y_t] + 0.86i_{t-1} \tag{22}$$

$$1991 - 2000 \quad : \quad i_t = (1 - 0.84)[2.08E_{(t)}\pi_{t+1} + 0.13y_t] + 0.84i_{t-1} \tag{23}$$

All reported parameters are statistically significant at least at the 5% confidence level. To gain stability, I constrain the parameter ω_E to zero, although at various times exchange rate concerns played some role in the setting of Canadian monetary policy (see also Kahn and Parrish, 1998). In fact stable estimates of pre-1991 policy reaction function are difficult to obtain, since the Bank of Canada has in the past paid attention to a number of indicators, among which monetary aggregates, inflation, nominal exchange rate with the US dollar, nominal spending growth.

5.2. Counterfactual under the Alternative Monetary Policy

Can the switch to an inflation targeting regime account for the change in inflation dynamics and the Phillips curve which occurred in Canada after 1991? After building the model-consistent stochastic disturbances from the model where policy is described by eq. (23), I build a counterfactual using the estimated pre-1991 policy rule, eq. (22). In this way I can examine what would have been the behaviour of the economy if monetary policy had not switched to inflation targeting.

---

[7]Black et al. (1998) describe canadian monetary policy with a policy rule where the instrument is the slope of the term structure of interest rates: $i^{slope} = 1.6E_t\pi^4_{t+7} + 1.8E_t\pi^4_{t+8} + \epsilon_{M,t}$, with π^4 indicating the annual inflation rate. Once allowing for the fact that the estimated policy rule in eq. (22) targets the quarterly inflation rate, and take into account interest rate smoothing behaviour, the two policy reaction functions are roughly consistent.

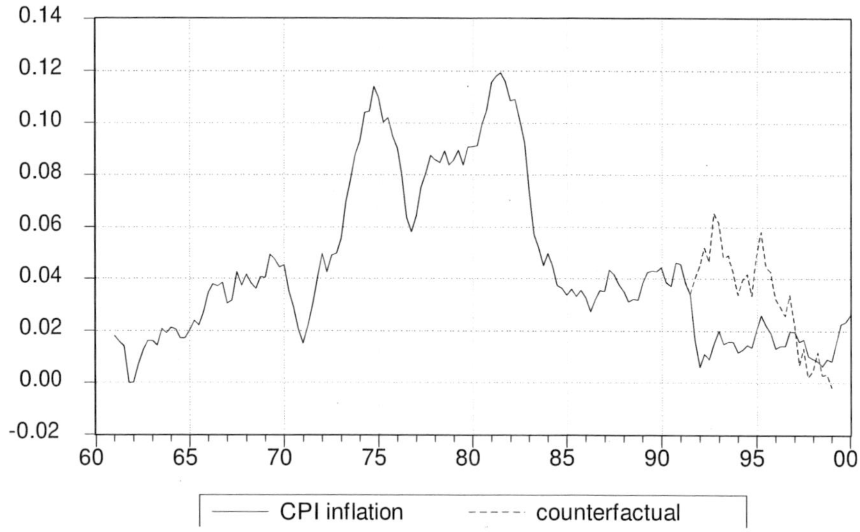

Figure 8. CPI annual inflation and counterfactual, 1960:1 - 1991:1.

5.2.1. Shifts in Inflation Dynamics and the Phillips Curve

Figure 8 shows the counterfactual path of CPI inflation under the pre-1991 monetary policy, together with the actual CPI inflation during the inflation targeting regime. Counterfactual inflation is built under two hypotheses. First, the shift in the steady state money growth (and the corresponding shift in the steady state inflation level) occurring at the time of the inflation target policy announcement did not happen. I set the average inflation rate at 4% , the level prevailing after the disinflation of the early eighties[8]. Second, the Bank of Canada feedback rule is given by eq. (22).

The old policy regime would have implied higher inflation by as much as four percentage points for most of the 1990s, and a much higher variability. Note that this does not mean the policy would have anyway implied higher and more variable inflation, but that conditional on the exogenous shocks affecting the Canadian economy in the 1990s this would have been the outcome.

Section 2 presented evidence that the inflation process became much less persistent in Canada in the inflation targeting era. Even if counterfactual inflation would have been higher and more variable conditional on the old policy regime, this does not necessarily imply Canada would have experienced higher persistence (or a unit root) inflation time-series. But this would have been the case indeed. Figure 9 shows the result of rolling sample ADF tests for the counterfactual CPI inflation series. It shows that a very different result would have obtained compared to the shift in the inflation persistence documented for the historical path of inflation after 1991 (figure 6). For nearly all samples, the test cannot

[8]Under the model assumptions a higher steady state inflation simply shifts the inflation, nominal interest rate and exchange rate paths, but has no effect on the dynamic behaviour of the economy. The results in this section are anyway robust to adding a shift in the mean inflation rate for the 1990s (although it is hard to argue that the mean inflation rate could have shifted without the explicit commitment of the central bank to lower inflation target).

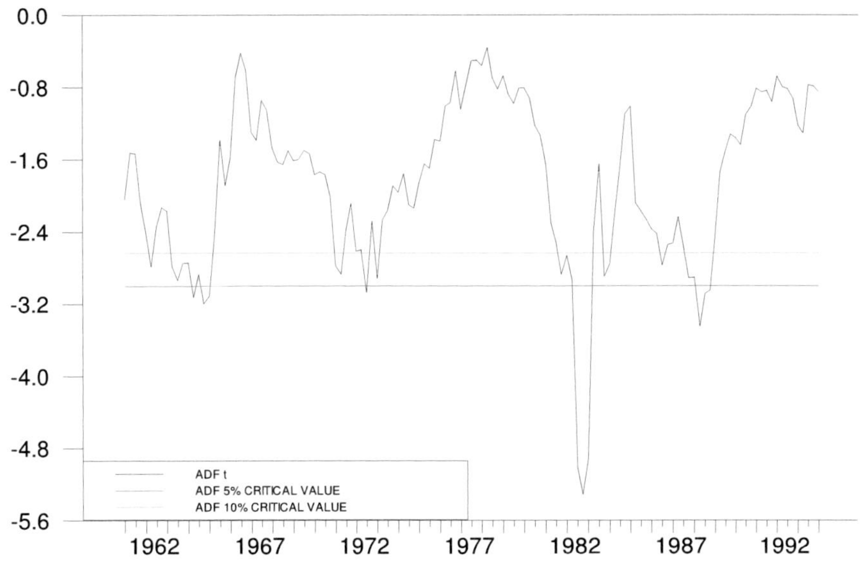

Figure 9. Rolling sample ADF tests on counterfactual inflation, n = 7 years - 2 lags included.

reject the hypothesis of a unit root after 1991. The result is robust to changing the rolling sample size adopted for the ADF test.

Can the shift to inflation targeting account for the structural break in the Phillips curve in 1991? I test this hypothesis by running rolling Chow tests on the Phillips curve (eq. 4) estimated on counterfactual inflation and detrended output. Results are reported in figure 10. Contrary to the results on the historical data (figure 3), the test on the counterfactual cannot detect a structural break in the Phillips curve equation at any point in the 1990s, while it detects the break in the 1980s at a higher confidence level. This result supports the claim that the shift to an inflation targeting regime not only occurred at the same time, but caused the favorable regime shift in the Phillips curve during the 1990s.

5.2.2. Inflation Stabilization and the 1992-1994 Recession

The Bank of Canada success in reducing inflation was associated by some critics with a high cost in terms of unemployment. But it is by no means clear that the level of unemployment reached in the early 1990s (around 10%) would have been avoidable if monetary policy had been different (Mishkin and Posen, 1997). In the same period world oil markets created inflationary pressures, while low commodity prices harmed Canadian exports.

The counterfactuals (figures 11 and 12) show that the allegation of a substantial disinflation cost is not far-fetched[9]. The counterfactual path of detrended output, had the monetary authority credibly followed the pre-1991 policy rule (eq. 22), implies that the output loss in the first half of the 1990s would have mostly been avoided. The pre-inflation targeting policy rule (22) implies a very output-stabilizing monetary policy: the standard deviation

[9]Note that the model is built to explain business cycle variations. As such it cannot help to draw conclusions about the costs or benefits of movements in the steady state inflation rate, but only about variations in the inflation rate induced by the central bank reaction function to the business cycle.

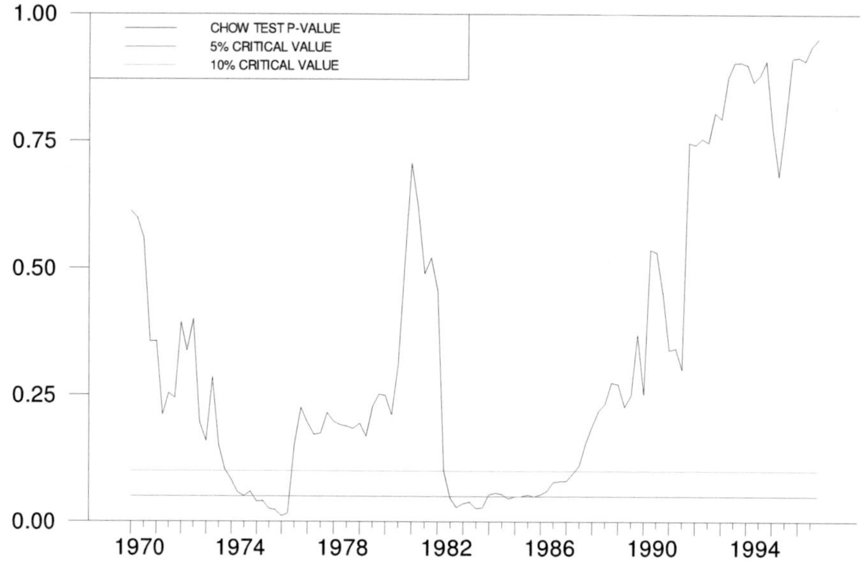

Figure 10. Phillips curve, counterfactual: Sequential Chow test (p-value of structural break).

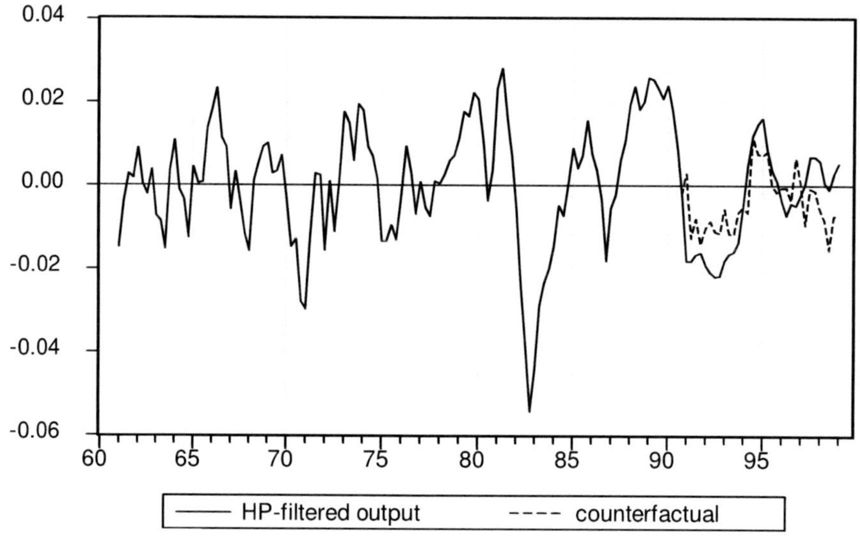

Figure 11. Output and counterfactual, 1960:1 - 1999:1. $\omega_y = 0.5$.

of counterfactual output would have been 0.71% , far lower than the standard deviation of output in any period in postwar Canadian history. The estimate of the pre-1991 policy rule is probably affected by the very accommodative policy of the 1970s. Since it seems unrealistic that in the 1980s the central bank followed such a policy, I calibrate the parameter ω_y to a value of 0.5, in line with the literature on Taylor rules. This policy rule brings the counterfactual output standard deviation to 1.12% , a value consistent with the standard deviation of output in the 1960s. Figures 11 and 12 show that even under this assumption, monetary

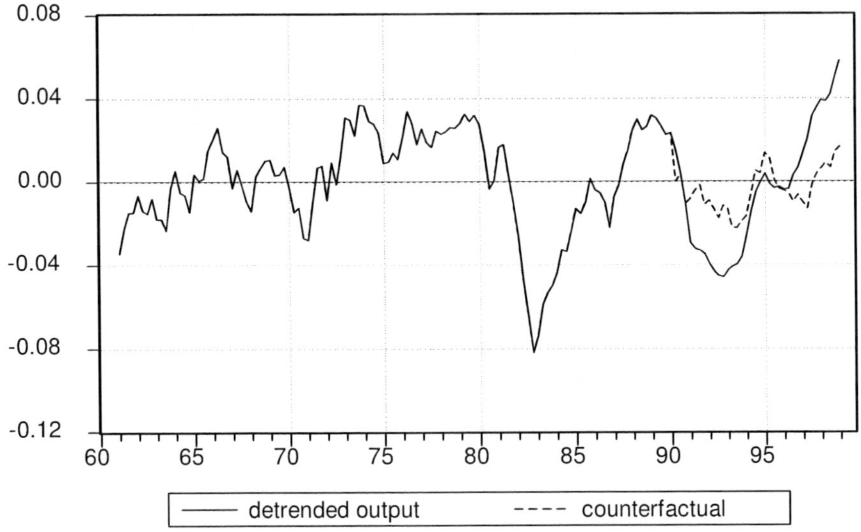

Figure 12. Output and counterfactual, 1960:1 - 1999:1. $\omega_y = 0.5$.

policy would have been much more stabilizing in the first half of the 1990s, had not the inflation targeting regime been introduced. The (excess) output loss averaged between 1% and 2% per year, depending on the measure of potential output used.

On the other hand, the counterfactual shows that the large expansion starting in 1997 would have been much dampened. This result may look awkward, but can be easily explained. First, it is reasonable to assume that the monetary authority reacts asymmetrically to recessions and expansions - it is much harder to get the blame for restraining the economy during an expansion which might overheat the economy, than to ease monetary policy during a recession. Second, the measure of the output gap is obtained by fitting a trend from 1960 to 2000. If Canadian potential output has surged in the last five years, the detrended output measure of output gap will indicate that the economy is at a peak in the business cycle. The rule (22) then calls for a tightening of monetary policy, which is unwarranted if potential output has increased together with output (as the Bank of Canada recently revised estimate of potential output in the 1990s acknowledges). In fact, repeating this experiment using Hodrick-Prescott filtered output as a measure of the output gap will solve the puzzle. Figure 11 shows that counterfactual output would have been below potential output by more than 1% after 1997, whereas under inflation targeting output would have been hovering around potential output in the same period. On the other hand, using HP-filtered data does not change the interpretation of the early '90s recession. If inflation targeting had not been adopted, the output loss would have been approximately halved between 1991 and 1994.

5.2.3. The Role of Monetary Policy Shocks in the 1992-1994 Recession

Figure 13 shows the time series for the model-consistent shock to the policy rule. It averages slightly below 1% , but has been very variable in the quarters between 1993 and 1996. I verify the impact of monetary policy shocks in the 1990s in Canada by simulating a

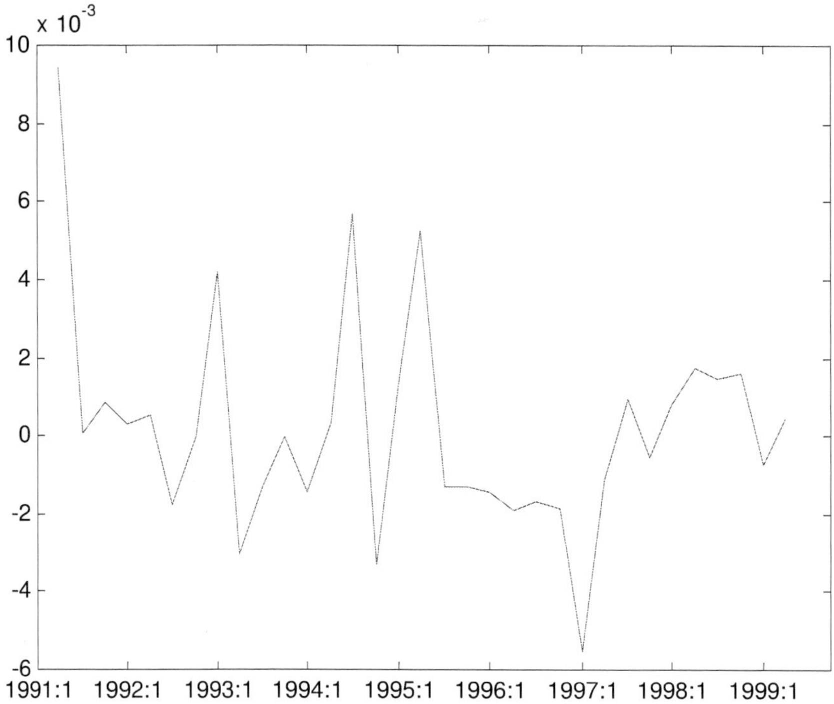

Figure 13. Monetary policy rule shock.

counterfactual economy where the policy rule is exactly the one estimated, but setting to zero the monetary policy disturbance.

The path of output (figure 14) would have deviated from the data, but not as significantly as it would have adopting a different systematic monetary policy (figure 9). Unexpected movements in monetary policy did not cause the 1993 - 1994 recession years. They contributed instead to the 1991 - 1992 portion of the downturn, accounting on average for an extra 2% output loss on an annual basis. In the second part of the 1990s policy shocks appear to have smoothed out the output path. The counterfactual shows that policy shocks did not play a relevant role in the expansion since 1998. Overall, the shape of the counterfactual path is not very different from the data.

5.2.4. Counterfactual Paths of the Policy Instrument and the Monetary Policy Transmission Mechanism

Figure 15 shows the actual path the policy instrument i_t in the 1990s together with the counterfactual paths under the assumption that monetary policy did not shift to inflation targeting (for ease of comparison the figure assumes the same 2% steady state inflation rate).

The nominal interest rate - which results from a combination of the policy reaction function to the state of the economy and the policy exogenous shocks - would not have been widely different from the data under the alternative monetary policy. This result is not at odds with the very different paths of output and inflation that the two monetary regimes

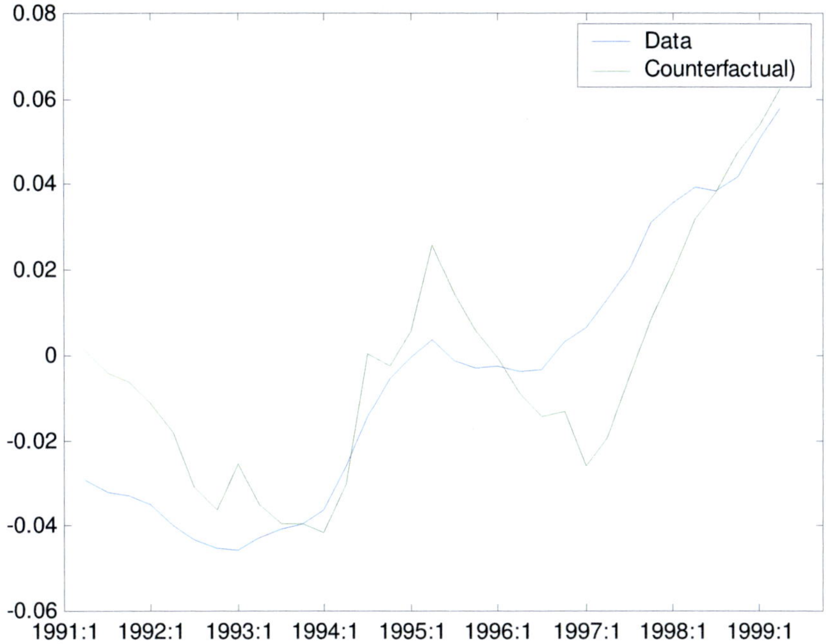

Figure 14. Output, data and counterfactual when the central bank does not deviate from the policy rule in any period.

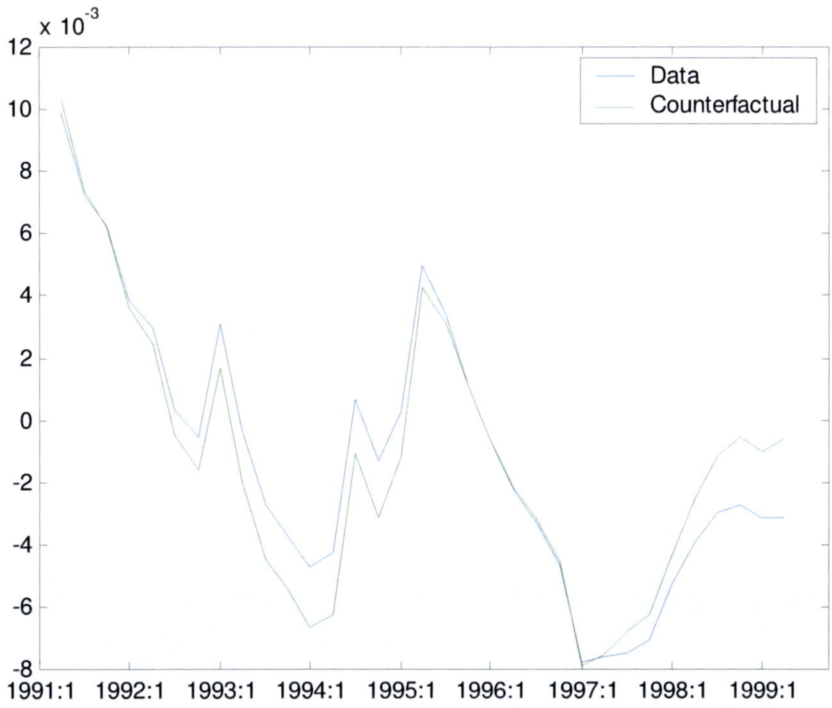

Figure 15. Nominal short-term interest rate, data and counterfactual, 1991:1 1999:1.

generate. It is rather a consequence of the fact that one way monetary policy in the model affects the economy is by changing the way the private sector form expectations. In other words, if the central bank has an aggressive stance towards inflation, the model predicts it will not have to move the policy rate very much. The expectation of the private sector that the monetary authority would do so if faced with raising inflation, is sufficient for the economy not to overheat and to curb inflationary pressure.

6. Conclusion

This chapter discussed the impact of the Canadian inflation targeting policy adopted in 1991 on the inflation-output gap trade-off, and the role it played in the recession over the 1992-1994 period. I document that the empirical relationship between the output gap and the inflation rate in Canada changed after the shift to the inflation targeting regime, and show that, conditional on the vector of business cycle shocks that hit the Canadian economy, the shift in the inflation process and in the inflation-output gap trade-off can be explained as the result of the inflation targeting monetary policy. This implies that the backward-looking Phillips curve is not a structural feature of the Canadian economy, but simply a useful reduced-form regularity contingent on the monetary policy regime. As a consequence, the policymaker was able to influence the recessionary impact of inflation stabilization.

This result is obtained by building counterfactual histories of the Canadian economy consistent with a stochastic general equilibrium model. Statistical tests performed on the counterfactual under the alternative monetary policy suggests that the shifts in the Phillips curve and inflation dynamics since 1991 would not have happened under the existing monetary policy. The regime shift cannot be explained simply by favorable macroeconomic conditions: the management of monetary policy played a key role.

But while the monctary authority may have achieved a better trade-off between inflation and output gap stabilization *on average*, the impact of policy for a particular historical sample also depends on the business cycle shocks realization. The chapter shows that the Canadian disinflation in the early 1990s occurred at the cost of a significant output loss. Therefore, conditional on the vector of shocks that affected the economy, the adoption of inflation targeting was among the causes of the 1992-1994 recession.

A. Appendix: Model Parametrization

A.1. Preferences and Technology

Given the assumptions on the steady state terms of trade, the parameter γ measuring the elasticity of substitution between the foreign and home goods aggregate is equal to the steady state share of imports on total consumption, and as well to the steady state share of exports on domestic production. I set the share γ equal to 0.33 , in accordance with most models calibrated on the Canadian economy. Following the estimates in Kollman (2001), the price elasticity of export demand ρ^* , and the domestic households' price elasticity of demand ρ , is set equal to 1.2. The habit formation parameter b is set equal to 0.6 , a value that optimizes the match of sticky price models with consumption data (Fuhrer, 2000). The steady state real interest rate is set at level of 1.21% per quarter (calculated from the average US 3-month T-Bill deflated by CPI inflation). As in Mendoza

(1991) and Kollmann (2001) models of the Canadian economy, the labor supply elasticity $(1/\eta)$ is set equal to 2 . The parameter ℓ is chosen to match steady state N , which is about 20% of the available time in the postwar data.

I set the steady state producers' markup $\mu = \vartheta/(\vartheta - 1) = 1.2$ (Bernanke and Gertler, 1999). I choose the same value for the steady state workers' markup $\phi/(\phi - 1)$, as other authors in the sticky price - sticky wage literature (Edge, 2000, 2002)[10]. As in most of the literature adopting the Calvo (1983) pricing adjustment, the probability θ_p faced by firms of not adjusting the price in any given period is set to 0.75 , implying that the average time between price adjustments for a producer is 1 year. The wage contract is supposed to adjust in the same fashion.

A.2. Exogenous Variables

The stochastic exogenous variables follow an AR(1) process. Its general form is:

$$\log Z_t = (1 - \rho_i) \log \overline{Z} + \rho_Z \log Z_{t-1} + \varepsilon_{Z,t} \qquad \varepsilon_{Z,t} \sim i.i.d.\ N(0; \sigma_Z^2)$$

where $\overline{Z}$ is the steady state value of the variable. I calibrate the technology autocorrelation parameter ρ_A to match the model's simulated output first order autocorrelation with Canadian postwar data, choosing a value of 0.9 . In the same fashion, the preference shock autocorrelation coefficient ρ_D is calibrated to a value of 0.8 . The foreign (US) interest rate autocorrelation parameter ρ_{I^*} is estimated and set equal to 0.7 . Following Kollman (2001), I set the foreign price autocorrelation $\rho_{P_F^*} = 0.8$.

Acknowledgment

I would like to thank Mark Gertler, Thomas Cooley, Pierpaolo Benigno, Fabrizio Perri, Bart Hobijn, Tommaso Monacelli and Harald Uhlig for very helpful comments and suggestions on an earlier draft of the paper.

References

[1] Amato, J. and Laubach, T., (1999), 'Monetary policy in an estimated optimization-based model with sticky prices and wages', *Federal Reserve Bank of Kansas City Research Working Paper* 99-09.

[2] Andersen, Torben, (1998), 'Persistency in sticky price models', *European Economic Review* **42**, 593-603.

[3] Backus, D., (1984), 'Exchange rate dynamics in a model with staggered contracts', *Working Paper* **561**, Queen's University, Kingston, Ontario.

[4] Banerjee, A., Lumsdaine, R. and Stock, J., (1992), 'Recursive and sequential tests of the unit-root and trend-break hypotheses: theory and international evidence', *Journal of Business and Economic Statistics* **10**(3): 270-90.

[10] Amato and Laubach (1999) estimate a sticky price - sticky wage model of the US economy and find a value for the steady state workers' markup $\phi/(\phi - 1)$ of 8.5 , with a standard deviation of 6.1 .

[5] Ball, L., and Sheridan, N., (2005), 'Does Inflation Targeting Matter?', in Bernanke, B. and Woodford, M., eds., *The Inflation Targeting Debate,* University of Chicago Press.

[6] Bernanke, B. and Gertler, M., (1999), 'Monetary policy and asset price volatility', *Federal Reserve Bank of Kansas City Economic Review,* **84**(4).

[7] Bernanke, B., Laubach, T., Mishkin, F. and Posen, A., (1999), Inflation Targeting: Lessons from the International Experience, Princeton: Princeton University Press.

[8] Black, R., Macklem, T. and Rose, D., (1997) 'On policy rules for price stability', Proceedings of the conference on Price Stability, Inflation Targets and Monetary Policy, Bank of Canada.

[9] Blanchard, O. and Kahn, (1980), 'The solution of linear difference models under rational expectations', *Econometrica* **48**: 1305-1311.

[10] Blankenau, W., Kose, M. and Yi, K., (2001), 'Can world real interest rates explain business cycles in a small open economy?', *Journal of Economic Dynamics & Control* **25**: 867-889.

[11] Boldrin, M., Christiano, L. and Fisher, J., (2001), 'Habit persistence, asset returns and the business cycle', *American Economic Review* **91**: 149-166.

[12] Chari, V., Kehoe, P. and McGrattan, E., (2006), 'Business Cycle Accounting', *Econometrica*, forthcoming..

[13] Clarida, R., Gali, J. and Gertler, Mark, (1999), 'The science of monetary policy: a New Keynesian perspective', *Journal of Economic Literature* **37**: 1661-1707.

[14] - (1998), 'Monetary policy in practice: some international evidence', *European Economic Review* **42**: 1033-1067.

[15] - (2000), 'Monetary policy rules and macroeconomic stability: evidence and some theory', *Quarterly Journal of Economics* **115**: 147-80.

[16] Calvo, G., (1983), 'Staggered prices in a utility-maximizing framework', *Journal of Monetary Economics* **12**: 383-98.

[17] Edge, R., (2002), 'The equivalence of wage and price staggering in monetary business cycle models', *Review of Economic Dynamics*, **5**: 559-585.

[18] - , (2000), 'Time-to-build, Time-to-plan, habit-persistence and the liquidity effect', *Board of Governors of the Federal Reserve System International Finance Discussion Paper* **673**.

[19] Erceg, C., Henderson, D. and Levin, A., (1999), 'Optimal monetary policy with staggered wage and price contracts', *Journal of Monetary Economics* **46**: 281-313.

[20] Estrella, A. and Fuhrer, J., (2000), 'Are deep parameters stable? The Lucas critique as an empirical hypothesis', mimeo, Federal Reserve Bank of New York.

[21] Fischer, S., (1977), 'Long term contracts, rational expectations and the optimal money supply rule', *Journal of Political Economy* **85**: 191-205.

[22] Fuhrer, J., (2000), 'Habit Formation in Consumption and Its Implications for Monetary-Policy Models', *American Economic Review* **90**(3): 367-90.

[23] Gali , J. and Gertler, Mark, (1999), 'Inflation dynamics : a structural analysis', *Journal of Monetary Economics* **44**: 195-222.

[24] Hall, G., (1996), 'Overtime, effort, and the propagation of business cycle shocks', Journal of Monetary Economics 38: 139-60.

[25] Hamilton, J., (1983), 'Oil price and the macroeconomy since World War II', *Journal of Political Economy* **XCI**: 228-48.

[26] Hostland, D., (1995), 'Changes in the inflation process in Canada: evidence and implications', *Bank of Canada Working Paper* 95-5.

[27] Kahn, G. and Parrish, K., (1998), 'Conducting monetary policy with inflation targets', *Federal Reserve Bank of Kansas City Economic Review,* **(3)** 1998: 5-32.

[28] King, R. and Rebelo, S., (1998) 'Resuscitating real business cycle', in Woodford, M. and Taylor, J., eds., *Handbook of Macroeconomics,* Amsterdam: North-Holland.

[29] Kollmann, R., (2001), 'The Exchange Rate in a Dynamic-Optimizing Business Cycle Model with Nominal Rigidities: A Quantitative Investigation', *Journal of International Economics* **55**: 243-262.

[30] Ingram, B., Kocherlakota, N. and Savin, N., (1994), 'Explaining business cycles: a multiple-shock approach', *Journal of Monetary Economics* **34**: 415-28.

[31] Levin, Andrew T., and Jeremy M. Piger, (2002), "Is Inflation Persistence Intrinsic in Industrialized Economies?" *FRB St. Louis Working Paper* 2002-023E.

[32] Levin, A., Natalucci, F., and Piger, J., (2004), 'The Macroeconomic Effect of Inflation Targeting', *Federal Reserve Bank of St. Louis Review* **86**(4): 51-81.

[33] Leybourne, S., Mills, T. and Newbold, P., (1998), 'Spurious rejections by Dickey-Fuller tests in the presence of a break under the null', *Journal of Econometrics* **87**, 191-203.

[34] Lucas, Robert E., Jr. and Thomas J. Sargent, (1978), "After Keynesian Macroeconomics", in After the Phillips Curve: Persistence of High Inflation and High Unemployment, *Federal Reserve Bank of Boston Conference Series* No. **19**, pp. 49-72.

[35] McCallum, B. and Nelson, E., (1999), 'Performance of operational policy rules in an estimated semiclassical structural model', in Taylor, ed., Monetary Policy Rules, Chicago: The University of Chicago Press.

[36] McGrattan, E., Rogerson, R. and Wright, R., (1997), 'An equilibrium model of the business cycle with household production and fiscal policy', *International Economic Review* **38**: 267-90.

[37] Mendoza, E.,(1991), 'Real business cycle in small open economy', *American Economic Review* **81**(4): 797-818.

[38] Mishkin, F. and Posen, A., (1997), 'Inflation targeting: lessons from four countries', *Economic Policy Review*, August.

[39] Obstfeld, M. and Rogoff, K., (2000), 'New directions for stochastic open economy models', *Journal of International Economics,* **50**(1): 117-53.

[40] Parkin, M., (1988), 'A method for determining whether parameters in aggregate models are structural', *Carnegie-Rochester Conference Series on Public Policy* **29**: 215-22.

[41] Perron, P., (1989), 'The great Crash, the oil price shock and the unit root hypothesis', *Econometrica* **57**, 1361-1401.

[42] - (1990), 'Testing for a unit root in a time series with a changing mean', *Jouranl of Business and Economic Statistics,* **8:** 153-162.

[43] - (1997), 'Further evidence on breaking trend functions in macroeconomic variables', *Journal of Econometrics*, **80**: 355-385.

[44] Pivetta, Frederic, and Ricardo Reis, (2007), "The Persistence of Inflation in the United States", *Journal of Economic Dynamics & Control,* forthcoming.

[45] Ravenna, F. (2007), 'Inflation Targeting: a Structural Approach', Santa Cruz Center for International Economics Working Paper.

[46] Ricketts, N. and Rose, D., (1995), 'Inflation, learning and monetary policy regimes in the G-7 economies', *Bank of Canada Working Paper* **95-6**.

[47] Rotemberg, J. and Woodford, M., (1998), 'An optimization-based econometric framework for the evaluation of monetary policy', in B. Bernanke and J. Rotemberg, eds., *NBER Macroeconomics Annual* 1997: 297-346.

[48] - (1999), 'Interest rate rules in an estimated sticky price model', in J. Taylor, ed., Monetary Policy Rules, NBER and Chicago University Press.

[49] Rudd, J. and Whelan, K., (2005), 'Does labor's share drive inflation?', *Journal of Money, Credit and Banking* **37**: 298-312.

[50] Sbordone, A., (2002), 'An optimizing Model of US wage and price dynamics', *Proceedings,* Federal Reserve Bank of San Francisco, March.

[51] Schmitt-Grohe, S., (1998), 'The international transmission of economic fluctuations: effects of US business cycles on the Canadian economy', *Journal of International Economics* **44**: 257-87.

[52] Schmitt-Grohe and Uribe, M., (2001), 'Stabilization policy and the costs of dollarization', Journal of Money, Credit, and Banking 33: 482-509.

[53] Taylor, J., (1979), 'Staggered wage setting in a macro model', *American Economic Review, Papers and Proceedings,* **69**: 108-113.

Reviewed by: Prof. Maurizio Iacopetta, School of Economics, Georgia Institute of Technology.

In: Recessions: Prospects and Developments
Editors: N.M. Pérez and J.A. Ortega, pp. 99-125
ISBN: 978-1-60456-866-0

Chapter 5

ON ACCURACY MEASURE OF RECESSION FORECASTS

Khurshid M. Kiani [*]
Department of Economics, The University of the West Indies,
Mona, Kingston, Jamaica, West Indies

Abstract

This research employs a number of economic and financial variables and their combinations to forecast recessions for Canada and the USA. These variables include real gross domestic product (GDP), industrial production, M1 money supply, spread between long term bond rates and risk free rates, Treasury bill rates, short-term bond rates, longterm bond rates, TSE300 stock prices index for Canada, and S&P500 stock price index for USA. The relationship between these economic and financial variables and recessions 1 − 10 quarters ahead out of sample is modeled using artificial neural networks (ANN) that are considered to be a highly flexible functional form of nonlinear models. The forecast approximated from these models are evaluated using SCORE accuracy measure of recession predictions.

From the fourteen ANN models that are approximated from the seven economic and financial or indicator variables and their combinations for each of the forecast horizons (i.e. 1 − 10 quarters ahead), the single indicator variables stock price index, Treasury bill rates, industrial production, short term bond rates, long term bond rates, and the spread between long term bond rates and Treasury bill rates are the candidate variables for predicting Canadian recessions. However, when these indicator variables are used for real time forecast of future recessions for Canada, no single indicator variable predicted Canadian recessions beyond 2005:Q2 which is the last observation in all the series. However, short term bond rate predicted American recessions two quarters ahead, whereas industrial production growth predicted American recessions one, three and four quarters ahead, although the combined indicator variables are able to predict American recessions up to nine quarters ahead.

Key phrases: artificial neural networks; out-of-sample forecasts; asymmetries; business cycles; recessions; forecast horizons

JEL Codes: C22, C32, C45

---

[*] E-mail address: mkkiani@yahoo.com, or khurshid.kiani@uwimona.edu.jm Tel: +1-876-512-3015; Fax: +1-876-977-1483.

1. Introduction

Recession forecasts have caught the attention of a wide body of empirical research with the advent of the 2001 USA recession. In this context many researchers focused on the spread between the long term bond rates and the risk free rates for forecasting recessions. Fabio (2005) concluded that 3-month interbank rates outperformed all other spreads for recession predictions in euro area. On the other hand Nyholm (2007) proposed a new approach for recession predictions and claimed that only the yield curve had been used to predict all NBER recession forecasts for USA from 1973 to 2004 at least eight months ahead in future. Similarly, Estrella (2005) showed that the yield curve has the ability to predicting output and inflation in most cases. Henri and Gerlach (1998) showed that the index of leading economic indicators outperformed the yield spread in the short run up to 4 months but the yield spread performed better at longer horizons. Alternatively, Beatriz and Galvão (2006) proposed a model to predict recessions that accounted for non- linearity and a structural break using the spread between the long-term and short-term interest rates as the leading indicator. Contrary to that, Lahiri and Wang (2006) showed that the probabilistic forecasts are often more useful in business than point forecasts. Alternately, Anderson and Vahid (2001), using nonlinear autoregressive models, concluded that conditional on the spread, the marginal contribution of M2 growth in predicting USA recessions is negligible.

A wide body of empirical research shows that business cycle fluctuations are asymmetric. In this context, studies including Neftci (1984), Brunner (1997), Beaudry and Koop (1993), Potter (1995), Ramsay and Rothman (1996), Bidarkota (2000), Andreano and Savio (2002), and Kiani and Bidarkota (2004) using univariate nonlinear time series models showed that asymmetric business cycle fluctuations do exist in macroeconomic time series. Likewise, Anderson and Vahid (1998), and Anderson and Ramsay (2002) using multivariate nonlinear time series models showed that asymmetries are prevalent in business cycle fluctuations. That is the reason why linear models cannot be used in business cycle research when the underlying data generating process is nonlinear.

Considering that business cycle asymmetries do prevail in most macro-financial time series data, Estrella and Mishkin (1998) employed nonlinear time series models in conjunction with a number of macro-financial time series for forecasting USA recessions. Qi (2001) employed artificial neural networks (ANN) and the data used by Estrella and Mishkin (1998) to predict USA recession, but despite using an alternative methodology her results were not better than Estrella and Mishkin (1998). Somewhat later, Kiani and Kastens (2006) using ANN and macro-financial variables from the Canadian economy predicted Canada recession 1 − 10 quarters ahead in future out-of-sample. Using Canada as well as USA macro-financial variables and ANN, the focus of the present study is to explore whether USA and Canada recessions can be predicted 1 − 10 quarters ahead in future out-of-sample when using accuracy measure and dynamic benchmark of recession forecasts due to Kiani and Kastens (2006).

ANN has been used successfully in engineering, finance, business and economics. However, there are very few examples of ANN being used in business cycle research or the recession forecasts. For example, Vishwakerma (1995), Kiani et al. (2005), and Kiani Savio (2002), and Kiani and Bidarkota (2004) using univariate nonlinear time series models showed that asymmetric business cycle fluctuations do exist in macroeconomic time series. Likewise,

Anderson and Vahid (1998), and Anderson and Ramsay (2002) using multivariate nonlinear time series models showed that asymmetries are prevalent in business cycle fluctuations. That is the reason why linear models cannot be used in business cycle research when the underlying data generating process is nonlinear.

Considering that business cycle asymmetries do prevail in most macro-financial time series data, Estrella and Mishkin (1998) employed nonlinear time series models in conjunction with a number of macro-financial time series for forecasting USA recessions. Qi (2001) employed artificial neural networks (ANN) and the data used by Estrella and Mishkin (1998) to predict USA recession, but despite using an alternative methodology her results were not better than Estrella and Mishkin (1998). Somewhat later, Kiani and Kastens (2006) using ANN and macro-financial variables from the Canadian economy predicted Canada recession 1 − 10 quarters ahead in future out-of-sample. Using Canada as well as USA macro-financial variables and ANN, the focus of the present study is to explore whether USA and Canada recessions can be predicted 1 − 10 quarters ahead in future out-of-sample when using accuracy measure and dynamic benchmark of recession forecasts due to Kiani and Kastens (2006).

ANN has been used successfully in engineering, finance, business and economics. However, there are very few examples of ANN being used in business cycle research or the recession forecasts. For example, Vishwakerma (1995), Kiani et al. (2005), and Kiani (2005) employed neural networks in business cycle research and Qi (2001), and Kiani and Kastens (2006) employed ANN for forecasting recessions. The contribution of the present study is two-fold. One, it employs ANN to approximate recession forecasts using USA and Canada macro-financial time series recursively 1 − 10 quarters ahead where neural networks are approximated out of sample using a combination of genetic algorithm (GA), and fminsearch routine from MATLAB, because the GA is the most reliable algorithm that can be used to estimate any nonlinear model. The accurately predicted forecasts from ANN 1 − 10 quarters ahead both for Canada and USA are evaluated using SCORE accuracy measure of recession forecasts. These results reveal a significant improvement in recession forecasts over the previous studies (Estrella and Mishkin (1998), and Qi (2001)).

2. Empirical Model

Artificial neural network (ANN) is a computational technique that is closely associated with the human brain's learning and decision making techniques. The ANN has an ability to mimic human brain for information processing to recognize pattern and make decisions based on these pattern recognitions. Because of their ability to process information, ANN can learn from examples and generalize these learnings to solve unknown problems (Reilly and Cooper 1990). The term "neural" stems from the three dimensional lattice of network among human brain cells that are known as "nodes" or "neurons". When compared to the human brain's superior ability to recognize and understand various patters, ANN are extremely primitive. However, these are capable of understanding and recognizing patterns in a large number of variables simultaneously in addition to being able to carrying out multiple operations as well as being able to detect correlation in a large number of variables but are able to recognize patterns only in a few variables.

Although a number of ANN have been proposed by cognitive scientists and researchers for econometric applications, one of the most influential ANN architecture is multilayer feed forward perception (MLP) that is able to approximate a large number of diverse functions arbitrarily (White 1989a). ANN are able to learn important features of the data, even when a data is noisy or it has irrelevant inputs, although these irrelevant inputs may contain useful information which can be extracted by ANN due to their patter recognition ability. This approach is useful in problems where data is available but the underlying data generating process is unknown. ANN are nonlinear, nonparametric statistical methods that are independent of the distribution of the data generating processes (White 1989b) that enables them to approximate any continuous function with desired level of precision (Hornick et al. 1989).

Despite their positive modeling aspects, ANN are under heavy criticism for overfilling the data (Kean 1993), and that they are "black boxes" meaning that it is difficult to visualize functional form of the ANN models. Additionally, Qi (1996) argues that due to multi-minima error surface, it is hard to ensure global minimum in the absence of an optimal estimating algorithm for approximating ANN. Unlike traditional econometric techniques, time series models are more widely used particularly for predictive purposes. However, the first step of time series modeling is a bit difficult because of the model that would fit to a given time series data appropriately in addition to appropriate order specifications. However, unlike time series models, ANN are not confronted with the data generating processes or the underlying distribution of the data generating process, instead ANN are data driven and can fit to any time series data adequately (Davies 1995). Moreover, unlike statistical models, ANN is adept to handling noise pertaining to most financial market data. For example, White (1989b) and Kuan and White (1994) showed that ANN performed better than the competing statistical models. A general form of artificial neural networks is shown in Equation.

$$f(x) = \psi\left[\alpha_0 + \sum_{j=1}^{n} a_j \psi\left(\sum_{i=1}^{k} \beta_{ij} x_i + \beta_{0j}\right)\right] + u \qquad (1)$$

where, n is the number of hidden nodes in the network, k the number of explanatory variables,(x) = 1/(1+e-x) is a transfer function that can either be sigmoid (logistic) or hyperbolic (tangent) cumulative distribution function, aj arepresents a vector of parameters or weights that link the hidden layers to output layers' units,(i = 1 , ... , k; j = 1 , ... , n) denotes a matrix of parameters linking input to the hidden layers' units, and is an error term.

ANN are considered to be non-parametric, and highly flexible form of nonlinear statistical methods and because of the complexity of these models, convergence of ANN can be an issue. To overcome this difficulty, the present study employs a combination of genetic algorithm (GA)[1] and fiminsearch routine from MATLAB that is coded in MATLAB software. The GA is employed for neural network approximations which are considered to be the most reliable algorithm to estimate any nonlinear functional form but it appeared to be very slow. Therefore, GA is used to start with but to increase the probability of obtaining a

[1] Initially, De Jong (1975) applied genetic algorithm, to mathematical optimization, whereas Goldberg, (1989) employed it in biology, engineering and operation research. Axelrod (1987) appears to be a pioneer to employ it in Economics. Somewhat later Marimon, McGratten and T. Sergeant (1990), and Dorsey and Walter (1995) also employed it in economics.

global minimum, 4 independent runs of the GA are considered. Out of these four random starts, the parameter vector that has the smallest sum of squared errors (SSE) is next used as the starting conditions for Matlab's fminsearch algorithm, which is a Nelder-Mead simplex algorithm that works well for closing in on the optima. Though the process is computationally intensive, these steps are essential to ensure that the model estimations could be repeatable.

3. Empirical Results

3.1. Data Sources

The present study employs Treasury bill (T-bill) rates, short-term bond rates (of less than three-year duration) long term bond rates (of more than ten-year duration), M1 money supply, real gross domestic product (GDP), and industrial production both for Canadian and USA economies from the November 2005 version of the International Financial Statistics' CD-ROM. On the other hand the S&P 500 USA stock price index and TSE 300 stock price index for Canada are obtained from DataStream. Data for all the series span from 1957:Q1 to 2006:Q2. Table 1 show the structure of various single and combined variables that are also called as indicator variables. The Table show fourteen indicator variables that comprise of seven single indicator variables and seven combined indicator variables that are employed for ANN approximations.

Table 1. Structure of the Variables Employed

Description of Variables	**Indicator Variables**	
Single Indicator Variables		
	Canada	*USA*
10-year Treasury bond rate less 3-month Treasury bill rate	*Spread*	*Spread*
3-month Treasury bill market equivalent bond rate	*T-bill*	*T-bill*
1-3 year Government bond rates	*BondLT*	*BondLT*
10-year Government Treasury bond rates	*BondST*	*BondST*
M1 Money Supply, seasonally adjusted	*M1*	*M1*
S&P 500 USA stock price Index		*index*
TSE300 Canada stock price Index	*Index*	
Industrial Production Growth	*IPG*	*IPG*
Combined Indicator Variables		
Government Treasury bill and three-year Government *Bond rates*	*T-bill&BondST*	*T-bill&BondST*
10-year Government Bond rates and three-year *Bond rates*	*BondLT&BondST*	*BondLT&BondST*
Spread and Stock Price Index	*Index&Spread*	*Index&Spread*
Government Treasury bill and *Spread*	*T-bill&Spread*	*T-bill&Spread*
Three-year Bond and *Spread*	*BondST&Spread*	*BondST&Spread*
Government Treasury bill and Long Term bond rates	*T-bill&BondLT*	*T-bill&BondLT*
Stock Price Index and *Government Treasury Bill*	*Index&T-bill*	*Index&T-bill*

3.2. Forecast Evaluations

This research focuses on accuracy measure of recession forecasts that would require adequate understanding of various measures of prediction evaluations. Therefore, to answer the research question of the present study an accurate measure of recession forecast would be required. To this end, it would be advantageous to work for a measure of prediction accuracy to start with. Thereafter, thinking of predicting recessions many quarters ahead of previous studies (e.g. Qi ,2001) would make the present empirical exercise useful for policymakers and researchers.

When considering forecasting methods, the important empirical question would be the choice of an error measure. Fildes (1983) shows that the commonly used measures are dependent on the magnitude of the series in question and often it is not possible to make direct comparisons of forecast accuracy. For example, Chatfield (1988) show that the mean square error (MSE) approach of evaluating forecasting method shows the intensity of the feelings involved, although according to Mehmoud (1987) it is the measure that is considered to be adequate for the applications such as inventory control. Alternative approaches include Gardner (1983) who used median error and Anderson (1983) and Fildes (1989) employed geometric mean as the measure of accuracy of forecasting models.

Inappropriate application of error measure can result in distorted view of forecast performance especially when real life rather than simulated data are used for analysis. There are a variety of views on how to select a measure of forecast evaluation. Armstrong (1985) and Mehmoud (1987) argued for an interrelationship among the various measures. The most common used measures of forecast evaluation of the forecasting models can be split into two broad categories or groups such as the ratio type accuracy measures and volume based accuracy measures. The measures, such as mean absolute error, mean squared error, root mean squared error, standard deviation of the error fall into the category of volume base accuracy measures whereas mean percentage error, mean absolute percentage error, adjusted absolute percentage error, average absolute percentage error, coefficient of variation, and accuracy ratio fall into the category of the ratio type accuracy measures, although some of the other measures such as mean error, Theil's U, and tracking signals do not fall in any of these two categories.

Estrella (1998) showed a list of various measures of goodness of fit that can again be categorized into two main groups i.e. probability based and moment based measures. The probability based measures are based on the maximum likelihood statistics but the moment based measures are based on the first and second moments of the actual values of the endogenous variables. However, the unconstrained likelihood for the dichotomous dependent variables is occasionally zero, which causes likelihood based goodness of fit to be occasionally unidentified. Therefore, Qi (2001) employed a measure due to Hamilton and Periz-Quiros (1996) in conjunction with a static benchmark of recession forecasts. However, contrary to Qi (2001), we employ root mean square error (RMSE) to evaluate recession forecasts approximated by ANN using single as well as combined indicator variables whose structure is shown in Table 1 in addition to using SCORE accuracy measure of recession predictions due to Kiani and Kastens (2006) for evaluating accuracy of recession forecasts for all the series.

3.3. Results on Recession Forecasts

The data series employed in this empirical exercise are represented by the sample period that spans from 1977: Q1 to 1995: Q1 which is henceforth called total sample period. The total sample is divided into two sample periods i.e. earlier sub-sample period and the later sub-sample period so that each sub-sample period corresponds to the Canadian recessions in 1980s (1981:Q1 to 1983:Q3) and 1990s (1990:Q2 to 1993:Q2). Having had judged the forecast performance of ANN models in conjunction with single as well combined indicator variables for predicting the abovementioned two Canadian recessions, these models are employed to predict future Canadian and USA recessions beyond year 2005, which is the end point of the data series employed for both the economies. USA recessions are henceforth denoted as American recessions.

The forecasts obtained from neural network models can be evaluated using a static benchmark of forecast accuracy as was done by Qi (2001), however, following Kiani and Kastens (2006) we employ dynamic benchmark of forecasting recession that changes with each of the additional observation used for forecasting recessions over time which varies with changes in forecast horizons. For example the static benchmark of recession forecast is the probability of recessions calculated using the entire data set employed whereas the dynamic benchmark of recessions forecast is the probability of recession forecast only up to a particular point whereupon inclusion of any additional observation in the series would change the benchmark at that point, and this process would continue until the final observation is employed entailing to a final value of benchmark of recessions. The results on recession forecast that are evaluated using various measure of forecast accuracy like RMSE and SCORE are shown in Tables 2.1 – 2.3, and Tables 3.1 – 3.3 respectively for the earlier and later sub-sample periods.

Table 2.1 show results for the earlier sub-sample period Canadian recession forecasts. In this Table, column 1 show the names of various single and combined indicator variable models and column 2-9 show recession forecasts approximated using ANN and all the indicator variables shown in Table 1. These recession forecasts are evaluated using RMSE for all horizons 1-8 quarters ahead. In this Table for example, in row 2, column 2, the number 0.540 1 show RMSE for the single indicator variable T-bill. This number (0.540 1) is smaller than the dynamic benchmark (0.5774) for horizon 1 .The dynamic benchmark for recession forecast for this horizon is shown in the last row of the second column. Since RMSE is lower than the dynamic benchmark of recession, the indicator variable T-bill is a candidate variable for predicting Canadian recession at forecast horizon 1 i.e. one quarter ahead. Similarly, column 3, row 2 shows RMSE at horizon 3 (0.6325) which is equal to the dynamic benchmark of recession (0.6325) reveals that T- bill is able to find turning points of Canadian recession at this horizon. Similarly, the combined indicator variable BondST&Spread predicts recessions at horizon 3 and T – bill&BondLT predicts recessions at horizon 4 i.e. 4 quarters ahead. These results show that inclusion of combined indicator variable in the analysis for predicting recession does not necessarily improve the forecasting results.

Notes on Tables 2-5

The numbers shown in Tables 2.1, 3.1, 4.1, and 5.1 reveal recession forecasts evaluated using root mean square error (RMSE). Tables 2.2, 3.2, 4.1, and 4.5 show recession forecast that are evaluated using SCORE measure of forecast accuracy where missing recessions and missing non-recessions are equally penalized. However, for the results shown in Tables 2.3, 3.3, 4.3, and 5.3, recession forecast are evaluated using SCORE accuracy measure of recession forecasts wherein missing recessions is penalized 10 times heavier than missing non-recessions. This shows that both missing recessions and missing non-recessions have equal error costing i.e.C=1. However, when C>1, unequal error costing results wherein missing recessions are penalized more than missing non-recessions.

In these Tables bold numbers show that recession forecast is able to beat the relevant dynamic benchmark of recession. The last row in each of these Tables shows dynamic benchmark of recessions for each of the forecast horizons.

When evaluating a recession forecast based on RMSE, the relevant indicator variable would qualify for predicting recessions only if the number shown in the Table against the variable is lower than the benchmark of recession prediction at that particular horizon.

For the recession forecasts that are evaluated using SCORE accuracy measure of prediction, a forecast of recession prediction higher than the benchmark would enable the relevant variable for recession predictions.

In these Tables bold face numbers show that the indicator variable is able to predict recession at that particular forecast horizon. Similarly, the underlined numbers show that the variable in question is able to locate the turning point of recession.

Table 2.1. Canada: Earlier Period Recession Forecast Evaluations Based on RMSE

Model	Horiz1	Horiz2	Horiz3	Horiz4	Horiz5	Horiz6	Horiz7	Horiz8
Spread	0.6124	0.6396	0.7071	0.7071	0.7071	0.7071	0.7071	0.6325
T-bill	**0.5401**	**0.5641**	0.6325	0.707 1	0.7500	0.707 1	0.6455	0.4472
BondLT	0.7071	0.6030	0.7416	0.7071	0.7500	0.6547	0.5774	0.5477
BondST	0.6770	0.7071	0.7071	0.7071	0.6614	0.6547	0.5774	0.3162
M1	0.6770	0.6030	0.6325	0.6667	0.7906	0.6547	0.5000	0.4472
index	**0.5401**	**0.5641**	0.7071	0.7454	0.8292	0.8018	0.8165	0.7071
IPG	0.5774	0.7385	**0.5916**	0.6667	0.7500	0.6547	0.6455	0.7071
T-bill& BondST	0.6455	0.7385	0.6708	0.707 1	0.7500	0.8018	0.6455	0.3 162
BondLT&BondST	0.6770	0.7071	0.6708	0.7071	0.6614	0.6547	0.7071	0.3162
Index&Spread	0.5774	0.6396	0.6708	0.6667	0.7500	0.7071	0.8660	0.8367
T-bill&Spread	0.5774	0.6030	0.7416	0.6667	0.7906	0.5976	0.7071	0.4472
BondST&Spread	0.6455	0.7071	**0.5916**	0.7071	0.7071	0.7559	0.6455	0.3162
T-bill&BondLT	0.5774	0.6030	0.6325	**0.6236**	0.707 1	0.6547	0.6455	0.4472
Index&T-bill	0.5774	0.6030	0.7416	0.7454	0.7906	0.7071	0.8660	0.6325
Benchmark	0.5774	0.6030	0.6325	0.6667	0.6614	0.5976	0.5000	0.3 162

Table 2.2. Canada: Earlier Period Recession Forecast Evaluations Based on Equal Error Costing (C=1)

Model	Horiz 1	Horiz2	Horiz3	Horiz4	Horiz5	Horiz6	Horiz7	Horiz8
Spread	0.6250	0.5909	0.5000	0.5000	0.5000	0.5000	0.5000	0.6000
T-bill	**0.7083**	**0.6818**	0.6000	0.5000	0.4375	0.5000	0.5833	0.8000
BondLT	0.5000	0.6364	0.4500	0.5000	0.4375	0.57 14	0.6667	0.7000
BondST	0.5417	0.5000	0.5000	0.5000	0.5625	0.5714	0.6667	0.9000
M1	0.5417	0.6364	0.6000	0.5556	0.3750	0.5714	0.7500	0.8000
index	**0.7083**	**0.6818**	0.5000	0.4444	0.3125	0.3571	0.3333	0.5000
IPG	0.6667	0.4545	**0.6500**	0.5556	0.4375	0.57 14	0.5833	0.5000
T-bill& BondST	0.5833	0.4545	0.5500	0.5000	0.4375	0.357 1	0.5833	0.9000
BondLT&BondST	0.5417	0.5000	0.5500	0.5000	0.5625	0.5714	0.5000	0.9000
Index&Spread	0.6667	0.5909	0.5500	0.5556	0.4375	0.5000	0.2500	0.3000
T-bill&Spread	0.6667	0.6364	0.4500	0.5556	0.3750	0.6429	0.5000	0.8000
BondST&Spread	0.5833	0.5000	**0.6500**	0.5000	0.5000	0.4286	0.5833	0.9000
T-bill&BondLT	0.6667	0.6364	0.6000	**0.6111**	0.5000	0.5714	0.5833	0.8000
Index&T-bill	0.7083	0.6364	0.4500	0.4444	0.3750	0.5000	0.2500	0.6000
Benchmark	0.6667	0.6364	0.6000	0.5556	0.5625	0.6429	0.7500	0.9000

Table 2.3. Canada: Earlier Period Recession Forecast Evaluations Based on Unequal Error Costing (*C*=10)

Model	Horiz1	Horiz2	Horiz3	Horiz4	Horiz5	Horiz6	Horiz7	Horiz8
Spread	**0.2500**	0.1383	0.1087	0.1000	0.1013	0.1186	0.1538	0.3158
T-bill	**0.2708**	**0.2553**	0.1304	**0.2000**	0.0886	0.1186	0.1795	0.4211
BondLT	**0.2188**	**0.2447**	0.0978	0.1000	0.0886	0.1356	0.2051	0.3684
BondST	0.1354	**0.2128**	0.1087	0.1000	0.1139	0.1356	0.2051	0.4737
M1	**0.2292**	**0.2447**	0.1304	0.1111	0.0759	0.1356	0.2308	0.4211
index	**0.3646**	**0.2553**	0.1087	0.0889	**0.1772**	0.0847	0.1026	0.2632
IPG	**0.2604**	0.1064	**0.2391**	0.1111	0.0886	0.1356	0.1795	0.2632
T-bill& BondST	**0.3333**	**0.2021**	0.1196	**0.2000**	0.0886	0.0847	0. 1795	0.4737
BondLT&BondST	**0.2292**	**0.2128**	0.1196	0.1000	0.1139	0.1356	0.1538	0.4737
Index&Spread	**0.2604**	**0.2340**	0.1196	**0.3111**	**0.2025**	0.1186	0.0769	0.1579
T-bill&Spread	**0.2604**	**0.2447**	0.0978	**0.2111**	0.0759	0.1525	0.1538	0.4211
BondST&Spread	**0.3333**	**0.2128**	**0.3370**	0.1000	0.1013	0.1017	0. 1795	0.4737
T-bill&BondLT	**0.3542**	**0.2447**	0.1304	**0.2222**	0.1013	0.1356	0.1795	0.4211
Index&T-bill	**0.2708**	**0.2447**	0.0978	**0.1889**	0.0759	0.1186	0.0769	0.3158
Benchmark	0.1667	0.1489	0.1304	0.1111	0.1139	0.1525	0.2308	0.4737

Table 3.1. Canada: Later Period Recession Forecast Evaluations Based on RMSE

Model	Horiz 1	Horiz2	Horiz3	Horiz4	Horiz5	Horiz6	Horiz7	Horiz8
Spread	**0.6325**	**0.6547**	**0.6794**	0.7360	**0.7385**	0.8062	0.9129	0.8660
T-bill	**0.5774**	**0.5976**	**0.6504**	0.7638	0.7977	0.8660	0.9129	0.8660
BondLT	0.6583	**0.6547**	**0.6794**	0.7360	**0.7385**	**0.7746**	0.8165	0.8292
BondST	0.6583	**0.6547**	0.7338	0.7638	0.7687	**0.7746**	0.8165	0.7906
M1	**0.6325**	**0.6547**	**0.6794**	0.7360	0.7687	0.8367	0.8498	0.8292
index	0.7071	0.7559	0.7071	0.7360	0.7687	0.8062	0.8165	0.7906
IPG	0.6583	0.7071	0.7596	0.7360	0.7687	0.8062	0.8165	**0.7500**
T-bill& BondST	0.683 1	**0.5669**	0.707 1	0.7360	0.8257	0.8367	0.9129	0.8292
BondLT&BondST	**0.5774**	**0.5345**	**0.5547**	**0.7071**	0.7687	0.8660	0.8498	0.8292
Index&Spread	**0.5477**	**0.6268**	0.7071	0.7906	**0.7385**	0.8062	0.8165	0.8660
T-bill&Spread	**0.6325**	**0.5976**	0.7071	0.8165	0.7687	0.8062	**0.7817**	0.8660
BondST&Spread	0.6583	0.6814	0.7338	**0.6455**	0.7977	0.8660	0.8819	0.8292
T-bill&BondLT	**0.6055**	**0.5000**	**0.6794**	0.7906	0.8790	0.9220	0.9129	0.8660
Index&T-bill	**0.5164**	**0.5976**	**0.6794**	0.8165	0.8528	0.8367	0.8819	0.8292
Benchmark	0.6583	0.6814	0.7071	0.7360	0.7687	0.8062	0.8165	0.7906

Table 3.2. Canada: Later Period Recession Forecast Evaluations Based on Equal Error Costing (*C*=1)

Model	Horiz 1	Horiz2	Horiz3	Horiz4	Horiz5	Horiz6	Horiz7	Horiz8
Spread	0.6000	**0.5714**	**0.5385**	0.4583	**0.4545**	0.3500	0.1667	0.2500
T-bill	0.6667	**0.6429**	**0.5769**	0.4167	0.3636	0.2500	0.1667	0.2500
BondLT	0.5667	**0.5714**	**0.5385**	0.4583	**0.4545**	**0.4000**	0.3333	0.3 125
BondST	0.5667	**0.5714**	0.4615	0.4167	0.4091	**0.4000**	0.3333	0.3750
M1	0.6000	**0.5714**	**0.5385**	0.4583	0.4091	0.3000	0.2778	0.3 125
index	0.5000	0.4286	0.5000	0.4583	0.4091	0.3500	0.3333	0.3750
IPG	0.5667	0.5000	0.423 1	0.4583	0.4091	0.3500	0.3333	0.4375
T-bill& BondST	0.5333	**0.6786**	0.5000	0.4583	0.3 182	0.3000	0.1667	0.3 125
BondLT&BondST	0.6667	**0.7143**	**0.6923**	**0.5000**	0.4091	0.2500	0.2778	0.3 125
Index&Spread	**0.7000**	**0.6071**	0.5000	0.3750	**0.4545**	0.3500	0.3333	0.2500
T-bill&Spread	0.6000	**0.6429**	0.5000	0.3333	0.4091	0.3500	**0.3889**	0.2500
BondST&Spread	0.5667	0.5357	0.4615	**0.5833**	0.3636	0.2500	0.2222	0.3 125
T-bill&BondLT	0.6333	**0.7500**	**0.5385**	0.3750	0.2273	0.1500	0.1667	0.2500
Index&T-bill	**0.7333**	**0.6429**	**0.5385**	0.3333	0.2727	0.3000	0.2222	0.3 125
Benchmark	0.6667	0.5357	0.5000	0.4583	0.4091	0.3500	0.3333	0.3750

Table 3.3. Canada: Later Period Recession Forecast Evaluations Based on Unequal Error Costing (*C*=10)

Model	Horiz1	Horiz2	Horiz3	Horiz4	Horiz5	Horiz6	Horiz7	Horiz8
Spread	**0.3061**	**0.2966**	**0.2867**	**0.2057**	**0.2662**	**0.1825**	0.0238	0.0377
T-bill	**0.4422**	**0.3724**	**0.3566**	**0.1986**	**0.1223**	**0.1022**	0.0238	0.0377
BondLT	0.1156	**0.1724**	**0.1608**	0.0780	**0.1367**	**0.1241**	0.0476	0.0472
BondST	**0.1769**	**0.1724**	0.0839	0.0709	0.0647	**0.1241**	0.0476	0.0566
M1	**0.1837**	**0.1724**	**0.1608**	0.0780	0.0647	0.0438	0.0397	0.0472
Index	**0.2245**	**0.1448**	0.0909	0.0780	0.0647	0.0511	0.0476	0.0566
IPG	**0.2993**	**0.2207**	0.0769	0.0780	0.0647	0.0511	0.0476	**0.1509**
T-bill& BondST	**0.2925**	**0.5034**	**0.2168**	**0.2695**	**0.1151**	**0.1095**	0.0238	0.0472
BondLT&BondST	**0.3810**	**0.4483**	**0.4406**	**0.2128**	**0.1942**	0.0365	0.0397	0.0472
Index&Spread	**0.5102**	**0.3034**	**0.2168**	**0.1277**	**0.2662**	**0.1825**	**0.1190**	**0.1226**
T-bill&Spread	**0.3061**	**0.4345**	**0.2168**	**0.1206**	**0.1295**	0.0511	**0.1270**	0.0377
BondST&Spread	**0.1769**	**0.3517**	**0.2098**	**0.2908**	**0.1871**	**0.1022**	0.03 17	0.0472
T-bill&BondLT	**0.3741**	**0.5793**	**0.2867**	**0.1277**	**0.1007**	0.0219	0.0238	0.0377
Index&T-bill	**0.5170**	**0.3724**	**0.2867**	0.0567	0.0432	**0.1752**	0.03 17	0.0472
Benchmark	0.1156	0.1034	0.0909	0.0780	0.0647	0.0511	0.0476	0.0566

For earlier sub-sample period, the single indicator variable T-bill is able to predict Canada recessions at horizon 2 and 3 . Likewise, the variable index predicts 1 – 2 quarters ahead and IPG predicts recessions 3 quarter ahead. The combined indicator variable BondST&Spread predicts recessions at horizon 3 whereas the variable Tbill&BondLT predicts Canadian recessions 4 quarters ahead. Unlike Qi (2001), these results do not show any improvement in recession forecasts when combined indicator variables are employed to predict Canadian recessions.

The Canadian recession forecasts results on earlier sub-sample period evaluated using SCORE accuracy measure due to Kiani and Kastens (2006) are presented in Table 2.2. These results are based on the value assigned to the variable C that penalizes missing recessions equal to missing non-recession when C is chosen to be . However, when C is chosen to be more than missing a recession is penalized more heavily than missing non-recessions. Thus, using SCORE[2] method of recession forecasts (for earlier sub-sample period), when both missing recessions and missing non-recessions are equally penalized for C=1), single indicator variable T-bill predicts recessions at forecast horizons 1 and 2. Likewise, single indicator variable index also predicts recessions at forecast horizon 1 and 2, however, the indicator variable IPG predicts recession 3 quarters ahead. Likewise the combined indicator variables BondST&Spread predict recession 3 quarters ahead, T - bill&BondLT predicts at horizon 4, and Index&T-bill predict Canada recessions 1 quarters ahead in future. However, Canadian recession forecasts that are evaluated using SCORE measure of forecast accuracy wherein missing recessions are penalized 10 times (C=10) higher than missing non-recessions are shown in Table 2.3. These results show that most single as well as combined indicator variables are candidate variables for predicting Canadian recessions.

Later sub-sample period forecasts for Canadian recessions that are evaluated based on RMSE (Table 3.1) show that the single indicator variable Spread predicts recessions 1, 2 , 3 , and 5 quarters ahead. The indicator variable T – bill predicts recessions at horizons 1, 2 and 3 BondLT predicts at horizons 2, 3, 5, and 6, BondST at horizons 2, 3, and 6, M1 at horizons 2 and 3, and IPG predicts Canadian recessions at horizon 8 i.e. 8 quarters ahead. Likewise, many combined indicator variable predict Canadian recessions at forecast horizons ranging from 1 to 7 quarters ahead in future. Thus, considering the results presented in Table 3.1 for later sub-sample period, inclusion of combined indicator variables improves the forecasting results over the single indicator variables when RMSE is used to evaluate recession forecasts. These results are in line with Qi (2001) who used root mean square prediction errors (RMSPE) for evaluating her recession forecasts.

---

[2] The SCORE measure of forecast accuracy due to Kiani and Kastens (2006) can be calculated as follows:

$$SCORE = 1 - \frac{C\left[\sum_t G_t - \sum_t G_t I(Y_t \geq 0.5)\right] + \left[\sum_t (1-G_t) - \sum_t (1-G_t) I(Y_t < 0.5)\right]}{C\sum_t G_t + \sum_t (1-G_t)}$$

where, Gt is 1 when period t is recession and 0 otherwise. Model prediction is Yt and $I(.)$ is an indicator that equals 1 if its argument is true and 0 otherwise. C is a constant that scales Type I errors pertaining to missed recessions and Type II errors are related to missed non-recessions. The two bracketed terms shown in the numerator of the above Equation show the number of incorrect recession predictions, and the number of incorrect non-recession predictions respectively from left to the right. The denominator show the maximum error cost assuming that every prediction is wrong. Finally the fraction is subtracted from so that a higher SCORE indicates a better model. The results evaluated using SCORE are presented in Tables 2.2, 3.2, 4.2, and 5.2 as well as those presented in Tables 2.3, 3.3, 4.3, and 5.3 show that the bold number that are higher than the relevant dynamic benchmark of prediction are the candidate variables for forecasting recessions.

Forecast evaluations for later sub-sample period are shown in Table 3.2. These forecasts are evaluated using SCORE measure of forecast accuracy when missing recessions are equally penalized to missing non-recessions choosing C equal to 1. The results show that single indicator variable Spread predicts recession at horizon 5, T − bill at horizon 3, BondLT at horizons 5 and 6, BondST at horizon 6, and IPG predicts Canadian recession at horizon 8. Similarly for single and combined indicator variables whose forecasting results are presented in Table 3.3, missing recessions is panelized 10 times higher than missing non-recessions. These results show that when a high penalty is imposed for missing recessions, more indicator variables would be able to predict recessions. However, when compared to the results that are evaluated using RMSE the results based on SCORE measure of forecast accuracy show that only a few indicator variables are able to predict Canadian recessions. Canadian recession predictions decline substantially when switching from RMSE to SCORE measure of forecast evaluations.

3.4. Results on Future Recession Forecasts

Recessions can be difficult to predict even by the experts for a number of reasons. For example, Loungani (2001) who studied survey forecasts of top economists pointed out that "the record of failure to predict is virtually unblemished." Likewise, Zarnowitz and Lambros (1987) noted that consensus forecast from economist might fail to predict recessions accurately even though it has a record of predicting better than individual forecasters. This can be attributed to the fact that forecaster often face real pressure not to predict downturns because of the fear that forecasting may lead to crises of confidence. However, with all these difficulties, the present study seeks to predict future Canadian, and American recessions using economic and financial time series from both the economies beyond the year 2005 where our data point end, the result of which are elaborated in the following sub-sections.

3.4.1. Results on Canadian Recessions

Tables 4.1 − 4.3 show future Canadian recession forecasts 1 − 10 quarters ahead that are approximated using ANN in conjunction with single and combined indicator variables whose structure is shown in Table1. The future recession forecast evaluated using RMSE are presented in Table 4.1 wherein column 1 show names of the indicator variables employed and columns 2 − 11 show predictions at forecast horizons that spans 1 − 10 quarters ahead. In this Table for example the forecasts from the single indicator variable *spread* (0.2338) is shown in column 2 row 1 and the relevant dynamic benchmark of recession forecasts (0.1919) for horizon 2 is shown in the last row of the column 2. However, the variable *spread* is not a candidate variable for predicting Canadian recessions because the forecast based on RMSE should be lower than the benchmark making the variable candidate for predicting recession. The forecasts shown in this Table for the remaining variables are evaluated and presented in the similar manner. These forecasts reveal that no single variable is able to predict Canadian recessions 1 − 10 quarters ahead. However, T − bill, predicts turning point of recessions 10 quarters ahead, BondST 5 quarters ahead, index 2 , and 8 quarters ahead, and IPG predicts recession turning points 3 quarters ahead. Alternately, when considering combined indicator variables, Index&Spread predicts recessions 8 quarters ahead, whereas T − bill&BondST predicts turning points of recession at horizon 10, and T − bill&Spread predicts recession turning points at forecast horizons 8 and 9.

Table 4.1. Canada Recession Forecast Evaluations Based on RMSE

Model	Horiz 1	Horiz2	Horiz3	Horiz4	Horiz5	Horiz6	Horiz7	Horiz8	Horiz9	Horiz10
Spread	0.2338	0.2680	0.2479	0.2255	0.2138	0.2150	0.2163	0.2176	0.2321	0.2582
T-bill	0.2338	0.2973	0.2479	0.1989	0.2138	0.2281	0.2294	0.2035	0.2321	0.1907
BondLT	0.2218	0.2575	0.2364	0.2255	0.2000	0.2012	0.2023	0.2308	0.2321	0.2060
BondST	0.2338	0.2102	0.2695	0.1989	0.1852	0.2012	0.2023	0.2035	0.2047	0.2202
M1	0.2338	0.2230	0.2114	0.1989	0.2507	0.2845	0.2757	0.2551	0.2047	0.2202
Index	0.2452	0.1967	0.1978	0.2126	0.2000	0.2404	0.2023	0.1884	0.2321	0.2060
IPG	0.2665	0.2575	0.1831	0.2377	0.2000	0.2522	0.2294	0.2433	0.2189	0.2335
T-bill& BondST	0.2338	0.2680	0.2479	0.2493	0.2619	0.2522	0.2023	0.2035	0.2189	0.1907
BondLT&BondST	0.2338	0.2781	0.2695	0.2604	0.2268	0.2281	0.2294	0.2551	0.2321	0.2582
Index&Spread	0.2452	0.2680	0.2797	0.2604	0.2138	0.2281	0.2023	**0.1720**	0.2447	0.2335
T-bill&Spread	0.2452	0.2680	0.2114	0.3007	0.2507	0.2281	0.2163	0.1884	0.1895	0.2060
BondST&Spread	0.3136	0.2879	0.2695	0.2812	0.2268	0.2522	0.2536	0.2308	0.2447	0.2462
T-bill&BondLT	0.2338	0.2680	0.2479	0.2812	0.2000	0.2150	0.2023	0.2035	0.2447	0.2462
Index&T-b ill	0.2665	0.2973	0.2589	0.2255	0.2268	0.2012	0.2163	0.2035	0.2321	0.2060
Benchmark	0.1919	0.1956	0.1831	0.1841	0.1852	0.1862	0.1873	0.1884	0.1895	0.1907

Table 4.2. Canada Recession Forecast Evaluations Based on Equal Error Costing (*C*=1)

Model	Horiz1	Horiz2	Horiz3	Horiz4	Horiz5	Horiz6	Horiz7	Horiz8	Horiz9	Horiz10
Spread	0.9454	0.9282	0.9385	0.9492	0.9543	0.9538	0.9532	0.9527	0.9461	0.9333
T-bill	0.9454	0.9116	0.9385	0.9605	0.9543	0.9480	0.9474	0.9586	0.9461	0.9636
BondLT	0.9508	0.9337	0.9441	0.9492	0.9600	0.9595	0.9591	0.9467	0.9461	0.9576
BondST	0.9454	0.9558	0.9274	0.9605	0.9657	0.9595	0.9591	0.9586	0.9581	0.9515
M1	0.9454	0.9503	0.9553	0.9605	0.9371	0.9191	0.9240	0.9349	0.9581	0.9515
Index	0.9399	0.9613	0.9609	0.9548	0.9600	0.9422	0.9591	0.9645	0.9461	0.9576
IPG	0.9290	0.9337	0.9665	0.9435	0.9600	0.9364	0.9474	0.9408	0.9521	0.9455
T-bill& BondST	0.9454	0.9282	0.9385	0.9379	0.93 14	0.9364	0.9591	0.9586	0.9521	0.9636
BondLT&BondST	0.9454	0.9227	0.9274	0.9322	0.9486	0.9480	0.9474	0.9349	0.9461	0.9333
Index&Spread	0.9399	0.9282	0.9218	0.9322	0.9543	0.9480	0.9591	**0.9704**	0.9401	0.9455
T-bill&Spread	0.9399	0.9282	0.9553	0.9096	0.9371	0.9480	0.9532	0.9645	0.9641	0.9576
BondST&Spread	0.9016	0.9171	0.9274	0.9209	0.9486	0.9364	0.9357	0.9467	0.9401	0.9394
T-bill&BondLT	0.9454	0.9282	0.9385	0.9209	0.9600	0.9538	0.9591	0.9586	0.9401	0.9394
Index&T-bill	0.9290	0.9116	0.9330	0.9492	0.9486	0.9595	0.9532	0.9586	0.9461	0.9576
Benchmark	0.9632	0.9617	0.9665	0.9661	0.9657	0.9653	0.9649	0.9645	0.9641	0.9636

Table 4.3. Canada Recession Forecast Evaluations Based on Unequal Error Costing (*C*=10)

Model	Horiz 1	Horiz2	Horiz3	Horiz4	Horiz5	Horiz6	Horiz7	Horiz8	Horiz9	Horiz10
Spread	0.7033	0.6885	0.7210	0.7273	0.7293	0.7269	0.7244	0.7220	0.7149	0.7032
T-bill	0.7033	0.6762	0.7210	0.7359	0.7293	0.7225	0.7200	0.7265	0.7149	0.7260
BondLT	0.7073	0.6926	0.7253	0.7273	0.7336	0.7313	0.7289	0.7175	0.7149	0.7215
BondST	0.7398	0.7090	0.7124	0.7359	0.7380	0.7313	0.7289	0.7265	0.7240	0.7169
M1	0.7033	0.7049	0.7339	0.7359	0.7162	0.7004	0.7022	0.7085	0.7240	0.7169
Index	**0.7358**	**0.7869**	**0.7768**	0.7316	0.7336	0.7181	0.7289	0.7309	0.7149	0.7215
IPG	**0.8008**	**0.7664**	**0.8197**	**0.7619**	0.7336	0.7137	0.7200	0.7130	0.7195	0.7123
T-bill& BondST	**0.7398**	0.6885	0.7210	0.7186	0.7118	0.7137	0.7289	0.7265	0.7195	0.7260
BondLT&BondST	**0.7398**	0.6844	0.7124	0.7143	0.7249	0.7225	0.7200	**0.7489**	0.7149	0.7032
Index&Spread	**0.7724**	**0.7254**	0.7082	0.7143	0.7293	0.7225	0.7289	**0.8161**	0.7104	0.7123
T-bill&Spread	0.6992	0.6885	**0.7725**	0.6970	**0.7555**	0.7225	0.7244	0.7309	0.7285	0.7215
BondST&Spread	0.7439	0.6803	0.7124	0.7056	0.7249	0.7137	0.7111	0.7175	0.7104	0.7078
T-bill&BondLT	0.7033	0.6885	0.7210	0.7056	0.7336	0.7269	0.7289	0.7265	0.7104	0.7078
Index&T-bill	**0.7276**	**0.7500**	0.7167	0.7273	0.7249	0.7313	0.7244	0.7265	0.7149	0.7215
Benchmark	0.7235	0.7154	0.7425	0.7403	0.7380	0.7357	0.7333	0.7309	0.7285	0.7260

Table 5.1. USA Recession Forecast Evaluations Based on RMSE

Model	Horiz 1	Horiz2	Horiz3	Horiz4	Horiz5	Horiz6	Horiz7	Horiz8	Horiz9	Horiz10
Spread	0.4616	0.4582	0.4294	0.4318	0.4209	0.4301	0.4326	**0.4213**	0.4308	0.4334
T-bill	0.4435	0.4334	0.4294	0.4185	0.4209	0.4233	0.4258	0.4351	0.4308	0.4404
BondLT	0.43 10	0.4270	0.4422	0.4633	0.4209	0.4433	0.4393	0.4485	0.4377	0.4606
BondST	0.4310	**0.4205**	0.4546	0.4510	0.4276	0.4498	0.4326	0.4351	0.4512	0.4472
M1	0.4616	0.4521	0.4485	0.4871	0.4536	0.4233	0.4776	0.4742	0.4770	0.4606
Index	0.4310	0.4334	0.4358	0.4318	0.4276	0.4233	**0.4189**	0.4351	0.4308	0.4334
IPG	**0.4049**	0.4270	**0.4162**	**0.4117**	0.4209	0.4498	0.4258	**0.4213**	0.4512	0.4472
T-bill& BondST	0.43 10	0.4642	0.4607	0.4694	**0.4071**	0.4368	0.4393	0.4283	0.4445	0.4334
BondLT&BondST	0.4435	0.4334	0.4844	0.4754	**0.4071**	0.4433	0.4588	0.4419	0.4512	0.4671
Index&Spread	0.4675	0.4270	0.4607	**0.3906**	0.4276	0.4368	0.4459	0.4283	0.4308	0.4472
T-bill&Spread	0.4497	0.4334	0.4485	0.4633	0.4342	0.4687	0.4326	**0.4142**	0.4512	0.4334
BondST&Spread	0.4435	0.4460	0.4294	0.4813	0.4472	0.4748	0.4326	0.4283	0.4377	0.4334
T-bill&BondLT	0.4435	0.4270	0.4358	0.4510	0.4472	0.4301	0.4459	0.4283	0.4238	0.4472
Index&T-b ill	0.4247	0.4205	0.4546	0.4510	0.4276	0.4498	0.4258	0.4283	0.4512	0.4472
Benchmark	0.4247	0.4270	0.4228	0.4185	0.4209	0.4233	0.4258	0.4283	0.4308	0.4334

Table 5.2. USA Recession Forecast Evaluations Based on Equal Error Costing (*C*=1)

Model	Horiz1	Horiz2	Horiz3	Horiz4	Horiz5	Horiz6	Horiz7	Horiz8	Horiz9	Horiz10
Spread	0.7869	0.7901	0.8156	0.8136	0.8229	0.8150	0.8129	**0.8225**	0.8144	0.8121
T-bill	0.8033	0.8122	0.8156	0.8249	0.8229	0.8208	0.8187	0.8107	0.8144	0.8061
BondLT	0.8142	0.8177	0.8045	0.7853	0.8229	0.8035	0.8070	0.7988	0.8084	0.7879
BondST	0.8142	**0.8232**	0.7933	0.7966	0.8171	0.8208	0.8129	0.8107	0.7964	0.8000
M1	0.7869	0.7956	0.7989	0.7627	0.7943	0.7977	0.7719	0.7751	0.7725	0.7879
Index	0.8142	0.8122	0.8101	0.8136	0.8171	0.8208	**0.8246**	0.8107	0.8144	0.8121
IPG	**0.8361**	0.8177	**0.8268**	**0.8305**	0.8229	0.8208	0.8187	**0.8225**	0.7964	0.8000
T-bill& BondST	0.8142	0.7845	0.7877	0.7797	**0.8343**	0.7977	0.8070	0.8166	0.8024	0.8121
BondLT&BondST	0.8033	0.8122	0.7654	0.7740	**0.8343**	0.8092	0.7895	0.8047	0.7964	0.7818
Index&Spread	0.7814	0.8177	0.7877	**0.8475**	0.8171	0.8035	0.8012	0.8166	0.8144	0.8000
T-bill&Spread	0.7978	0.8122	0.7989	0.7853	0.8114	0.8092	0.8129	0.8166	0.7964	0.8121
BondST&Spread	0.8033	0.8011	0.8156	0.7684	0.8000	0.7803	0.8129	**0.8284**	0.8084	0.8121
T-bill&BondLT	0.8033	0.8177	0.8101	0.7966	0.8000	0.7746	0.8012	0.8166	**0.8204**	0.8000
Index&T-b ill	0.8197	**0.8232**	0.7933	0.7966	0.8171	0.8150	0.8187	0.8166	0.7964	0.8000
Benchmark	0.8197	0.8177	0.8212	0.8249	0.8229	0.8208	0.8187	0.8166	0.8144	0.8121

Table 5.3. USA Recession Forecast Evaluations Based on Unequal Error Costing (C=10)

Model	Horiz1	Horiz2	Horiz3	Horiz4	Horiz5	Horiz6	Horiz7	Horiz8	Horiz9	Horiz10
Spread	0.3000	0.2992	**0.3319**	0.3158	0.3172	0.3119	0.3089	**0.3304**	0.3049	0.3018
T-bill	0.3063	**0.3264**	0.3126	0.3202	0.3172	0.3142	0.3111	**0.3259**	0.3049	0.2995
BondLT	0.3 104	**0.3473**	**0.3469**	0.3048	0.3 172	0.3075	0.3067	**0.3214**	0.3027	0.2928
BondST	0.3292	**0.3305**	**0.3233**	0.3092	0.3 150	0.3 142	0.3089	0.3058	0.2982	**0.3581**
M1	0.3000	0.3013	0.3062	0.2961	**0.3458**	**0.3650**	0.2933	0.2924	**0.3094**	0.2928
Index	0.3292	**0.3452**	**0.3298**	**0.3355**	0.3150	0.3142	**0.3333**	0.3058	0.3049	0.3018
IPG	**0.3750**	**0.3285**	**0.3362**	**0.3618**	0.3 172	0.3 142	**0.3311**	**0.3304**	0.2982	0.2973
T-bill& BondST	0.3 104	**0.3159**	**0.3212**	**0.3026**	**0.3811**	0.3053	0.3067	**0.3482**	0.3004	**0.3221**
BondLT&BondST	**0.3250**	**0.3828**	0.3 126	0.3004	**0.3612**	0.3097	0.3000	0.3036	0.2982	0.3 108
Index&Spread	**0.3354**	**0.3661**	**0.3597**	**0.4671**	0.3 150	**0.3473**	0.3044	**0.3482**	**0.3453**	**0.3581**
T-bill&Spread	**0.3229**	**0.3452**	**0.3255**	0.3048	0.3 128	0.3097	**0.3289**	**0.3281**	0.2982	**0.3626**
BondST&Spread	**0.3250**	**0.3222**	**0.3512**	0.2982	0.3084	0.2987	**0.3289**	**0.3728**	**0.3229**	**0.3423**
T-bill&BondLT	**0.3438**	**0.3661**	**0.3876**	0.3092	**0.3282**	0.2965	**0.3244**	**0.3482**	**0.3475**	**0.3176**
Index&T-b ill	**0.3875**	**0.4059**	**0.3619**	**0.3289**	**0.3348**	**0.3319**	**0.3511**	0.3080	0.2982	0.2973
Benchmark	0.3125	0.3096	0.3148	0.3202	0.3172	0.3142	0.3111	0.3080	0.3049	0.3018

Canadian recession forecast results shown in Table 4.2 are evaluated using SCORE accuracy measure of recession forecasts when missing recessions and missing non-recessions are equally penalized choosing C equal to 1. These results show that none of the single indicator variable is able to predict Canadian recession; however, the combined indicator variable Index&Spread is able to predict Canadian recession only at forecast horizon 8 i.e. 8 quarters ahead. Likewise, the single indicators T − bill&BondST predicts turning point of recession 10 quarter ahead whereas the variable T − bill&Spread is able to predict turning points at horizons 8 and 9. Alternately, when the SCORE measure penalizes missing recessions 10 times higher than missing non- recession (choosing C = 1), many additional single as well as combined indicator variables become candidate for predicting recessions. These results are shown in Table4.3. This choice of higher penalty imposed on missing recessions is quite arbitrary which would allow policymakers to ensure the magnitude of the penalty they would need based on a particular situation for accurately predicting recessions.

3.4.2. Results on American Recessions

USA recession forecasts that are approximated from ANN models using various single and combined indicator variables across forecast horizons 1 − 10 that are evaluated using RMSE as a measure of forecast evaluations are shown in Table 5.1. The results presented in this Table show that the single indicator variable Spread is able to predict American recessions 8 quarters ahead, BondST 2 quarters ahead, Index 7 quarters ahead, and IPG predicts recessions 1, 3, 4, and 8 quarters ahead. Moreover, the single variables Spread, T − bill, BondLT, BondST, M1, Index, and IPG are able to predict American recession turning points at various forecast horizons 1 − 10 quarters ahead. On the other hand, the combined indicator variable T − bill&BondST as well as BondLT&BondST is able to predict American recessions 5 quarters ahead, and Index&Spread 4 quarters ahead, Index&T − bill 2 quarters ahead, whereas T − bill&Spread is able to predict American recessions 8 quarters ahead. Similarly, the combined indicator variable T − bill&BondST , BondST&BondLT , Index&Spread T − bill&Spread , BondST&Spread, T − bill&BondLT, Index&T − bill, and Index&T − bill are able to find turning points of American recessions at various forecast horizons 1 − 10 quarters ahead in future.

When considering the SCORE accuracy measure of recession forecast for USA (Table 5.2) wherein missing recessions and missing non-recessions are equally penalized, the single indicator variable BondST is a candidate variable for predicting American recession 2 quarters ahead, Index predicts American recessions 7 quarters ahead, in addition to IPG that predicts recessions 1, 3 , 4 and 8 quarters ahead, and variable Spread that is a candidate variable for predicting American recessions 8 quarters ahead. Likewise, all the single indicator variables are able to point out turning point of American recession for up to 3 forecast horizons from horizons 2 − 10 ahead. The combined indicator variables T − bill&BondST predicts American recession 5 quarters ahead, likewise, BondLT&BondST also predicts American recessions five quarters ahead, Index&Spread 4 quarters ahead, T − bill&BondLT 9 quarters ahead and Index&T − bill predicts American recessions 2 quarters ahead. Like single indicator variables, most combined indicator variables are able to predict turning point of American recession for up to 3 forecast horizons from horizons 1 − 10 ahead. However, when considering SCORE measure of recession forecasts wherein missing recessions is penalized 10 times higher than missing non-recessions (Table 5.3), most single as well as combined indicator variable are able to predict American recessions 1 – 10 quarters ahead. This type of error costing would help policymakers to choose their own penalty appropriate to a particular situation.

3.5. Discussions

The results on recession forecast for the Canadian economy reveal that the forecast performance of ANN was much better in predicting later sub-sample period Canada recessions when comparing earlier sub-sample period and total sample period. The use of combined indicator variable does not improve forecasting results or the length of forecast horizon.

When considering future Canadian recession forecasts, no single indicator variable predicted Canadian recessions at any forecast horizon from 1 – 10 quarters ahead when the recession forecasts from these variables were evaluated using SCORE measure of forecast accuracy assuming that both missing recessions and missing non-recessions have equal costs (C = 1). However, one of the combined indicator variables was able to predict Canadian recession although a number of single as well as combined indicator variables were able to predict turning points of Canadian recessions. The situation for American recession forecasts is quite different where at least 3 single and 2 combined indicator variables are able to predict American recession 3 to 4 quarters ahead. The results on forecasting Canadian as well American recessions when using combined indicator variables did not improve the forecasting results substantially. This comparison might be useful for those who would be in quest of exploring comparison of the economic and financial health of these economies.

Comparing the recession forecast of the present study with the previous studies, i.e. Estrella and Mishken (1998) and Qi (2001), the present study predicted American recession up 10 quarters ahead whereas the previous studies successfully predicted American recessions only up to 4 quarters ahead, but our results for Canadian recession forecast are in line with Kiani and Kastens (2006). However, the results from the present study on the candidacy of the indicator variable Spread as accurate predictor of recessions are in sharp contrast with some earlier studies that include Nyholm (2007), Estrella (2005), and Henri and Gerlach (1998).

4. Conclusions

In this research a number of macro-financial variables and their combinations are employed to forecast Canadian and American recessions 1 - 10 quarters ahead in future recursively using forecast approximated from artificial neural networks (ANN) in conjunction with single and combined indicator variables. These forecasts are evaluated using root mean square error (RMSE) that is a summary or volume based measure of forecast evaluation and SCORE that is an accuracy measure of forecast evaluation due to Kiani and Kastens (2006).

The study results do not show any of the fourteen models (constructed from single and combined indicator variables) predicting Canadian recessions at any of the forecast horizons 1 – 10 quarters ahead in the future when using SCORE measure of forecast accuracy, wherein missing recessions and missing non-recessions have equal costs, i.e. they are equally penalized. However, it would be interesting to note that the combined indicator variable Index&Spread is able to predict Canadian recessions at forecasting horizon 8 using RMSE as well as score measure of forecast accuracy. No other variable appears to predict Canadian recessions.

When considering the American economy, single indicator variables BondST and IPG as well as a number of other indicator variables are able to predict American recessions at forecast horizons 1 – 8 quarters ahead when these forecast are evaluated using RMSE. On the other hand using SCORE measure of forecast accuracy, single indicator variable BondST predicts American recessions 2 quarters ahead whereas IPG predicts American recessions 1, 3, and 4 quarters ahead in future. Likewise, combined indicator variables appear to predict American recessions at 7 different forecast horizons from 1 – 9 quarters ahead in future. This shows that SCORE measure performs better than the RMSE as measure of forecast accuracy. Indeed, these results reveal that the macro- financial variable predicting recessions are showing financial health of the American economy when compared to neighboring Canadian economy.

In general recession forecasts evaluated using RMSE are not able to predict Canadian and American recessions as many quarters ahead as is predicted using SCORE measure of forecast accuracy i.e. 1 – 10 quarters ahead in the future. This helped predicting both Canadian and American recessions up to 10 quarters ahead. Such forecast would be useful especially for policymakers for various policy actions. This is because the SCORE accuracy measure of the recession forecasts provides an opportunity for the policymakers and researchers to exercise the desired level of flexibility to penalize either missing recessions or missing non-recessions arbitrarily. Such flexibility helps in gauging accurate forecasts of recessions when compared to most other measures that are employed for evaluating recession forecasts. Therefore, future research on recession forecasts might employ similar models with additional indicator variables and their combinations for predicting recession forecasts for the forecast horizons even beyond 10 quarters ahead.

References

Anderson, H. M. and F. Vahid. (1998). Testing Multiple Equation Systems for Common Nonlinear Components. *Journal of Econometrics*, **84**(1), 1-36.

Anderson, H. M. and J. B. Ramsey. (2002). U.S. and Canadian Industrial Production Indices as Coupled Oscillators. *Journal of Economic Dynamics and Control*, **26**(1), 33- 67.

Anderson, H. M. and F. Vahid (2001), Predicting the probability of a recession with nonlinear autoregressive leading-indicator models, *Macroeconomic Dynamics,* **5**, 482- 505

Anderson, A. (1983). Viewpoint of Box-Jenkins Analyst in the M-competition, *Journal of Forecasting,* **2**, 286-7.

Armstrong, J. S. (1985), Long Range Forecasting: From Crystal Ball to Computer, John Wiley.

Andreano, M. and G. Savio. (2002). Further Evidence on Business Cycle Asymmetries in G7 Countries. *Applied Economics,* **34**, 895-904.

Axelrod, R. (1987). The Evolution of the Strategies in the Iterated Prisoner's Dilemma. In Laurence Davis (ed.), *Genetic Algorithms and Simulated Annealing.* Los Altos, CA: Morgan Kaufmann, 32-41.

Beatriz, A., and C. Galvão. (2006). Structural break threshold VARs for predicting US recessions using the spread. *Journal of Applied Econometrics.* **21**, 463-487.

Beaudry, P. and G. Koop. (1993). "Do Recessions Permanently Change Output? *Journal of Monetary Economics,* **31**(2), 149-163.

Bidarkota, P. V. (2000). Asymmetries in the Conditional Mean Dynamics of Real GNP: Robust Evidence. *The Review of Economics and Statistics,* **82**(1), 153-157.

Brunner, A. D. (1997). On the dynamic properties of asymmetric models of real GNP. *The Review of Economics and Statistics,* **79**(2), 321-326.

Chatfield, C. (1988). Apples, oranges and mean square error. *International Journal of Forecasting,* **4**, 515-18.

Davies, P. C. (1995). Neural network techniques for financial time series analysis in virtual trading, Lederman J., and Klein, R. A. ed. Probus Publishing, 81-87.

De Jong, K., (1975). An analysis of the behaviour of a class of Genative Adaptive System unpublished Ph.D. dissertation, *University of Michigan, Department of Computer Science.*

Dorsey, R., and J. Walter. (1995). Algorithm for Estimation Problems with Multiple Optima, Nondifferenti ability, and other Irregular Features. *Journal of Business Economics and Statistics,* **13**, 53-66.

Estrella, A. (2005). "Why Does the Yield Curve Predict Output and Inflation?" *The Economic Journal,* **115**(505), 722-744.

Estrella, A. and F. S. Mishkin. (1998). Predicting U.S. Recessions: Financial Variables as Leading Indicators. *Review of Economics and Statistics,* **80**(1), 45-61.

Estrella, A. (1998). A new measure of fit for equations with dichotomous dependent variables. *Journal of Business Economics and Statistics,* **16**(2), 198-205.

Fabio, M. (2005) Does the Yield Spread Predict Recessions in the Euro Area? Internati*onal Finance,* **8** (2), 263–301.

Fi ldes, R. (1983). A posteriori opinions of a Bayesian Forecasters. *Journal of Forecasting,* **2**, 289-91.

Gardener, A.A. (1983). The trade off in choosing a time series model. *Journal of Forecasting,* **2**, 263-267.

Goldberg, D. E. (1989). *Genetic Algorithms in Search, Optimization and Machine Learning.* Reading, MA: Addison Wesley.

Hamilton, James D. and Perez-Quiros. (1996). What do leading indicators lead? *Journal of Business,* **69**(1), 27-49.

Henri, B. and S. Gerlach. (1998) "Does the term structure predict recessions? The international evidence" International Journal of Finance & Economics, Volume 3, Issue 3, Pages 195 – 215.

Hornik, K., M. Stinchcombe, and H. White. (1989). Multilayer feed forward networks are universal approximators. *Neural Networks,* **2**, 359-366.

Kaun, C. and H. White. (1994). Artificial Neural Networks: An Econometric Perspective. *Econometric Review,* **13**(1), 1-91.

Kean, J. (1993). Neural Nets and Stocks. *PCAI,* **7**(6), 16. (September – October).

Kiani, K. M. and P. V. Bidarkota. (2004). On Business Cycle Asymmetries in G7 Countries. *Oxford Bulletin of Economics and Statistics,* **66**(3), 333-353.

Kiani, K. M. (2005). Detecting Business Cycle Asymmetries Using Artificial Neural Network and Time Series Models. *Computational Economics,* **26**(1), 65-85.

Kiani, K. M. P. V. B idarkota, and T. L. Kastens. (2005). Forecast Performance of Neural Networks and Business Cycle Asymmetries. *Applied Financial Economics Letters,* **1**(4), 205-21 0.

Kiani, K. M. and Kastens, T. L. (2006), Using macro-financial variables to forecast recessions (a case of Canada, 1957-2002). *Applied Econometrics and International Development,* **6**(3), 97-106.

Lahiri, K. and J G. Wang. (2006). Subjective Probability Forecasts for Recessions. *Business Economics*, **41**(2), 26-36.

Loungani, P. (2001). How Accurate are Private Sector Forecasts? Cross-Country Evidence from Consensus Forecasts of Economic Growth. *International Journal of Forecasting,* **17**, 419-432.

Mahmoud, E. (1989). The Evolution of Forecasts, in S. Makridakis (ed), *The Handbook of Forecasting,* New York, Wiley, Interscience.

Marimon, R., McGratten, E., and T. Sergeant, (1990). Money as Medium of exchange in an economy with artificially intelligent agents. *Journal of Economics Dynamics and Control,* **14**, 329-373.

Neftci, S. (1984). Are economic time series asymmetric over the business cycle? *Journal of Political Economy,* **92**, 307-328.

Nyholm, K. (2007). A new approach to predicting recessions. *Economic Notes*, **36**(1) 27- 42.

Potter, S.M., (1995). A non-linear approach to U.S. GNP. *Journal of Applied Econometrics,* **10**, 109-125.

Qi, M. (2001). Predicting US Recessions via Leading Indicators via Neural Network Models. *International Journal of Forecasting,* **17**(3), 383-401.

Qi, M. (1996). Financial Applications of artificial neural networks. In: Madala, G.S. and Rao, C.R. (Eds.), Handbook of Statistics: Statistical Methods in Finance, Vol. 14, Elsevier, Amsterdam, pp 529-552.

Ramsey, J. B., and P. Rothman. (1996). Time Irreversibility and Business Cycle Asymmetry. *Journal of Money Credit and Banking,* **28**(1): 1-21.

Reilly, D. L. and L. N. Cooper. (1990). An Overview of Neural Networks: Early Models to Real World Systems. In Steven F. Zornetzer, Joel L. Davis, and Clifford Lau (eds.). *An Introduction to Neural and Electronic Networks*, New York: Academic Press, 227-248.

Vishwakarma, K. P. (1995). A Neural Network to Forecast Business Cycle Indicators. *Elsevier Science, Mathematics, and Computers in Simulations*, **39**(3-4), 287-29 1.

White, H. (1989a). Connectionist nonparametric regression: multilayer feel forward can learn arbitrary mapping. *Neural Networks,* **3**, 535-549.

White, H. (1989b). Learning in Artificial Neural Networks: A Statistical Perspective. *Neural Computations,* **1**(4), 425-464.

Zarnowitz, V. and L. A. Lambros, (1987). Consensus and Uncertainty in Economic Prediction. *Journal of Political Economy*, **95**(3), 59 1-621.

In: Recessions: Prospects and Developments
Editors: N.M. Prez and J.A. Ortega, pp. 127-137
ISBN 978-1-60456-866-0

Chapter 6

PREDICTING RECESSIONS USING FINANCIAL VARIABLES

Fabio Moneta*
Carroll School of Management, Boston College,
140 Commonwealth Avenue, Chestnut Hill, MA 02467-3808

Abstract

Forecasting when a recession is approaching is important for policy makers and market participants. The focus of this literature review is on predicting binary recession events rather than predicting output growth itself. This article includes a review of the econometric methods used in the literature to forecast recessions. The main predictors used in the literature are examined. In particular, considerable research used financial variables as predictors since they are forward-looking variables and have the main advantage of being instantaneously available and precisely measured. The main financial variables that have been identified as leading indicators of future expansions and contractions include: interest rates, and in particular interest rate spread such as the term spreads (the difference between long-term interest rates and short-term interest rates) and default spreads (the difference between the interest rates on matched maturity with different degrees of default risk), and stock returns. I review the empirical evidence of predicting recessions for the United States and for selected developed countries. The term spread appears to contain important predictive content for future recessions and to outperform other indicators although its predictability has diminished in the most recent period.

1. Introduction

Over the last decade, several empirical studies have examined the usefulness of financial variables for predicting future macroeconomic conditions and, in particular, recessions. Estrella and Mishkin (1998) documented that the spread between the ten-year Treasury bond rate and the three-month Treasury bill rate performs better than composite indices of leading indicators in predicting economic recessions in the US, especially at a horizon

*E-mail address: moneta@bc.edu

beyond one quarter. The existing literature provides additional evidence of this for some other developed economies. Other financial indicators also appear to contain some useful information for forecasting recessions although less consistently. The attractiveness of these indicators stems from the fact that they are instantaneously available and observed with negligible measurement error.

In this paper, the information content of financial variables will be studied in order to predict recessions. Hence, the focus of this paper is to review studies that predict recessions rather than a quantitative measure of output growth.[1] In a sense, this forecasting exercise appears more stable and tends to perform better than the latter approach (see Estrella et al., 2003). Moreover, there is evidence that the economy behaves differently according to the current regime (see for example Hamilton, 1989). Therefore, forecasting when a recession is approaching can be useful for policy makers and market participants. The main difficulty associated with predicting recessions is that recessions are rare events which are difficult to fit to a model. It is also difficult to test its stability.

The term spread appears to contain important predictive content for future recessions and to outperform other indicators. The term spread is defined as the difference between a long-term and a short-term Treasury yield. The best results are obtained empirically using ten-year and three-month Treasury yields (see Estrella and Trubin 2006). However, its forecasting power seems to have diminished or at least changed in the most recent period whereas a credit spread (the difference between yields on high-yield corporate bonds and on safe bonds such as AAA or Treasury bonds with similar maturity) appears to have become more important than in the past.

First, I will review the main econometric models which have been used in the literature for predicting recessions. The most popular model is a probit regression. The forecast accuracy of a model can be evaluated using an in-sample or out-of-sample approach. Next, I will present the empirical evidence of predicting recessions and describe several predictors have been identified in the literature. In particular, I will focus on the term spread. Finally, I will examine the international evidence.

2. Methods for Predicting Recessions

The main framework that has been used for predicting recession is a probit or logit model used among others by Estrella and Hardouvelis (1991) and Estrella and Mishkin (1998). In the probit model, the variable being predicted is a dummy variable R_t where $R_t = 1$ if the economy is in recession in period t and $R_t = 0$ otherwise. The probability of recession at time t, with a forecast horizon of k periods is given by the following equation:

$$\Pr(R_t = 1) = \phi(c_0 + c_1 X_{t-k}), \tag{1}$$

where X_{t-k} is the set of explanatory variables used to forecast the recessions observable

[1]Numerous studies provide evidence of the predictive content of financial variables for real output in the US and in the major developed economies. See Stock and Watson (2003a) for a survey of this literature.

at time $t-k$, $\phi(.)$ is the cumulative standard normal density function

$$\phi\left(x\right)=\frac{1}{\sqrt{2\pi}}\int_{-\infty}^{x}\exp\left(-\frac{u^2}{2}\right)du$$

The model can be estimated maximizing the log-likelihood function that in the case of the probit model is given by

$$\log L=\sum_{R_t=1}\log\phi\left(c_0+c_1X_{t-k}\right)+\sum_{R_t=0}\log\phi\left(1-c_0-c_1X_{t-k}\right)$$

One of the main assumptions of the probit model is that the random shocks u are independent, identically distributed normal random variables with mean zero. However, as observed by Estrella and Rodrigues (1998), when the forecast horizons are overlapped the prediction errors are generally autocorrelated. This bias can be corrected using the Newey-West (1987) technique and presenting a t-statistics calculated using robust errors adjusted for the autocorrelation problem. In the traditional time series approach, the autocorrelation of the errors can be eliminated or at least reduced using an autoregressive moving average filter. Since the shocks u are unobservable, this technique does not apply. Therefore, Dueker (1997) suggested a technique to remove the serial correlation in u by adding a lag of R_t (the indicator variable of the state of the economy). Hence, the model now uses information contained in the autocorrelation structure of the dependent variable to form predictions. The probit equation becomes:

$$\Pr(R_t=1)=\phi(c_0+c_1X_{t-k}+c_2R_{t-k}). \tag{2}$$

In this context, it is important to test whether X has predictive content beyond the information already contained in the autoregressive structure of the binary time series as performed by Moneta (2005).

Two main approaches have been used to evaluate the forecasting power of a variable of interest. One is an in-sample approach and the second one is a pseudo out-of-sample approach. The first approach uses all the data available for the forecast. A test on the null hypothesis that c_1 is equal to zero is performed. A measure of significance of X_{t-k} as a predictor can be assessed using a goodness of fit measure. In terms of goodness of fit, in a probit model it is no more likely to yield an R^2 close to 1 as in the classical regression model. Therefore, Estrella (1998) suggested to use a pseudo-R^2 in which the log-likelihood of an unconstrained model, L_u, is compared to the log-likelihood of a nested model, L_c[2]:

$$pseudo-R^2=1-\left(\frac{L_u}{L_c}\right)^{-(2/n)L_c} \tag{3}$$

The main drawback of an in-sample forecast is that it is calculated using information that was not available at the time of the forecast. For example, the estimated probability of a recession sometime in the past is calculated estimating the model for the whole period. By contrast, an out-of-sample forecast simulates a real-time forecasting exercise

[2]The constrained model comes from a model with c_1, in equation (1), is equal to zero.

using only information available to market participants at the time of the forecast. Moreover, an in-sample forecast can always be improved by adding a new explanatory variable. This however can lead to an "overfitting problem". To avoid a possible misleading indication of the true ability of the term spread to forecast a recession, it is important to carry out an exercise of out-of-sample forecasting. In general, the sample period is divided by two. The first part of the sample is used to estimate the model and the second part is used for the out-of-sample forecasting exercise simulating as it was in real-time. At every period a forecast is obtained and the model is recursively estimated. The forecasting performance can be evaluated by calculating the forecast error of a model under analysis against the forecast error of a benchmark. One problem is that the dependent variable is not observable. However, considering that an ideal model should give a probability of one in the recession period and zero otherwise, the forecast error can be calculated as the difference between the estimated probability and the indicator of recession (the dummy variable R_t). A loss function can be calculated such as a quadratic or absolute value.[3] Different models can be compared. For example, Moneta (2005) compares three models: a probit model with only the term spread as an explanatory variable, a probit model in which just the lag of the dependent variable is used as an independent variable and the probit model that includes both the term spread and a lagged dependent variable. The Diebold and Mariano (1995) test is generally implemented to compare the forecasting ability of the different models.[4] The null hypothesis of this test is that of equal accuracy for two forecasts.

The probit model has the advantage of being parsimonious and simple to estimate but it suffers some shortcomings. As suggested by Ivanova *et al.* (2000) it requires that a fixed lead time for the predictor be chosen and to restrict this lead to not vary over time. Moreover, the probit model relies on ex post realized recession dates that make its predictions dependent on the choice of business cycle dating. Finally, the probit model assumes that the predictive index is a linear function of the predictors and has a parametric distribution.

Other econometric models which try to address some of these shortcomings have been used in the literature. Lahiri and Wang (1996), Layton (1996) and Ahrens (1999 and 2002) among others use the Markov-switching model developed by Hamilton (1989). Ahrens (2002) shows, however, that on average the Markov-switching model does not improve the forecasting ability of the term spread obtained using a probit model. Similar results are found by Birchenhall *et al.* (1994). By contrast, Layton and Katsuura (2001) compare three different models (probit model, logit model and a Markov regime switching model) to forecast US business cycles and find that the regime-switching model performs the best. Shaaf (2000) investigates the power of the yield curve to predict recessions using an artificial intelligence model ("neural networks"). The author documents a more accurate prediction, especially in out-of-sample simulations of this nonparametric model, in comparison to traditional econometric models. Sephton (2001) adopts a nonparametric model called multivariate adaptive regression splines (MARS) obtaining a better result than the probit

[3]Brier (1950) proposed a statistic to measure the accuracy of probability predictions that has been used by Diebold and Rudebusch (1989). The measure is known as the *quadratic probability score* (QPS) and is defined as follows: $\text{QPS} = \frac{1}{T}\sum_{t=1}^{T} 2\left(p_t - r_t\right)^2$, where p_t is the predicted probability (of a recession in our case) and r_t is the realization (in our case, it is the indicator of recession). The QPS statistics can range between 0 and 2, with 0 implying a perfect forecast.

[4]West (1996) Giacomini and White (2006) propose a test which generalizes the Diebold and Mariano test taking into account for estimation errors of the unknown vector of parameters.

model especially for in-sample recession forecasting. Chauvet and Potter (2001) compare forecasts of recessions using four different specifications of the probit models: a time invariant conditionally independent version; a business cycle specific conditionally independent model; a time invariant probit with autocorrelated errors; and a business cycle specific probit with autocorrelated errors. They provide evidence in favor of the last and more sophisticated model. Dueker (2005) applies a vector autoregression (VAR) model to forecast qualitative variables such as a recession in the US. A Bayesian VAR is presented by Del Negro (2001), but it does not perform better than the Estrella-Mishkin model. Galvão (2006) proposes a VAR model to predict recessions that accounts for non-linearity and a structural break using the term spread as a predictor. Anderson and Vahid (2001) develop a bivariate non-linear autoregressive leading-indicator model to predict the probability of recession. In conclusion, many other econometric models have been proposed in the literature. However, there is not yet a clear and robust alternative to the probit model.

3. Empirical Evidence

This section provides a review of studies that use financial variables to predict recessions in the United States and for some other developed countries. Defining a recession is fundamental for constructing the binary time series R_t. The National Bureau of Economic Research (NBER) officially dates the beginning (the peak of the business cycle) and end of US recessions (the trough of the business cycle) and it defines a recession as "a significant decline in activity spread across the economy, lasting more than a few months, visible in industrial production, employment, real income and wholesale retail trade". To derive a recession indicator, every month (or quarter) between the peak and the subsequent trough, as well as the trough itself, is classified as a recession. For other countries that do not have an equivalent to the NBER, the rule of thumb that defines recessions by at least two consecutive quarters of declining GDP is often adopted.

As mentioned previously, the term spread appears to be the most reliable predictor of recessions. Why might the yield curve contain information about future recessions? In general, the relationship between the slope of the yield curve and real economic growth is positive and, essentially, reflects the expectations of financial market participants regarding future economic growth. A positive spread between long-term and short-term interest rates (a steepening of the yield curve) is associated with an increase in real economic activity, while a negative spread (a flattening of the yield curve) is associated with a decline in real activity. In particular, the yield curve inverted (the term spread became negative) before all the US recessions since 1960.

First, the expectations hypothesis of the term structure of interest rates states that long-term interest rates reflect the expected path of future short-term interest rates. In particular, it claims that, for any choice of holding period, investors do not expect to realize different returns from holding bonds of different maturity dates. The long-term rates can be considered a weighted average of expected future short-term rates.[5] An anticipation of

[5]In some formulations of the expectation hypothesis a term premium (i. e. risk and/or liquidity premium) is included. Hamilton and Kim (2002) show that both expectations effect and a term premium effect are relevant for predicting real GDP growth although the contribution of the former is more important.

a recession implies an expectation of decline of future interest rates, which is translated into a decrease in long-term interest rates. These expected reductions in interest rates may stem from countercyclical monetary policy designed to stimulate the economy. In addition, they may reflect low rates of return during recessions, explainable, among other factors, by credit market conditions[6] and by lower expectations of inflation. Indeed, the slope of the yield curve is calculated on nominal interest rates and therefore embodies a term representing expected inflation. Since recessions are generally associated with low inflation rates, assuming for example that a downward Phillips-curve relationship holds, this can play a role in explaining the expectation of low rates of return during recessions. Alternatively, if market participants anticipate an economic boom and future higher rates of return on their investments, then expected future short rates exceed the current short rate, and the yield on long-term bonds should rise relative to short-term yields according to the expectations hypothesis.

Another explanation for the relationship between the slope of the yield curve and real economic growth is related to the effects of monetary policy. For example, when monetary policy is tightened, short-term interest rates rise; long-term rates also typically rise but usually by less than the current short rate. This leads to a downward-sloping term structure[7]. The monetary contraction can eventually reduce spending in sensitive sectors of the economy, causing economic growth to slow and, thus, the probability of a recession to increase. Estrella and Mishkin (1997) show that the monetary policy is an important determinant of term structure spread[8]. In particular, they observe that the credibility of the central bank affects the extent of the flattening of the yield curve in response to an increase in the central bank rate.

For the United States, Estrella and Hardouvelis (1991) and Estrella and Mishkin (1998) document, by estimating a probit model, that the term spread significantly outperforms other indicators in predicting recessions. Dueker (1997) confirms this result using a modified probit model which includes a lagged dependent variable. Moreover, he introduces a Markov-switching coefficient variation in the model. Other studies have documented a weakening in the predictive power of the term spread (see, e. g., Dotsey, 1998). In particular, the term spread did not forecast the U. S. recession of 1990 well (e.g., Filardo, 1999) and provided a weak signal for the 2001 recession. (see, e.g., Stock and Watson 2003b).

Other useful predictors used in the literature to forecast recessions include other measures of spread, such as a default spread and the commercial paper spread, and stock prices. A default spread is the difference between interest rates on bonds with different degrees of default risk but with similar rates of maturity. This can be a good measure of overall financial conditions which play an increasing role in shaping aggregate economic activity.[9] In particular Gertler and Lown (1999) show that the high yield spread has had significant

[6]In particular, if a recession is forthcoming a reduction in demand of credit is expected which will tend to lower the long-term interest rates.

[7]In fact, as Bernard and Gerlach (1998) point out, since monetary contractions are temporary, agents raise their expectations of future short-term rates by less than the change in the current short rate.

[8]Estrella (1997) also presents a theoretical rational expectations model that shows how the monetary policy is likely to be a key determinant of the relationship between the term structure of interest rates and future real output and inflation.

[9]Indeed, financial factors may amplify and propagate business cycles according to a mechanism called 'financial accelerator' (for a macroeconomic theoretical model see for example Bernanke *et al.* 2000).

explanatory power for the business cycle. They also show that over this period the high yield spread outperforms other leading financial indicators, including the term spread, the paper-bill spread and the Federal Funds rate. Stock and Watson (2003b) also show that the high yield spread was one of the strongest predictors of the 2001 recession although it incorrectly predicted a slowdown in the economy during 1998.[10] Friedman and Kuttner (1993) found that the spread between commercial paper and U.S. Treasury bills of the same maturity was a good predictor of real growth. This spread appeared to widen in advance of recessions and narrow before recoveries. However, the commercial paper spread failed to forecast the 1990-1991 recession (Friedman and Kuttner, 1998) and the 2001 recession (Stock and Watson, 2003b). Stock prices should reflect the expected present discounted value of future earnings. Therefore, stock returns can contain useful information for future earning growth and output at the aggregate level. For the US data, Estrella and Mishkin (1998) found that stock prices are useful predictors of recessions, particularly one through three quarters ahead. However, this evidence appears weak. Campbell et al. (2001) suggested using the variance of stock returns to predict output growth finding some evidence of predictability. An application of this indicator to recession predictions is still missing.

Building on the above studies, some papers studied the predictive power of financial variables and in particular the term spread for the main industrialized countries outside the U.S. These papers include Bernard and Gerlach (1998), which provide cross-country evidence of the usefulness of the term spreads to predict the probability of recessions within eight quarters ahead. Estrella and Mishkin (1997) focus on a sample of major European economies (France, Germany, Italy and the United Kingdom). These authors found that for Germany the yield spread has the best fit and the largest coefficient. Sédillot (2001) provides empirical evidence for France, Germany and the U. S. Moneta (2005) provides evidence that the term spread helps to predict recessions in the euro area outperforming other competitor indicators. Ahrens (2002) evaluates the informational content of the term structure as a predictor of recession in eight OECD countries. Birchenhall et al. (2001) document that a real M4 variable is consistently found to have predictive content for UK business cycle regimes.

4. Concluding Remarks

Stock and Watson (2003a) compare many predictors of output growth and find considerable instability (over time and/or across countries) in the predictability. However, the term spread appears to be the indicator that "comes closest " to being a reliable predictor. This appears to be even closer when a recession is predicted. Some instability is expected considering the changes in the economy and financial markets experienced in the last two decades. There is also ample evidence that the business cycle characteristics have changed over time. For example, McConnell and Perez-Quiros (2000) documents the presence of a structural break in output volatility. Chauvet and Potter (2002) also document the presence of a structural break in the predictive power of the yield spread. However, as suggested by Estrella (2006), "this evidence does not necessarily imply that the predictive power of the yield curve has

[10]The high yield (also known as 'junk') market was only developed in the 1980s. Outside the U.S. this market started only more recently.

disappeared all together, only the values of the parameters in the formal models may have changed". Stock and Watson (2003a) advocate the need "to develop methods better geared to the intermittent and evolving nature of these predictive regressions". The authors also suggest that combining the information in the various predictors can improve the reliability of the output growth prediction. Similarly, in the context of predicting regressions, King *et al.* (2007) find that a bivariate model that includes the default and term spread provides much better forecasting performance than any combination of univariate models. They also find that a Bayesian model combination is preferable to simply averaging forecasts coming from different models. A bivariate model is also used by Wright (2006) with the difference that the default spread is replaced with the level of the federal funds rate. This model shows better out-of-sample predictive performance than just using the term spread alone. I expect the approach of combining the information from several predictors to yield interesting insights in the futures.

References

Ahrens, R. (1999), 'Examining Predictors of U.S. Recessions: A Regime-Switching Approach', *Swiss Journal of Economics and Statistics* **135** (1), 97-124.

Ahrens, R. (2002), 'Predicting Recessions with Interest Rate Spreads: A Multicountry Regime-Switching Analysis', *Journal of International Money and Finance* **21**, 519-537.

Anderson, H. M., F. Vahid (2001), 'Predicting the probability of a recession with nonlinear autoregressive leading-indicator models'. *Macroeconomic Dynamics* **5**: 482-505.

Bernanke, B., M. Gertler, and S. Gilchrist (2000), 'The financial accelerator in a quantitative business cycle framework' in J. Taylor and M. Woodford, eds., Handbook of Macroeconomics. Amsterdam: North-Holland, 1341-93.

Bernard, H., and S. Gerlach (1998), 'Does the Term Structure Predict Recessions? The International Evidence', *International Journal of Finance and Economics* **3**, 195-215.

Birchenhall, C. R., H. Jessen, D. R. Osborn, and P. Simpson (1994), 'Predicting U.S. business cycle regimes' *Journal of Business and Economic Statistics* **17**, 313–323.

Birchenhall, C. R., D. R. Osborn, and M. Sensier (2001), 'Predicting UK Business Cycle Regimes', *Scottish Journal of Political Economy* **48** (2), 179-195.

Bonser-Neal, C., and T. R. Morley (1997), 'Does the Yield Spread Predict Real Economic Activity? A Multicountry Analysis', *Federal Reserve Bank of Kansas City Economic Review* **82**, 37-53.

Brier, G. W. (1950), 'Verification of Forecasts Expressed in Terms of Probabilities', *Monthly Weather Review*, **78**, 1-3.

Bry, G., and C. Boschan (1971), 'Cyclical Analysis of Time Series: Selected Procedures and Computer Programs', *NBER Technical Paper*, no. **20**.

Campbell, J., M. Lettau, B. Malkiel, and Y. Xu (2001), 'Have Individual Stocks Become More Volatile? An Empirical Exploration of Idiosyncratic Risk', *Journal of Finance* **56**, 1-43.

Chauvet, M., and S. Potter (2001), 'Forecasting Recessions Using the Yield Curve', *Federal Reserve Bank of New York, Staff Reports,* no. **134**, August.

Chauvet, M., and S. Potter (2002), 'Predicting Recession: Evidence from the Yield Curve in the Presence of Structural Breaks', *Economics Letters* **77** (2), 245-253.

Del Negro, M. (2001), 'Turn, Turn, Turn: Predicting Turning Points in Economic Activity', *Federal Reserve Bank of Atlanta, Economic Review*, second quarter, 1-12.

Diebold, F. X, and R. S. Mariano (1995), 'Comparing Predictive Accuracy', *Journal of Business and Economic Statistics* **13**, 253-263.

Diebold, F. X, and G. D. Rudebusch (1989), 'Scoring the Leading Indicators'. *Journal of Business* **62**, 369-391.

Dotsey, M. (1998), 'The Predictive Content of the Interest Rate Term Spread for Future Economic Growth', *Federal Reserve Bank of Richmond Economic Quarterly* **84**, 31-51.

Dueker, M. J. (1997), 'Strengthening the Case for the Yield Curve as Predictor of U.S. Recessions', *Federal Reserve Bank St. Louis Review* **79**, 41-51.

Dueker, M. (2005), 'Forecasting Qualitative Variables with Vector Autoregressions: A Qual VAR Model of U.S recessions', *Journal of Business & Economic Statistics* **23**.

Estrella, A., and G. A. Hardouvelis (1991), 'The Term Structure as a Predictor of Real Economic Activity', *Journal of Finance*, **46**, 555-576.

Estrella, A., and F. Mishkin (1997), 'The Predictive Power of the Term Structure of Interest Rates in Europe and the United States: Implications for the European Central Bank', *European Economic Review* **41**, 1375-1401.

Estrella, A. (1997), 'Why Do Interest Rates Predict Macro Outcomes? A Unified Theory of Inflation, Output, Interest and Policy', *Federal Reserve Bank of New York Research Paper,* no. **9717**, May.

Estrella, A. (1998), 'A New Measure of Fit for Equations with Dichotomous Dependent Variables', *Journal of Business and Economic Statistics* **16**, 198-205.

Estrella, A., and F. Mishkin (1998), 'Predicting U.S. Recessions: Financial Variables as Leading Indicators', *Review of Economics and Statistics* **80** (1), 45-61.

Estrella, A., and A. P. Rodrigues (1998), 'Consistent Covariance Matrix Estimation in Probit Models with Autocorrelated Disturbances', Federal Bank of New York Research Paper, April.

Estrella, A., A. P. Rodrigues and S. Schich (2003), 'How Stable is the Predictive Power of the Yield Curve? Evidence from Germany and the United States', *Review of Economics and Statistics* **85**, 629-644.

Estrella, A., and M. R. Trubin (2006), 'The Yield Curve as a Leading Indicator: Some Practical Issues', *Current Issues in Economics and Finance,* Federal Reserve Bank of New York.

Estrella. A. (2006), 'The Yield Curve as a Leading Indicator: Frequently Asked Questions', Federal Bank of New York manuscript.

Filardo, A. J. (1999), 'How Reliable are Recession Prediction Models?', *Federal Reserve Bank of Kansas City, Economic Review*, 2nd quarter, 35-55.

Friedman, B. M., and K. N. Kuttner (1993), 'Why Does the Paper-Bill Spread Predict Real Economic Activity?', in Business Cycles, Indicators, and Forecasting. J. H. Stock and M. W. Watson, U. Chicago Press.

Friedman, B. M., and K. N. Kuttner (1998), 'Indicator properties of the paper-bill spread: Lessons from recent experience', *Review of Economics and Statistics* **80**, 34-44.

Galvão, A. B. (2006) 'Structural break threshold VARs for predicting US recessions using the spread'. *Journal of Applied Econometrics* **21**, 463-481.

Gertler M., Lown C. S. (1999), 'The information in the high-yield bond spread for the business cycle: Evidence and some implications', *Oxford Review Economic Policy* **15**, 132-150.

Giacomini, R. and H. White (2006), 'Tests of Conditional Predictive Ability', *Econometrica* **74**, 1545-1578.

Hamilton, J. D. (1989), 'A New Approach to the Economic Analysis of Nonstationarity Time Series and the Business Cycle', *Econometrica* **57** (2), 357-384.

Hamilton, J. D., and D. H. Kim (2002), 'A Reexamination of the Predictability of Economic Activity Using the Yield Spread', *Journal of Money, Credit, and Banking*, **34** (2),340-360.

Ivanova, D., K. Lahiri and F. Seitz (2000), 'Interest Rate Spreads as Predictors of German Inflation and Business Cycles', *International Journal of Forecasting* **16**, 39-58.

King, T. B., A. T. Levin, and R. Perli (2007) 'Financial Market Perceptions of Recession Risk' *Finance and Economics Discussion Series,* Federal Reserve Board, Washington, D.C.

Lahiri K., Wang J.G. (1996), 'Interest rate spreads as predictors of business cycles'. In Handbook of Statistics, Vol. 14, Maddala GS, Rao CR (eds). Elsevier: Amsterdam; 297–315.

Layton, A. P., and M. Katsuura (2001), 'Comparison of Regime Switching, Probit and Logit Models in Dating and Forecasting US Business Cycles', *International Journal of Forecasting* **17**, 403-417.

Layton, A.P., (1996), 'Dating and predicting phase changes in the US business cycle'. *International Journal of Forecasting* **12**, pp. 417–428.

McConnell, M. M. and G. Perez-Quiros (2000), 'Output Fluctuations in the United States: What Has Changed Since the Early 1980's?' *The American Economic Review* **90**, 1464-1476.

Moneta, F. (2005), 'Does the Yield Spread Predict Recessions in the Euro Area?', *International Finance* **8**, 263-301.

Newey, W., and K. West (1987), 'A Simple Positive Semi-Definite Heteroskedasticity and Autocorrelation Consistent Covariance Matrix', *Econometrica* **55**, 703-78.

Shaaf, M. (2000), 'Predicting Recession Using the Yield Curve: an Artificial Intelligence and Econometric Comparison', *Eastern Econometric Journal* **26** (2), 171-90.

Sédillot, F. (2001), 'La Pente des Taux Contient-elle de l'Information sur l'Activité Économique Future?', *Economie et Prévision* **147**, 141-157.

Sephton, P. (2001), 'Forecasting Recessions: Can we Do Better on MARS?', *Federal Reserve Bank St. Louis Review* **83** (2).

Stock, J. H., and M. W. Watson (2003a), 'Forecasting Output and Inflation: The Role of Asset Prices', *Journal of Economic Literature* **41**, 788-829.

Stock, J. H., and M. W. Watson (2003b), 'How did leading indicator forecasts do during the 2001 recession', manuscript, Harvard University.

West, K. D. (1996), 'Asymptotic Inference about Predictive Ability', *Econometrica,* **52**, 143-162.

Wright, J. H. (2006). 'The Yield Curve and Predicting Recessions', Finance and Economics Discussion Series, Federal Reserve Board, Washington, D.C.

In: Recessions: Prospects and Developments
Editors: N.M. Pérez and J.A. Ortega, pp. 139-152
ISBN: 978-1-60456-866-0

Chapter 7

MYSTERIOUS SOCIO-ECONOMIC DISTURBANCES AND CYCLICAL FLUCTUATIONS

Ayub Mehar
Institute of Business and Technology, Karachi, Pakistan

Abstract

The mysterious and relatively less predictable cyclical fluctuations are known as 'Business Cycle' – one of the blackist in many black boxes in Economics. The patterns and ordering of the cyclical effects may vary for different economies. They depend on the socio-economic and political structure of the countries. The corporate arrangements, ownership structures, cash flows and employment are always affected in the recessions. The industrial and financial institutions – particularly, insurance companies, banks and securities firms - should always plan for their business with consideration of the patterns of business cycles.

I. Nature and Scope of Business Cycles

The direction and growth of the economies can be decomposed in four different types of movements: seasonal variations, cyclical fluctuations, long-term trend and the accidental changes. Seasonal trends are short-term fluctuations depend on the fundamental characteristics of the different economies: patterns of crops, production of seasonal industries, periodical collection of public revenues, flow of remittances and periodical socio-economic activities during the year. Those predictable seasonal variations determine the short-terms up and down in the economy. Such fluctuations are varied from country to country. So far as long-term trends are concerned they are reflectors of the economic planning and policies of the authorities.

The mysterious and relatively less predictable are the cyclical fluctuations – ignoring the accidental changes, which are the consequences of unpredictable events. The cyclical fluctuations are the regular and continuous ups and downs in the world economy without apparent reasons. This regular fluctuation is known as 'Business Cycle' – one of the blackist in many black boxes in Economics.

The term 'Business Cycle' indicates the fluctuations in economic activity, which forms a regular pattern, with an expansion of business activity followed by contraction succeeded by further expansion. Such cycles occur about the secular or long-term trend path of output. The expansion and contraction phases of the cycles appear in all over the world. The world economies face the same side of cycle simultaneously. The term "Cycle" gives the misleading impression of a regular, up-and-down pattern in the economy. Yet cycles come in many different shapes and size. Since the Second World War, the shortest expansion has lasted only 12 months, the longest, in the 1960, 106 months. It is this variation that makes downturn of hard to predict. However, it is clear that economic expansions have become longer and contraction shorter. According to the International Business Cycle Research Center at Columbia University, between 1854 and 1945 the average expansion slated 29 months and the average contraction 21 months. But, since the Second World War, expansion has lasted almost twice a long, an average of 50 months, while contractions have shorter to an average of only 11 months.

Why do these cyclical fluctuations occur? The economists describe different theories. However, a fairly large majority of economists are agreed on the existence of the business cycles. Many hypotheses have been advances as to the cause of the business cycle. Following theories in explanation of the causes of business cycles have been identified in the literature:

1. Purely monetary;
2. Over investment;
3. Changes in cost, horizontal maladjustments, and over indebtness;
4. Under consumption;
5. Psychological factors; and
6. The harvest theories (relating agriculture and the business cycles, including the sun spot theories).

The recession is a phase of business cycle, which follows a peak and ends with the trough. A recession is considered a mild version of the phase unlike the slump, which is a severe version. It is important that recession, technical correction in the stock market, economic crisis and disasters are absolutely different phenomena. So, they have different characteristics.

The National Bureau of Economic Research in USA has measured the duration of US business cycles, from turning point to turning point from 1854 to the current date. These data are shown in table 1. The length, strength and gravity of different cycles are varied. Sometimes accidental events - 1st world war, 2nd world war, US civil war, Korean and Vietnam wars, Y2K and 9/11 effects – have also been added in the cyclical effects of recession periods.

The recession in 1929-33 is considered the most sever recession in the known history, famously identified as 'great depression'. A series of financial panics converted the recession into a great depression in 1930. A fiscal crisis in Hungary had been observed in 1930. The government of Hungary adopted a badly managed price support scheme for wheat, which led to a loss of confidence by foreigners, who withdrew deposits and thus weakened the banking system. At same time, in Austria, where there was a serious fiscal problem, the Australian largest bank was unable to publish its annual accounts. This was an indicator of the bank's losses. As a result, withdrawals of the deposits from the banks are begun. Ultimately, the bank's assets have to be liquidated at vastly reduced depression prices. The government believed that it could not simply let Austria's largest bank fail. As the bank's losses become greater, the fiscal consequences of supporting it became graver. Austria, too, now had a fiscal problem. Germany that was next door yet had little capital participation in Austria. But depositors in German banks became nervous about Germany's banks and the currency.

Table 1. Business Cycles Since Freedom Movement of 1857

No.	Reference Time		Duration (Months)	
	Peak	Trough (Depression)	Contraction (Peak to Trough)	Expansion (Trough to Next Peak)
1	June 1857	December, 1858	18	30
2	October 1860	June, 1861	8	22
3	April 1865	December, 1867	32[a]	46[a]
4	June 1869	December, 1870	18	18
5	October 1873	March 1879	65	34
6	March 1882	May 1885	38	36
7	March 1887	April 1888	13	22
8	July 1890	May 1891	10	27
9	January 1893	June 1894	17	20
10	December 1895	June 1897	18	18
11	June 1899	December, 1900	18	24
12	September 1902	August 1904	23	21
13	May 1907	June 1908	13	33
14	January 1910	January 1912	24	19
15	January 1913	December 1914	23	12
16	August 1918	March 1919	7[a]	44[a]
17	January 1920	July 1921	18	10
18	May 1923	July 1924	14	22
19	October 1926	November 1927	13	27
20	August 1929	March 1933	43	21
21	May 1937	June 1938	13	50
22	February 1945	October 1945	8[b]	80[b]
23	November 1948	October 1949	11	37
24	July 1953	May 1954	10	45
25	August 1957	April 1958	8	39
26	April 1960	February 1961	10	24
27	December 1969	November 1970	11c	106c
28	November 1973	March 1975	16	36
29	January 1980	July 1980	6	58
30	July 1981	November 1982	16	12
31	July 1990	March 1991	8	92
32	March 2001	November 2001	8	120

a: Civil War period

b: World War I and II

c: Korean War and Vietnam War

d: Excluding Y2K' effect

In the great depression, the crises in the capital-importing countries of Central Europe and South America were followed by crises in industrialized countries. Britain had no fundamental banking problem, but British institutions suffered because some of their assets (Short-term loans to the borrowing countries) were frozen. So the speculations turned against the British currency. In September 1931 sterling was forced off the gold standard. Then the speculation affected the United States, where it led to a loss of international reserves as funds shifted out of dollars. Wave after wave of bank panics and closures followed until President Franklin Delano Roosevelt took the dollar off gold in March 1933. Then the remaining gold standard countries, Belgium, France, and Switzerland became vulnerable.

The existence and strength of the recession is usually gauged by the growth in GDP. However, GDP is not the only yardstick. The pattern of investment, stock market indexes, rate of inflation, rate of interest, exchange rate parity, employment situation, distribution of income, the level of poverty and the other economic and financial indicators are also affected in the recession. However, the pattern and ordering of the cyclical effects may be different for different economies. They depend on the socio economic and political structure of the countries. If a stock market is highly efficient, the cyclical change will be reflected in stock prices immediately. Otherwise, the reflection will be observed after the change in the corporate sales and profits.

Historical trends of international financial markets show that fluctuations in the stock markets are correlated with the economic boom and slump. But, the timing of bull in the stock market and the boom in the economy may not be coincided in some economies. Table 4 analyzes the correlation between worldwide cyclical fluctuations with the local stock markets. A bear market is defined as any decline of 15 percent or more in the all-share index. Similarly, a market is defined as a bull if the all-share index increased by 15 percent or more. In the light of this analysis, we concluded that recession in the world economies and bear in the world stock markets are appeared simultaneously. The stock markets of the United States and Britain show bearish trend at the time of economic recession. But the same is not observed in the Japanese stock market. Similarly, in the United States and Britain's stock markets bull appears before or on the time of economic boom. But, bull appears in the Japanese market after economic boom (or recovery).

II. Non-recessionary Economic Disturbances

Some analysts confuse the economic disaster and crises with the recession. The recession is a regular economic phenomenon and it is different from the economic and financial crises. The economic crises may be a result of the bad economic and political policies, but recession is not. Similarly, a recession is possible even in the presence of extremely good economic management and policies. If an economic problem is observed in a country at the boom or recovery stage in the global market, it will not be classified an impact of the recession or slump. Similarly, a decline in the business or observable weak indicators in the business and financial performance of a sector – local or worldwide – will not be considered as a part of recession. Recession affects all the sectors simultaneously.

Although, it has become a common practice that economic managers of a country and business managers of a firm blame the recession for every shortcoming in the economic and business policy or fundamental weaknesses. So, a clear difference between recession and structural problems should be identified for analysis and quantification of the impacts of a recession.

The decomposition of the impacts of a recession and an accidental event is too difficult – almost impossible – when they occurred simultaneously, like 1st and 2nd world wars, Korean and Vietnam wars, US civil war, Y2K, and 9/11 etc. However, a clear distinction is possible when an undesired event is happened in a non-recessionary period. Like, worldwide crises in the stock markets in March 1995 could not be considered as a recession; it was simply a crisis in the world economy, created by the cumulative effects of the following events:

1. The inflation in Mexican economy had increased to 42 percent from 7 percent, where the GDP growth rate had been reached at negative two percent from 3.5 percent in 1994. The economy had faced a trade deficit of $29 billion as compared to $2 billion in 1994. The local stock market index had been dropped at 1539 from 2094 in 1994. While, the exchange rate of Mexican peso in term of US dollar had increased to 7.85 from 5.0.
2. A heavy decline was observed in the Japanese Stock Market after the earthquake in Kobe.
3. The Barring Securities had been collapsed due to a famous transaction in derivatives in Singapore.
4. The low savings and deficit financing have been shown in the United States' budget.

As a result, the index of the New York Stock Exchange has been declined by 0.15 percent. The index declined by 2.56 percent in Hong Kong, 2.46 percent in Bangkok, 2 percent in Tokyo and 1.7 percent in Singapore. However, the index of London Stock Exchange rose by 0.5 percent. All the above events created a worldwide economic crisis, so a worldwide decline in the stock markets was observed. But, world economic growth was not declined, because this temporary crisis was not a part of business cycle. So it was not identified as a recession.

Similarly, the worldwide impact of the Asian Crises in 1997 was not recognized as a part of the cyclical fluctuation. Until the middle of 1997 Asia was the growth center of the global economy. However, currency crises, which were triggered in Thailand in July 1997, spread immediately to other countries. Record-breaking minus figures were registered in Indonesia, Thailand, Malaysia and Korea, which were considerably affected by currency crises. Russian economic crises have also been reflected in its currency crisis. Russia financed its deficit account through public borrowing. The Russian bonds have been launched in the international market. The Namura Securities of Japan played a key role in the sale of Russian bonds. However, a huge loss of $1 billion has to be born by the Namura. This loss transferred the effects of the crises into Japan.

In both the above-mentioned cases, banking and fiscal problems were eventually merged. All the troubles eventually had some thing in common __ falling commodity prices and fundamentally flawed banking systems and then changes in monetary and fiscal policies. The cobweb of commodity prices, unsold inventories, banking flaws, financial markets' turmoil and changes in macro economic policies have produced panic in both the cases.

Table 2. A Bird Eye's View of Cut in the Employment

Country /Company	Persons terminated
World	10,000,000
Russia	8,400,000
USA	625,000
China: Textile	450,000
South Korea	217,000
Philips (International)	80,000
USA: Boeing	48,000
Sweden (Ericsson)	10,000
Pakistan: Sindh Municipalities	6,500
Merrill Lynch	3,400
USA: Texaco Oil	2,000
Pakistan: Hino Pak	250
Pakistan: Shell	145
Pakistan: Phillips	140

The impact of Asian Crisis in 1997 can be measured by the phenomenon that the numbers of absolute poor in the world have been increased by 6 million, because of that recession. This non-recessionary crisis had added 10 million unemployed in the pool of 140 million jobless people in world. The unemployment was classified as a number one economic problem in the world. Social unrest has also increased in many countries. Ten millions people have lost their jobs and even their homes in that turmoil. The large chunks of the middle class in Asia (excluding Russia and Brazil) have lost their sense of ownership of their political system.

It is important that trade is not the only and not the primary transmission mechanism for international shocks. Even if we consider the effect of Asian crises on global trade, the United States economy was affected seriously. Thirty percent of the United States' total exports at that time had gone to the Asian economies. This share was 40 percent if we add the US exports of farm's products.

This was an interesting phenomenon that the 1997 crisis had badly affected the large companies in the United States of America, but the smaller companies in Indian economy. It had been claimed that the United States had a protection mechanism against the adverse effects of a recession. However, the United States economy was not ready to handle the adverse effects of the Asian crisis in1997. The corporate management in the United States faced a severe liquidity trap. However, the sales and profits of Indian companies have increased during the crisis. The Indian companies had managed the problem of large inventories' volume through lower growth in industrial production.

The economic, financial and social impacts of the Asian Crisis in1997 have been summarized in table 3. The recommended or implemented policies by the governments have also been indicated in this table. Different economies have been affected by this crisis in different ways. The economic managers have also adopted different policies to deal with the problem. However, the role of the International Monetary Fund (IMF) during the Asian Crisis has some question marks. The Fund had recommended the demand management policies in a large number of cases. This type of policies emphasize on the tight fiscal control and contraction in the money supply. They ultimately lead the unemployment in short-term. The IMF director for Asia has admitted that the fund would not had recommended such tightening policies during the crisis. The IMF admitted that it had drastically underestimated the extent of the crisis.

III. Contemplation of the Policy Measures

World depressions destroy economic and political stability. In the past, the depressions have been changing the economic and political map of the world. They frequently led to a vicious circle of wars, regionalism, the disintegration of states, and income disparities. The corporate set up, ownership structure and employment are always affected in the recessions. Since 1930s government intervention has been used to try to influence the timing and help dampen the intensity of business cycles. To deal with the recession the World Bank adopts a twin-track approach, which focuses on restructuring financial and corporate sectors and on social protection of the vulnerable groups during the crisis.

It is important for the planners that economies go into the slump with a higher speed as compare to their speed during the recovery. So, a V-shaped recovery should not be expected. There is no particular magic policy but we should not wait for a miracle. The changes take time and we will have to rebuild the confidence.

There are several recommendations for the softening of a business cycle. They include the shift in output from manufacturing to services, which tend to be less cyclical; the bigger role of governments, which unlike firms, do not slash job during recessions, unemployment benefits, that protect the poor in downturns; government deposit insurance, which help to prevent banking crises; and better inventory control through just-in-time technique.

It is obvious that the industries or suppliers of inelastic goods are less affected in the recession. But, luxurious of life and capital goods' industries are affected at large. The services industries – especially financial institution – are badly affected in recession period. The insurance companies, banks and securities firms should always plan for their business with consideration of the pattern of business cycles.

Economists always favor the expansionary policies to overcome the negative impacts of the recession. The government spending should be increased during the recession. More employment opportunities should be created in the public sector; more subsidies and allowances, low interest rate and soft credit facilities should be offered during the recession. India, Japan, China, Taiwan and South Korea have been adopting these policies during the last recession. But, in Pakistan, the privatization, downsizing, control over budget deficit and tight monetary polices have been adopted. The World Bank categorically recommended that control over the inflation during the recession by the government of Pakistan would create the lower investment growth in the economy. The World Bank indicated that anti-inflationary polices during the recession would be a cause of lower growth, while the higher growth in GDP is one of the required outcomes for Pakistan. A 7 percent GDP growth was recommended to reduce the poverty in South Asia.

It is important that recession is not always bad. Some economies and companies get benefits from it. For instance, India had got large economic benefits from the recession in 2001. A positive and higher growth rate during the recession had attracted the investors at the time when there were no good opportunities in other avenues. The credit of this growth is no doubt, goes the India economic mangers and policy makers. Sooner the recession started India adopted an expansionary policy. The Reserve Bank of India had announced the lower interest rate and soft credit terms in its credit policy. The United States and other countries had also adopted the expansionary policies. But it was surprising that a contractionary policy had been adopted in Pakistan and even the International Monetary Fund (IMF) emphasized the implementation of this policy in Pakistan.

Economic managers in Pakistan have always been blaming the recession and other exogenous factors for the economic problems. But, the last recession has produced, at least, three positive consequences for the economy of Pakistan:

1. The cost of imports has decreased because of the reduction in oil prices. As a result, the balance of trade was improved.
2. The benefit of reduction in oil prices was not transferred to the consumers. So, public revenue had increased despite of a worldwide recession.
3. The lower demand for goods and services reduced the rate of inflation.

Table 5 envisages that the economic growth in Pakistan has not been directly correlated with the worldwide recessions over the time. It was observed that the economy of Pakistan goes into a slump before a worldwide recession and into recovery phase before a worldwide expansion. This phenomenon is based on the following two propositions:

1. The worldwide recession does not affect the production, supply and demand of agricultural products, which are the major component of the Gross Domestic Product in Pakistan.
2. When the world economy goes into recession, the consumers shift to low priced commodities. So, the volume of exports from Pakistan is not affected as compared to the exports from industrialized countries.

The economic managers and large financial institutions should organize the research to forecast the time and strength of the business cycles. Not only the disclosure of the expected time and strength of the recession but financial planning to control over its effects is also required. The need of economic research is enhanced in recession, because of the preparation of a strategy for survival, situation analysis for short-term and planning for long-term. However, it is a common observation that confused management of the financial institutions reduces – or even shut downs – their research activities. If research activities were genuinely being performed, the losses will be enhanced by the closure of research activities. However, if research activities substitute the public relations' functioning through distribution and reproduction of the publicly provided data and information to the prospective clients, then such expenditures must be curtailed in the recession period. Because, there are less chances to make new clients during the recession.

Table 3. Worldwide Impacts of the Asian Crisis: A Bird's Eye View

Country	Economic Impacts	Financial Impacts	Social Impacts	Policy adopted by the government
USA	Record high growth in inventories ($1.00 billion) Significant decrease in exports GDP growth decrease to 2% from 8%	Share prices decreased by 15-20% Outflow of Investment Large number of mergers Profits of top 1500 decreased	Large firms stopped the cash bonus payments to the employees	Utilization of the surplus revenue
Russia	Negative (-10%) growth rate 56% inflation	High devaluation in currency 60% interest rate	1,13,000 children have been left by their parents 8.6 million persons became job less. 1,500 persons has suicide	Moratorium and then default
Japan	All the economic indicators show a worst position.	Huge losses in business Namura Securities earned a loss of $1 billion Decline in stock index	Mass unemployment	Tax cut policy A huge package for business sector Issuance of coupons for the protection of poor
China	Deflation (1.1%) Growth in industrial production is higher than GDP growth	___________	Unemployment rate has increased	Unemployment fund and developing work financed by public borrowing

Table 3. Continued

Country	Economic Impacts	Financial Impacts	Social Impacts	Policy adopted by the government
Hong Kong	Negative (-5.2%) growth in GDP Negative trade balance	________	Unemployment rate has been reached at 5.5% from 2.5 %	________
India	16% inflation Depreciation in currency	Small companies have been more affected 50% listed companies had faced a risk of survival	Un-employment and deporting of Indian immigrants from UAE	Expansionary Monetary policy Capital Adequacy ratio has been increased Cut in interest rate
South Korea	Negative growth rate (-6.8%)	Currency devaluation	Mass unemployment	Arrangement of Temporary work for 1.54 million jobless.
Taiwan	Forex reserves have decreased	________	6,000 firms have been shut down	T$120 billion loan for local business sector
Kuwait, UAE & Saudi Arabia	Decrease in oil prices Decrease in Public revenues	________	Unemployment Lower profits	Deport of immigrants Deficit financing Incentives for local investors

Table 4. Time Correlation Between Business Cycles and Stock Markets

Year	Boom in World Economies	Bull in the Stock Market				Recession in World Economies	Bear in the Stock Market			
		World	Japan	UK	USA		World	Japan	UK	USA
1944		+++								
1945										
1946					+++					
1947				+++						
1948	+++									
1949			+++			+++	+++		+++	+++
1950								+++		
1951				+++						
1952									+++	
1953	+++		+++					+++		
1954						+++				
1955				+++						
1956					+++					
1957	+++		+++					+++		+++
1958						+++			+++	
1959										
1960	+++									
1961		+++	+++	+++	+++	+++				
1962							+++		+++	+++
1963										
1964										

Table 4. Continued

Year	Boom in World Economies	Bull in the Stock Market				Recession in World Economies	Bear in the Stock Market			
		World	Japan	UK	USA		World	Japan	UK	USA
1965								+++		
1966				+++	+++				+++	+++
1967										
1968					+++					
1969	+++	+++		+++						
1970			+++			+++	+++	+++	+++	+++
1971										
1972				+++						
1973	+++	+++	+++		+++					
1974							+++	+++	+++	+++
1975						+++				
1976				+++	+++				+++	
1977										
1978										+++
1979				+++					+++	
1980	+++				+++	+++				
1981	+++	+++		+++					+++	
1982						+++	+++			+++
1983										
1984										
1985										

Table 4. Continued

Year	Boom in World Economies	Bull in the Stock Market				Recession in World Economies	Bear in the Stock Market			
		World	Japan	UK	USA		World	Japan	UK	USA
1986										
1987		+++	+++	+++	+++		+++		+++	+++
1988								+++		
1989			+++	+++						
1990	+++	+++			+++		+++		+++	+++
1991						+++				
1992				+++					+++	
1993										
1994				+++					+++	
1995								+++		
1996			+++							
1997										
1998		+++		+++	+++	+++	+++	+++	+++	+++
1999		+++	+++	+++	+++					
2000								+++		
2001	+++					+++	+++	+++	+++	+++
2002							+++	+++	+++	+++
2003										
2004							+++	+++	+++	+++
Total	10	9	10	16	12	11	11	13	18	14

Table 5. The Pakistan Economy During the Worldwide Recession

Recession (Trough)	Annual Growth in GDP in the year of:		
	Before trough	Trough	After trough
May 1954	1.72	10.22	2.03
April 1958	2.98	2.54	2.47
February 1961	0.88	4.89	6.01
November 1970	6.49	9.79	1.23
March 1975	7.45	3.88	3.25
July 1980	5.53	7.33	6.40
November 1982	6.40	7.20	6.72
March 1991	6.00	5.57	7.71
November 2001	3.9	2.2	3.4

References

Nelson, C.R (1987); " Investors' Guide to Economic Indicators"; New York: John Wiley and Sons, 1987

Auerbach, A.J. (1982); "The Index of Leading Indicators: Measurement Without Theory 35 Years Later"; The Review of Economic and Statistics; November 1982

Hildebrand, G (1992); "Business Cycles: Indicators and Measures"; Chicago, Bank Administration Institute, 1992

Mitchell, W.C. (1927); Business Cycles: The Problems and Its Setting"; Berkeley: University of California Press, 1927

Mitchell, W.C. (1951); "What Happens During Business Cycles: A Progress Report"; Berkeley: University of California Press, 1951

Schumpeter, J.A. (1981); "Business Cycles: A Theoretical, Historical and Statistical Analysis of the Capitalist Process"; Philadelphia: Porcupine Press Inc., 1981

Mehar, Ayub (1999); "History and Nature of Economic Recession"; Business Recorder Karachi, 1999

National Bureau of Economic Research (2003); " Business Cycles Information"; Cambridge Public Information Office, 2003

In: Recessions: Prospects and Developments
Editors: N.M. Pérez and J.A. Ortega, pp. 153-162
ISBN: 978-1-60456-866-0

Expert Commentary

DYNAMIC INVESTOR RISK PREMIA AND RECESSIONS

Jiangze Bian[1,a] ***and Michael E. Fuerst***[2,b]
[1]School of Finance and Banking, University of International Business and Economics, Beijing, China 100029
[2]Department of Finance, School of Business Administration, University of Miami, Coral Gables, FL 33124

Introduction

A critical consideration in understanding business cycles is the amplification and propagation of shocks to the economic system. Many recessions seem to arise without a clearly identifiable cause—or at least one of significant magnitude to justify an economy-wide recession. How can a small shock cause large changes in the economy? What are the mechanisms that amplify a modest shock such that a serious recession ensues?

Despite the persistent search for a mechanism for business cycle amplification and propagation, much research in business cycles seems to ignore the likely role of the financial system. If a shock to the economy inhibits the capital allocation capability of an economy, then a seemingly mild shock may be amplified through its impact on new investment thereby snuffing out economic growth and causing a recession.

This line of thinking is by no means without precedent. At least as early as the 1930s, Irving Fisher recognized that the Great Depression was due in no small part to the deflationary forces that inhibited the U.S. banking system from lending new capital. Deflation increased the real value of borrowers' liabilities (stated in nominal terms) that led to widespread default. In addition to a decline in banks' loan portfolios, banks' deposits (nominal liabilities for banks) increased in real value. Hence, the banking system was placed in peril; new lending drastically fell and an economic contraction ensued.

[a] E-mail address: bian_jiangze@yahoo.com. Tel.: +86 10 64492533.
[b] E-mail address: mfuerst@miami.edu. Tel.: +1 305 284 5289; fax: +1 305 284 4800

More recent research (see, e.g., Bernanke, 1993, and Gertler and Gilchrist, 1994) shows that contractionary Federal Reserve monetary policy is effected through both a firm balance sheet channel and a bank credit channel. In both channels, access to new capital for *small* firms is central. Through the firm balance sheet channel, when the Fed raises the fed funds rate, the higher cost of capital impairs the collateral value of firm balance sheets, reduces firms' ability to borrow, and thereby reduces new investment. Through the bank credit channel, a tightening of monetary policy reduces the number of new loans banks make as banks invest more in securities (as opposed to loans to firms) in order to meet reserve requirements. Although the Fed's goal is not to cause a recession, this line of reasoning lends support for a bank finance channel for recession propagation.

Hardouvelis and Wizman (1992) compare the variation in the required return on new investment over the business cycle by firm size and find a flight to quality: *The cost of capital for small firms shows greater cyclicality than that for large firms.* In asset-pricing terms, the risk premium for size shows strong countercyclical variation. Hardouvelis and Wizman conclude that this size effect may be a significant propagation mechanism of business cycles.

Our recent research (Bian, 2007, and Fuerst, 2006) recognizes the role of a dynamic risk premium in the capital investment decisions of firms. We provide empirical support for still another financial system mechanism: a market channel for recession propagation. Like the economics underlying the bank mechanisms of monetary policy transmission, an increase in the risk premium on market finance raises the cost of capital and induces contractions in the economy. This research links the premium that investors demand as compensation for risky investment to real macroeconomic fluctuations. This risk premium is an economy-wide factor that affects firms when making investment decisions. Moreover, this premium is countercyclical: as the economy enters a recession—perhaps in response to a modest real shock—the premium for risk rises and thereby amplifies the severity of the economic downturn through a reduction in new investment.

In this commentary, we draw heavily from our prior work, outlining the underlying economic logic of the risk premium as a propagation mechanism and providing empirical support for our view. We describe this analysis conceptually and refer the interested reader to Fuerst (2006) for additional technical details. In addition, we discuss issues addressed in companion research, Bian and Fuerst (2008).

The Investment Decisions of Firms

In making investment decisions, firms both project the future cash flows that a project will generate and discount those cash flows at an interest rate adjusted for risk. Clearly, when an economy is entering a recession, the projected cash flows for many projects will fall and, otherwise economically feasible projects will be rejected by a firm. This is a direct reflection of falling industrial production in the economy.

Unrecognized in most business cycle research, however, is the change to the discount rate over such cycles and its impact on investment decisions by firms. Hence, the financial sector of the economy, through the required return of investors in the capital markets, has the potential to accelerate and amplify recessions. An economy entering a recession experiences a significant increase in the risk premium that lowers firms assessed net present value for proposed projects and leads to the rejection of projects that otherwise would be accepted.

The implication is straightforward: due to a rising risk premium, an economy entering a recession will fund still fewer projects, hire still fewer workers, and produce still fewer goods than if the risk premium stayed constant. Hence, a dynamic risk premium is an amplifying mechanism for business cycles.

Theoretical Dynamics of the Risk Premium

Several general equilibrium asset-pricing models endogenize the equity premium and allow it to vary as a function of past, current, and expected future consumption levels and volatility. For reasonable model parameterizations, the risk premium in Black (1990) and Abel (1988) rises as current consumption falls, a consequence of a rising marginal utility for current consumption. The equilibrium factor model of Connor and Korajczyk (1989) also exhibits a risk premium that varies inversely with current output (under the assumption of constant absolute risk aversion and serially uncorrelated production). In addition, the models of Abel (1988, 1999) find a risk premium that rises as expected future consumption rises and expected future consumption volatility increases. Subject to parameter restrictions, all these models imply a risk premium that varies countercyclically with the business cycle and even leads it.

At business cycle peaks, when current consumption and output are high, investors have a relatively lower marginal utility for consumption and therefore require less compensation for bearing risk. At business cycle troughs, investors suffer from lower current consumption and anticipate higher future consumption levels and volatility (Kandel and Stambaugh, 1990). Therefore, the risk premium is at its greatest at the depths of a recession.

Consideration of habit formation, has allowed asset pricing models to better explain the unrealistic implications of earlier models including the well-documented equity premium puzzle of Mehra and Prescott (1985). In the Constantinides (1990) and Campbell and Cochrane (1999) models, for example, current consumption enters the utility function net of a benchmark or habit level of consumption. Empirically, this implies that the equity risk premium is also a function of current and lagged consumption. In simulations of their model, Campbell and Cochrane find a slowly time-varying countercyclical risk premium.

Other empirical evidence indicates that expected excess returns vary countercyclically with current business conditions. Chen (1991) examines the expected excess returns on the value-weighted portfolio of NYSE stocks relative to recent GNP growth and expected future GNP growth and growth volatility. He finds the expected excess return is countercyclical, rising as recent output growth falls. Recent work by Pástor and Stambaugh (2001) supports this countercyclicality. They find the equity risk premium reaches its highest level during the Great Depression and the stagflationary recession of the early 1970s. Its steepest decline is likewise during the long economic expansion of the 1990s. Fama and French (1989), who show similar results, offer an interpretation based on the consumption-smoothing hypothesis (Hall, 1978, and Modigliani, 1986): expected excess returns rise and fall opposite to economic prosperity because investors require a higher return during periods of low income. To induce investment in risky equity during recessions, firms have to offer a higher risk premium to entice investment, as current consumption is more highly valued. Moreover, Chen confirms the theoretical results of Abel (1988, 1999) and finds conditional expected excess returns rise as expected future GNP growth rises (to the contrary, however, he finds expected growth volatility has little explanatory power).

Asset Pricing Models and the Risk Premium

Fuerst (2006) and Bian (2007) frame the risk premium within the asset pricing literature. The advantage of this approach is that the Capital Asset-Pricing Model (CAPM) and, more recently, the intertemporal CAPM (ICAPM) and the Arbitrage Pricing Theory (APT) form the standard framework managers use to calculate the risk-adjusted cost of capital. As standard practice dictates, the decision to invest is made by either comparing the investment's internal rate of return against this hurdle rate or calculating the investment's net present value by discounting at this rate. A second advantage is that in the ICAPM framework valid state variables must act as predictors of changing consumption-investment opportunities. A priori, such a model is well suited to the study of linkages between asset pricing and future macroeconomic fluctuations.

We assume an asset i's *realized* return at time t may be described by the Fama-French (1993) three-factor model:

$$r_{it} = r_{0t} + \beta_{i,MRF}\mathrm{MRF}_t + \beta_{i,SMB}\mathrm{SMB}_t + \beta_{i,HML}\mathrm{HML}_t + \varepsilon_{it}.$$

where r_{0t} is the riskless return on the zero-beta portfolio. MRF_t, SMB_t, and HML_t are the factor realizations at time t; $\beta_{i,MRF}$, $\beta_{i,SMB}$, and $\beta_{i,HML}$ are the factor sensitivities of asset i; and ε_{it} is an (idiosyncratic) error term. (Fama and French view their three-factor model as a version of the ICAPM.)

Fama and French construct the MRF factor by taking the difference in returns between a (value-weighted) broad market index and a riskless rate. They construct SMB by taking the difference in returns between a portfolio of small stocks and a portfolio of big stocks each having the same weighted-average book-to-market equity ratio. They construct HML by taking the difference in returns on a portfolio of high and a portfolio of low book-to-market equity portfolios each having the same weight-averaged size. We use these factors as provided by the authors.

According to the Fama-French model, the *expected* return on an asset may be represented by:

$$\mathrm{E}_{t-1}[r_{it}] = \mathrm{E}_{t-1}[r_{0t}] + \gamma_{t-1,MRF}\beta_{i,MRF} + \gamma_{t-1,SMB}\beta_{i,SMB} + \gamma_{t-1,HML}\beta_{i,HML}.$$

where $\gamma_{t-1,MRF}$, $\gamma_{t-1,SMB}$, and $\gamma_{t-1,HML}$ are the risk premia on the respective factors. *We note that there are three separate risk premia in the economy, each represented by a distinct gamma*; consequently, the overall risk premium for some portfolio i is: $\gamma_{t-1,MRF}\beta_{i,MRF} + \gamma_{t-1,SMB}\beta_{i,SMB} + \gamma_{t-1,HML}\beta_{i,HML}$. Investors conditionally set each gamma based on all information available *in advance of the realization of the factors and, hence, the asset's return*. We emphasize the risk premia are dynamic and forward looking; they need not be functions of current and past macroeconomic state variables alone.

We form 27 portfolios by sorting all stocks available from the Center for Research in Security Prices (CRSP) database into treciles for each of the three factor sensitivities ($\beta_{i,MRF}$, $\beta_{i,SMB}$, and $\beta_{i,HML}$) for each year of the sample period. We then estimate the risk premia by cross-sectionally regressing the realized returns of the 27 portfolios on each portfolio's previously estimated factor betas month by month, July 1958 through June 1999, using the following regression equation:

$$r_{it} = r_{0t} + \gamma_{t-1,MRF}\hat{\beta}_{i,MRF} + \gamma_{t-1,SMB}\hat{\beta}_{i,SMB} + \gamma_{t-1,HML}\hat{\beta}_{i,HML} + \tilde{\varepsilon}_{it}$$

The coefficient for each beta is the respective factor's risk premium (plus an unanticipated factor shock) for a given month. Consequently, this analysis produces a monthly time series of the *estimated* risk premia that we could denote as $\hat{\gamma}_{t-1,MRF}$, $\hat{\gamma}_{t-1,SMB}$, and $\hat{\gamma}_{t-1,HML}$. From now on, however, we refer to the risk premia for factors MRF, SMB, and HML as RISKMRF, RISKSMB, and RISKHML, respectively.

The Macroeconomic Model

In light of the findings of Patelis (1997) and Thorbecke (1997, 2000), who show a link between monetary policy and stock returns, and Elder (2001), who shows a link between federal funds rate volatility and the Treasury bill risk premium, we cast our analysis within the well-established framework of monetary policy vector autoregressions. The benefit of this approach is the direct comparability of the effects of monetary policy on real macroeconomic variables with the effects of our risk premia on those same measures. Monetary models analyze the impact on the economy of changes in the cost banks incur to borrow for reserve shortfalls (i.e., the fed funds rate). Similarly, we analyze the impact on the economy of changes in the cost firms incur to borrow risky capital.

The base monetary model we use is very similar to those found in Bernanke and Blinder (1992) and Strongin (1995). In our analysis, we include the fed funds rate like Bernanke and Blinder and total reserves (relative to lagged total reserves) and nonborrowed reserves (relative to lagged total reserves) like Strongin. We then augment this standard monetary model with asset pricing factors and risk premia.

As with many common monetary models, we achieve identification by assuming a lower triangular matrix for the contemporaneous interactions among the variables (i.e., we use a Choleski decomposition). The first series in each system is *one* of the real macroeconomic series appearing in Bernanke and Blinder (1992) (namely, new durable orders, consumption, employment, housing, income, industrial production, and retail sales). The remaining variables in *each* system are inflation; a commodity price index; total reserves relative to lagged total reserves; nonborrowed reserves relative to lagged borrowed reserves; the fed funds rate; MRF, SMB, and HML; and RISKMRF, RISKSMB, and RISKHML, in this order.

We estimate all systems as vector autoregressions in levels for the period January 1959 through September 1998:

$$\mathbf{y}_t = \boldsymbol{\mu} + \sum_{i=1}^{k} \boldsymbol{\Gamma}_i \mathbf{y}_{t-i} + \tilde{\boldsymbol{\varepsilon}}_t$$

$\mathbf{y}_t$ is a p-vector of one real macroeconomic variable, the monetary policy variables, the risk factors, and their respective premia. $\boldsymbol{\mu}$ is a vector of drift constants (we let $\hat{\boldsymbol{\mu}}$ represent the *estimated* vector), and $\mathbf{\Gamma}_i$ is the *p* x *p* matrix of coefficients at lag *i* (we let $\hat{\mathbf{\Gamma}}_i$ represent the *estimated p* x *p* matrix at lag *i*). $\boldsymbol{\varepsilon}_t$~nid($\mathbf{0}$, Σ) is the vector of innovations. For each system, we specify the number of lags based on likelihood ratio tests, and in each case, these tests select a lag length of 12. We plot impulse-response functions using the moving average representation of (4) and include 95%-confidence bands that we generate using Monte Carlo techniques and 0.025 and 0.975 fractiles.

Macroeconomic Fluctuations and the Fama-French Risk Premia

We turn now to the central issue of this research: the responses of real economic variables to impulses in the risk premia. We emphasize new durable goods orders (NEWDUR) because this series measures future demand for production and employment. Durable goods include capital equipment such as industrial machinery, computers, electrical control instruments, trucks, aircraft, and ships, and new orders of durables often precede new investment in plant and equipment. Consequently, a rise in new orders for durable goods indicates firms expect a subsequent rise in demand for their products. As a result, NEWDUR should be a strong measure of real economic activity.

Figure 1 shows that NEWDUR is very quick to respond to a one-standard deviation increase in RISKSMB inducing a –0.75% drop in new durable orders at the two-month horizon. Moreover, the effects persist. In general, new durable orders are lower by about –0.50% over the three- to twelve-month horizon. The subsequent impulse-response pattern is similar to that of the standard VAR with stationary time series attenuating to almost no effect within 18 months. We see in Figure 1 that despite ordering the risk premia after inflation, all the monetary variables, and the factors, the risk premium on SMB remains informative about future states of the economy. Somewhat surprising, at least on the surface, is the lack of any significant effect of innovations in the risk premia on the MRF and HML factors. This issue is discussed in detail below. In unreported results, we also find the general lack of informativeness of RISKMRF (RISKHML) persists even when ordered first among the risk premia.

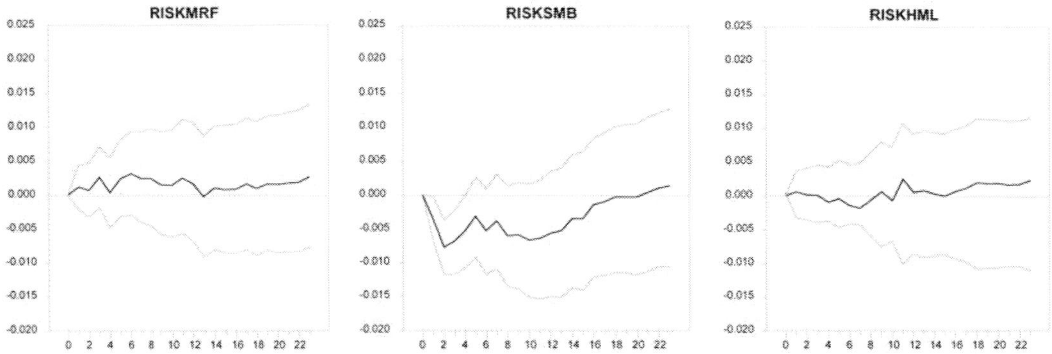

Figure 1. Responses of NEWDUR to Risk Premia Shocks.

Several other real variables respond significantly to innovations in RISKSMB. For example, Figure 2 shows employment (EMPLOY) falls significantly in response to a shock to

RISKSMB. EMPLOY decreases by about 0.15% following a one-standard deviation shock to RISKSMB, a reduction that persists over a 10- to 24-month horizon.

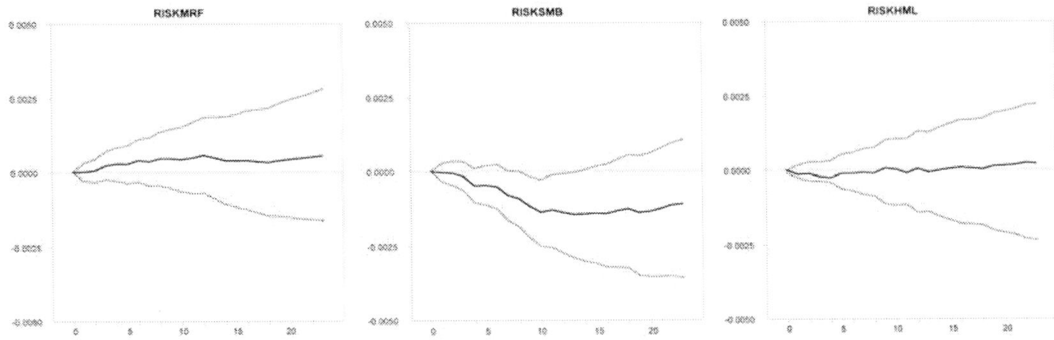

Figure 2. Responses of EMPLOY to Risk Premia Shocks.

Discussion and Interpretation

The lack of significance of the risk premium on MRF may reflect the perennial lack of significance of this factor's premium in Fama-MacBeth tests of the CAPM that include some measure of size (see, e.g., Banz, 1981, and Fama and French, 1992). In accordance with this research, we find that shocks to the risk premium for size are meaningful and contractionary. This result is also consistent with Hardouvelis and Wizman (1992), who study the risk premium on size over the business cycle using the firm-size augmented CAPM. Moreover, we observe similarities between our capital-budgeting story, the strength of the response functions to innovations in the small firm premium, and mechanisms of monetary policy transmission.

In the balance sheet and the credit channel views of monetary policy (see, e.g., Bernanke, 1993, and Gertler and Gilchrist, 1994), restrictions on the access to new capital and limitations on new investment are central. When the Fed reduces money supply and raises the fed funds rate, in addition to curbing inflation, the action impairs the collateral value of firms' balance sheets, reduces their ability to borrow at favorable rates, and lowers their capital expenditures. The firms most dependent on their balance sheets to attain credit, typically through bank loans, are small firms—the very firms that load most heavily on SMB according to Fama and French (1996).

In the credit channel of monetary policy transmission, it is the unwillingness of banks to lend that is at issue, not the lack of creditworthiness of borrowers. Following a tightening of monetary policy, banks reduce the number of new loans they make and invest more in securities as they rebalance their loan portfolios to meet reserve requirements. Again, as bank loans are made disproportionately to small firms—these firms have limited access to the capital markets—the effect of tighter monetary policy is propagated through the denial of new credit to small firms.

Like the economics underlying these mechanisms of monetary policy transmission and the work of Hardouvelis and Wizman, our results imply that an increase in the risk premium on the SMB factor raises the cost of capital to small firms and induces contractions in the economy. It is the small and vulnerable firms that induce macroeconomic fluctuations, not the established firms that constitute the lion's share of financial market capitalization.

In addition, our results for the SMB risk premium resonate strongly with the implications of the theoretical model of Rampini (2004). That model shows entrepreneurial activity is procyclical, and the dynamics of that activity are largely induced by a countercyclical willingness of entrepreneurs to bear risk (though that risk is project-specific, not systemic as in an asset pricing model). Hence, productivity shocks are amplified and propagated through an "entrepreneur channel" similar to the logic described in this commentary for the SMB factor.

New Directions in Research

It appears that a fundamental task in understanding business cycles is the consideration of heterogeneity of firm and investor types in macroeconomic models. Like the economics underlying the mechanisms of monetary policy transmission, the theoretical model of macroeconomic fluctuations in Rampini (2004), and the empirical work of Hardouvelis and Wizman, our results imply that an increase in the risk premium on the SMB factor raises the cost of capital to small firms and induces contractions in the economy. It is the small and vulnerable firms that amplify and propagate macroeconomic fluctuations, not the established firms that constitute the lion's share of financial market capitalization.

In addition, leading indicators that ignore the crucial role of access to capital and the cost of capital for small firms are inherently flawed. They ignore, perhaps, the single most important mechanism and, hence, best indicator of future economic conditions. As a start in this direction, we (Bian and Fuerst, 2008) analyze how dynamic risk premia act as new measures of optimism and, consequently, leading indicators of recessions and recoveries. Our hypothesis is that risk premia act as sensitive barometers of investors' expectations of future prosperity for the most vulnerable firms, the firms that drive fluctuations in the macroeconomy. The hope is that this new measure will complement existing indicators of consumer and investor confidence and improve our ability to forecast economic downturns.

References

Abel, A. B. 1988. Stock Prices under Time-Varying Dividend Risk: An Exact Solution in an Infinite-Horizon General Equilibrium Model. *Journal of Monetary Economics* **22**, 375-393.

Abel, A. B. 1999. Risk Premia and Term Premia in General Equilibrium. *Journal of Monetary Economics* **43**, 3-33.

Banz, R. 1981. The Relationship Between Return and Market Value of Common Stocks. *Journal of Financial Economics* **14**, 359-376.

Bernanke, B. S. 1993. Credit in the Macroeconomy. *Quarterly Review of Federal Reserve Bank of New York* **18**, 50-70.

Bernanke, B. S. and A. S. Blinder. 1992. The Federal Funds Rate and the Channels of Monetary Transmission. *American Economic Review* **82**, 901-921.

Bian, J., 2007, *The Causal Relationship between the Risk Premium and Macroeconomic Fluctuations,* unpublished dissertation, University of Miami.

Bian, J. and Fuerst, M., 2008, *Investor Risk Premia and Leading Economic Indicators*, working paper, University of International Business and Finance and University of Miami.

Black, F. 1972. Capital Market Equilibrium with Restricted Borrowing. *Journal of Business* **45**, 444-55.

Black, F. 1990. Mean Reversion and Consumption Smoothing. *Review of Financial Studies* **3,** 107-114.

Campbell, J. Y. and J. H. Cochrane. 1999. By Force of Habit: A Consumption-Based Explanation of Aggregate Stock Market Behavior. *Journal of Political Economy* **107**, 205-251.

Chen, N.-F. 1991. Financial Investment Opportunities and the Macroeconomy. *Journal of Finance* **46**, 529-54.

Connor, G. and R. Korajczyk. 1989. An Intertemporal Equilibrium Beta Pricing Model. *Review of Financial Studies* **2,** 373-92.

Constantinides, G. M. 1990. Habit Formation: A Resolution of the Equity Premium Puzzle. *Journal of Political Economy* **98**, 519-43.

Dimson, E. 1979. Risk Measurement When Shares are Subject to Infrequent Trading. *Journal of Financial Economics* **7**, 197-226.

Elder, J. 2001. Can the Volatility of the Federal Funds Rate Explain the Time-Varying Risk Premium in Treasury Bill Returns? *Journal of Macroeconomics* **23**, 73-97.

Elder, J. and P. E. Kennedy. 2001. F versus t Tests for Unit Roots. Economics Bulletin 3, 1-6.

Fama, E. F. 1996. Common Risk Factors in the Returns on Stocks and Bonds. *Journal of Financial and Quantitative Analysis* **31**, 441-65.

Fama, E. F. and K. R. French. 1989. Business Conditions and Expected Returns on Stocks and Bonds. *Journal of Financial Economics* **25**, 23-49.

Fama, E. F. and K. R. French. 1992. The Cross-Section of Expected Stock Returns. *Journal of Finance* **47**, 427-65.

Fama, E. F. and K. R. French. 1993. Common Risk Factors in the Returns on Stocks and Bonds. *Journal of Financial Economics* **25**, 3-56.

Fama, E. F. and K. R. French. 1996. Multifactor Explanations of Asset Pricing Anomalies. *Journal of Finance* **51**, 55-84.

Fama, E. F. and J. MacBeth. 1973. Risk, Return, and Equilibrium: Empirical Tests. *Journal of Political Economy* **81**, 607-36.

Fuerst, M., 2006, Investor Risk Premia and Real Macroeconomic Fluctuations. *Journal of Macroeconomics* v28, n3: 540-63.

Gertler, M. and S. Gilchrist. 1994. Monetary Policy, Business Cycles, and the Behavior of Small Manufacturing Firms. *Quarterly Journal of Economics* **109**, 309-40.

Hardouvelis, G. A. and T. A. Wizman. 1992. The Relative Cost of Capital for Marginal Firms over the Business Cycle. Federal Reserve Bank of New York *Quarterly Review Autumn,* 44-58.

Heaton, J. and D. Lucas. 2000. Portfolio Choice and Asset Prices: The Importance of Entrepreneurial Risk. *Journal of Finance* **55**, 1163-98.

Johansen, S. 1995. Likelihood-Based Inference in Cointegrated Vector Autoregressive Models. Oxford University Press, New York.

Kandel, S. and R. F. Stambaugh. 1990. Expectations and Volatility of Consumption and Asset Returns. *Review of Financial Studies* **3**, 207-232.

Kothari, S. P., J. Shanken, and R. G. Sloan. 1995. Another Look at the Cross-section of Expected Stock Returns. *Journal of Finance* **50**, 185-224.

Lettau, M. and S. Ludvigson. 2001. Resurrecting the (C)CAPM: A Cross-Sectional Test When Risk Premia Are Time-Varying. *Journal of Political Economy* **109**, 1238-87.

Lettau, M. and S. Ludvigson. 2002. Time-varying Risk Premia and the Cost of Capital: An Alternative Implication of the Q Theory of Investment. *Journal of Monetary Economics* **49**, 31-66.

Mehra, R. and E. C. Prescott. 1985. The Equity Premium: A Puzzle. *Journal of Monetary Economics* **15**, 145-61.

Patelis, A. D. 1997. Stock Return Predictability and the Role of Monetary Policy. *Journal of Finance* **52**, 1951-72.

Strongin, S. 1995. The Identification of Monetary Policy Disturbances: Explaining the Liquidity Puzzle. *Journal of Monetary Economics* **34**, 463-97.

Thorbecke, W. 2000. Monetary Policy, Time-varying Risk, and the Bond Market Debacle of 1994. *Journal of Macroeconomics* **22**, 159-74.

Thorbecke, W. 1997. On Stock Market Returns and Monetary Policy. *Journal of Finance* **52**, 635-54.

INDEX

C

D

E

F

G

H

I

J

K

L

Q

R

S

T

U

V

W

Y